UNIVERSITY OF NOTTINGHAM

WITHDRAWN

FROM LIBRARY

D0236422

HALLWARD SHORT LOAN COLLECTION

UNIVERSITY LIBRARY

18/1/93

Malle on Malle

Malle on Malle

Edited by
Philip French

NOTTINGHAM UNIVERSITY LIBRARY

ff

faber and faber

First published in 1993
by Faber and Faber Limited
3 Queen Square London WC1N 3AU

Photoset by Parker Typesetting Service, Leicester
Printed in England by Clays Ltd, St Ives plc

All rights reserved

© Louis Malle, 1993
Introduction and editorial commentary © Philip French, 1993

Louis Malle and Philip French are hereby identified as authors
of this work in accordance with Section 77 of the Copyright,
Designs and Patents Act 1988

A CIP record for this book is available
from the British Library
ISBN 0–571–16237–1

1000206165

2 4 6 8 10 9 7 5 3 1

Contents

Illustrations

Acknowledgements

My initial thanks are to Walter Donohue who had the idea for this book and has seen it through to publication. In 1989 he invited me to write an essay on the French cinema of and about the Occupation to accompany the published screenplays of *Lacombe, Lucien* and *Au revoir les enfants*, and the following year brought me together with Louis Malle, whom I also thank for his patient collaboration. I spent four hugely enjoyable days with Malle at his house near Limogne-en-Quercy in November 1990 eating truffles, talking about politics, literature and cinema, and recording the conversation which forms the bulk of this book. In June 1991 he came to London to take part in a television programme I presented to introduce Channel Four's ten-week season of his movies. Our conversation about *Damage* was taped over lunch one rainy Sunday in March 1992, surrounded by extras, in a location catering bus parked off Hanover Square in London's West End. Malle had spent the morning shooting a scene involving Juliette Binoche in the street outside Sotheby's and on the way to lunch dropped in on Jeremy Irons's caravan to discuss a scene to be shot that afternoon near the Embankment.

Thanks must also go to Marie-Christine Breton of Nouvelles Éditions de Films in Paris, to Tracey Scoffield at Faber and, most especially, to Kersti French for her editorial advice and invaluable role as translator.

The stills and other photographs appear by courtesy of the British Film Institute, the Rank Organization, Nouvelles Éditions de Films, Artificial Eye, Curzon Films, United Artists, PEA, Selta Films, Paramount, Universal, Tri Star-Delphi III, Skreba, and SYGMA. Stills from *Milou en mai* by Jeanne-Louise Bulliard; stills from *Damage* by Sophie Baker; portraits of Louis Malle by the Douglas Brothers.

Introduction

Louis Malle celebrated his sixtieth birthday in 1992, shortly after completing post-production on his thirtieth feature-length film, *Damage*, and thirty-six years after he shared with Jacques Cousteau the Palme d'Or at Cannes and a Hollywood Oscar for best full-length documentary as co-director of *Le Monde du silence*.

He was born in Thumeries, a small town south of Lille, in the dreary northern industrial area of France near the Belgian border, on 30 October 1932. The region resembles the dispiriting South Lancashire of my boyhood, that series of mining and manufacturing towns like Widnes, Warrington, Leigh and St Helens strung out in the countryside between Liverpool and Manchester.

Thumeries was then, and still is, a company town dominated by a single factory, one of the largest of its kind in Europe, processing sugar from the locally grown beet, which is piled high all around. Alongside the one local bank is the town's only restaurant, called appropriately enough La Sucrière (the sugar-bowl). The smoke belching out of the factory means prosperity, and the company belonged to the haut-bourgeois Béghin family. Malle's mother, Françoise, was a Béghin and her husband, Pierre, a former naval officer from Alsace, managed the factory. Their four sons (of whom Louis was the third) and three daughters were raised in a nearby mansion in a strict Catholic faith and as small children were taught by private tutors.

Thumeries has no feature of distinction and, despite its 1,000 years of existence, little claim to fame beyond being the source of Béghin sugar and the birthplace of Louis Malle. You would only visit it on business or pass through it by chance, a journey that takes little more than a couple of minutes. Moviegoers taking a detour by way of homage will be rewarded as they traverse the main road, renamed after the Second World War in honour of the great socialist statesman and three-times premier Léon Blum (1872–1950). They will recall the wartime words of Julien Quentin's mother in *Au revoir les enfants*, which are, almost verbatim, those of Malle's own Catholic mother: 'Mind you, I have nothing against Jews. On the contrary. Except for that Léon Blum, of course. He deserves hanging.'

In 1940, when the Occupation began, the family moved to Paris, where Louis and his brothers were educated by Jesuits before going on to a boarding school run by Carmelites in Fontainebleau. He has yet to set a movie in the region of his birth, though in *Le Voleur*, the late-Victorian gentleman-thief hero stops off to rob a complacent Belgian haut-bourgeois household just across the border. Malle subsequently studied the humanities at the Institut d'Études Politiques at the Sorbonne and the cinema at the Institut des Hautes Études Cinématographiques (IDHEC). At the end of his first year at IDHEC he was recruited by Commandant Cousteau and after three demanding years aboard the *Calypso* he was launched into a movie career. Brief service under Jacques Tati (a matter of days rather than weeks) and Robert Bresson (a matter of weeks rather than months) preceded his own entry into feature films with *Ascenseur pour l'échafaud*.

His début preceded those of the movie-critics-turned-directors who formed the hard core of the self-promoting Nouvelle Vague (a term coined by the magazine *L'Express*) and he never publicly castigated the then fashionable French directors of an older generation, the representatives of the so-called Cinéma de Papa. But his cinematographer, Henri Decaë, shot the first films of both Claude Chabrol and François Truffaut, and he was at first lumped together with them by critics and gossip columnists. The *Cahiers du Cinéma* writers welcomed Malle as one of their number and Truffaut wrote with particular appreciation of *Zazie dans le Métro*. But his work did not attract the sustained critical attention that Godard's and Truffaut's did and he was widely held to be a traditionalist rather than an iconoclast. True, the frequent controversies surrounding his work have been over its matter rather than its manner, but this fastidious craftsman would be better thought of as a renewer of tradition rather than as an uncritical follower.

Most of his contemporaries stumbled and lost their way, the majority of them fairly early on. Between 1959 and 1963, 170 French directors made their feature-film débuts and only a handful have been heard of since. Writing of this state of affairs in 'Nouvelle Vague or Jeune Cinéma?' (*Sight and Sound*, Winter 1964–5), the French critic Gilles Jacob wrote, prophetically:

A system of natural selection has operated among this flush of new and uneven talents, and today it is possible to draw up some sort of balance sheet. One director, Resnais, of international class, certain to leave his name in history; another, Godard, self-indulgent and maddening, but with a style and a world of his own, and perhaps the most gifted of the younger generation; seven more – Astruc, Démy, Franju, Malle, Marker, Truffaut, Varda – who probably haven't yet revealed their potential; and finally a number of question marks – Jessua, Rozier, Sautet, Enrico, etc. – for, no matter how talented, a first film is likely to be, if not autobiographical, at least extremely personal, almost a confession.

Malle has experienced few serious setbacks or major failures – or so it appears in retrospect. From the beginning he has been in control of his career to an unusual degree. And while the variety of his subject matter and the absence of a consistent style have often puzzled critics, Malle's work has a rare coherence of which he himself was not initially aware. There are three points worth making here.

First, after starting out with *Le Monde du silence* and *Ascenseur pour l'échafaud* he has pursued two careers, or rather has interwoven two strands of the same one, as feature-film-maker and documentarist. This pattern did not emerge until the screening of the innovative *L'Inde fantôme* series in 1970.

Second, *Ascenseur pour l'échafaud* contains most of the characteristic themes, tropes and preoccupations, if only in embryonic form, that were to get more considered treatment later – a fascinated contempt for the hypocrisies of the middle class; jazz music; suicide; the adult world observed by the dangerously innocent young; a political background that frames and is reflected in the protagonists' conduct; characters trapped in some web of fate; the destructive power of sexual passion; a gift for seizing a society at a precise moment of social change; the urge to disrupt and disconcert; a refusal to make direct moral judgements. Anti-clericalism is one of the few missing elements.

Third, in 1958 he acquired Nouvelles Éditions de Films, the company which Jean Thuillier had set up to produce Robert Bresson's *Un Condamné à mort s'est échappé* and which backed *Ascenseur pour l'échafaud* and *Les Amants*. This small company with a Paris office on the rue du Louvre has co-produced the majority of the pictures Malle has made. Initially one of the partners in the firm was an elder brother and it was at NEF that Louis introduced his younger brother Vincent, his junior by twelve years, to the cinema as an assistant on *Le Voleur*. Vincent went on to become a producer, working with Marco Ferreri on *La Grande Bouffe* and Robert Bresson on *Lancelot du lac*, as well as collaborating on numerous films directed by Louis.

There are only three films over which Malle has not had more or less complete control – *Vie privée*, his segment of *Histoires extraordinaires* and *Crackers*. Thus to see a steady progress and development in his work is simply to recognize the career of a man who has been, to a degree unusual in the cinema, the master of his fate. That makes the chronological breakdown of this book into six main chapters quite logical.

After *Le Monde du silence* Malle settled back in Paris, and the city is central to his first five feature films, even to *Les Amants* and *Vie privée*, the two not primarily set there. This chapter in his life ends with *Le Feu follet*, his first masterpiece and the high point of his early period. For the remainder of the 1960s he concentrated on large-scale costume pictures with major stars, in colour and widescreen. He then retreated to India, a sub-continent with a different past, a different present, a different culture.

Following two years largely devoted to editing the Indian material, he made three films of provincial life, two set in the recent past, the third, *Black Moon*, in a dystopian near future. He then crossed the Atlantic and spent the next decade in America making five features and two long documentaries. Only one of the features was offered him by a studio and only *Pretty Baby* is set in the past. With the exception of the cerebral conversation piece *My Dinner with André*, these movies took him into an area of society – the blue-collar and low-life world – that he knew little of from first-hand experience and had scarcely touched on in his previous work. He also played variations on American forms – the gangster film, the heist movie, the Warner Brothers social-conscience picture. His French documentaries had never asked the fundamental social questions he posed in *And the Pursuit of Happiness* and *God's Country*, the very titles of which define peculiarly American concerns. At the end of a decade in the States, he returned to Europe and to subjects of his own past which he had set aside. Chapter 6 concerns his latest film, *Damage*.

Inevitably, events in Malle's private life play some part at certain junctions of his career. So, while this book is not a biography or auto-biography, a few facts might clarify some references he makes.

Malle's first marriage was to Anne-Marie Deschodt, who had been close to him in the late 1950s before marrying an American and moving to New York. (The wife of Alain, the hero of *Le Feu follet*, had left him to live in New York.) Malle met her again in 1964 and after her divorce she married him in Mexico during the shooting of *Viva Maria*. They broke up three years later without having children. His first child, a son, was born in Mexico in 1971, and called Manuel Cuotemoc after Montezuma's nephew and the last Aztec emperor. His mother is the German actress Gila von Weitershausen, who played the prostitute chosen by Laurent's brothers for his sexual initiation in *Le Souffle au coeur*. He was brought up in Munich and educated at Brown University, Rhode Island. Malle's second child, a daughter, Justine, was born in 1974 to the Canadian actress Alexandra Stewart, who appeared in *Le Feu follet* and *Black Moon*. She has grown up in Paris. In 1980 Malle married the American actress Candice Bergen. Their daughter Chloë was born in 1985 in New York. At the end of the opening credit titles of *Au revoir les enfants*, just at the point where the children troop into the school, there comes up on the screen a dedication – 'Pour Cuotemoc, Justine et Chloë'.

Malle and Candice Bergen were married by the Mayor of Lugagnac, a small town on the Causse de Limogne, a limestone plateau south of the River Lot and east of Cahors in south-west France. Since the mid-1960s Malle has owned a large, rambling country house in this area way off the beaten track. Its oldest parts date back to the fifteenth century but the many additions give it a curiously surreal atmosphere. Stone staircases of various widths bend and twist. Rooms open off rooms, some of them baronial, others cell-like. The visitor's disturbing sense of *déjà vu* is explained by the fact that the house was the setting for *Black Moon*. *Lacombe, Lucien* was also shot in the vicinity and *Milou en mai* was made not far away at a château in Le Gers. Much of Malle's writing has been done here over the past quarter of a century and he is very attached to the region. He has in mind a documentary about the local truffle hunters. It was at this house that we recorded most of our conversation, so when Malle refers to 'this part of France' and 'here' he means this region or sometimes the particular house and not Paris.

The cinema has been Malle's sole occupation since he left IDHEC to work with Cousteau, but he has kept in close touch with the currents of life through his work as a documentarist, getting ever more intimate with his subjects as he has taken to operating the camera himself. Not all his plans have been realized and not every picture by any means has pleased him. But in most cases he has abandoned or postponed projects through his own volition. He is without rancour, something rare in a film-maker, and his enthusiasm for both life and the movies remains undiminished. As he remarks at the beginning of *God's Country*: 'It felt good to be on the road again, shooting film and making friends.' This amiable man makes friends as he works and likes working with friends, hence the continuing associations he has had over the years with various collaborators on both sides of the camera. In addition to making movies he loves watching them. A few years ago he emerged from seeing Andrei Tarkovsky's three-hour *Andrei Rublëv* in such a state of excitement that he saw it again the same night, persuading the people he had planned to dine with to snatch a sandwich instead and join him. There can be few directors so well acquainted with the new work of younger cinéastes on both sides of the Atlantic.

I hope that I have caught the excitement of talking with Malle. He is an engaging, thoughtful conversationalist and, though speaking with a marked accent, he is more articulate in his second language than many a monolingual English-speaking movie-maker. Anyone who has heard him broadcast or speak in public will be able to provide the voice and perhaps even note the points at which he is drawing pensively on his pipe or flourishing a cigar as he talks.

Philip French, March 1992

CHAPTER I

Paris and the Road to Maturity

PHILIP FRENCH: *Your partially autobiographical adolescent characters in* Le Souffle au coeur *and* Au revoir les enfants *are principally interested in literature and in jazz, not in the movies. Does that reflect your own situation growing up?*

LOUIS MALLE: No. I really had three great passions. Music was one. I went very quickly from Beethoven to Louis Armstrong and Charlie Parker at the age of fourteen, fifteen and sixteen. And literature, certainly. It just happened that, like the character in *Le Souffle au coeur*, my life was interrupted for almost two years because of a heart murmur – I was taken out of boarding school and I studied at home. I was not supposed to do very active sports or anything like that, so it was a time when I read enormously. The characters in *Au revoir les enfants* and *Le Souffle au coeur* come from that early time in my life when I was very much immersed in literature. I read almost anything – I even read Nietzsche when I was fourteen. That was ridiculous! My passion for the cinema came a little after that. I remember going to cinéclubs in Paris in those years, and discovering, for instance, *La Règle du jeu*, or that particular film which I've always thought triggered my decision to make films – *Les Dernières vacances*, directed by Roger Leenhardt;[1] I think it was made when I was fifteen or sixteen, right after the war. It must have been the first French film to suggest what would eventually become the Nouvelle Vague. I felt very close to Leenhardt's sensibility and to this film about a bourgeois family and all the little intrigues during the summer holidays. I have not seen it more than a couple of times, and it has not been an actual reference point, but I think *Les Dernières vacances* triggered a strong desire, almost an urge, to make films. I wish it was re-released. It was a very important film, not only for me, but for all members of the New Wave.

PF: *Godard introduced Roger Leenhardt into* Une Femme mariée, *didn't he?*

LM: Yes. Leenhardt was much admired and, although I think he directed only one other feature film, he made great shorts, wonderful shorts, for which he was famous.

PF: *What was the attitude to the cinema on the part of your parents and your family circle? Did they take it as seriously as the other arts?*
LM: No, they didn't. I don't remember having discussions about films with my parents. With my brothers, yes. I had two brothers, who were three and six years older than I was. My brother Bernard – the one who was three years older – has always influenced me: he was always telling me what to read and what not to read, and what to see and what not to see. We often talked about the future. He wanted to write, and so did I, but once he said to me, 'You're very active, you shouldn't be a writer, you should make films.' It obviously made an impression on me. My parents were quite cultivated but they were no film buffs. The idea of a great film for my mother would be *Monsieur Vincent*.[2] She was a very, very religious woman. She didn't keep us from seeing films, but she was really shocked when I told her that I wanted to become a film-maker. She came from a very traditional, upper-class background, and she imagined that I would be the one who would go into the family business. I don't know why she picked me – maybe it was because my brothers were hopeless students! They'd been kicked out of various schools. My mother had decided that I was going to an élite school, like the Polytechnique, as my grandfather had done, and then enter the family business. I was not even fourteen when I told my mother I wanted to direct films, and she was absolutely horrified.

PF: *Were you able to go to the cinema in Thumeries, or were you cut off from the local community while growing up?*
LM: No, I think there was what we call a *patronage* cinema – screenings organized by the parish – but I'm not sure there was a commercial cinema in Thumeries, because it was very close to Lille, and if we were going to the movies we would go to Lille. But I did not really live in Thumeries after 1940; I was not even eight when we settled in Paris, and for the rest of my school years I was based in Paris, and Fontainebleau, just going back to the family house in Thumeries for the holidays.

PF: *Growing up during the Occupation, were you aware of being denied the popular cinema of Hollywood, and seeing a rather special, very restricted sort of French cinema?*

LM: I remember seeing French cinema, of course, which was flourishing in those days, and it was, in fact, one of the great periods of French cinema. There were German films, including German propaganda films. I vividly remember seeing *Baron Münchhausen*[3] as a child, in 1943 or 1944, in the Champs Élysées. I cannot say that we were very aware of the absence of American films, because I'd never been exposed to the American cinema. Before the war I was just a child. I remember seeing *Snow White* in Lille, that must have been in 1938. Then came the war and we were cut off from the American cinema, but I do remember the sudden appearance after the war of American films from those five years. I didn't see *Citizen Kane* when it came out – I was probably at boarding school – but I saw it at a film society when it was already a classic. We saw lots of documentaries during the days of Vichy, and I suppose our parents encouraged that because it was educational. There was a cinema on the Champs Élysées that showed only documentaries, which I remember vividly – it's next to the Normandie. A friend of mine, who is the same age, said to me, 'Those films must have influenced your interest in documentary.' And I said, 'Well, it must have been subconscious, because I really don't remember them, except that sometimes they were very boring!'

PF: *When you went to Paris in 1940, was there a sense of relief at getting away from Thumeries? There is a pattern in your work, from* Les Amants *to* Atlantic City *and* Alamo Bay, *of people escaping from the restrictions of small-town life.*
LM: Well, in those years we were children. When my parents decided we would be better off in Paris, we moved into my grandfather's apartment, which was huge, but we were a large family, so we were cramped. None the less we had a great sense of freedom in Paris. And, of course, my elder brothers led the way. From the outset we were very rebellious. For two years I went to a Jesuit school which was about fifteen minutes' walk from where we lived. My father stayed in Thumeries because he was director of the family sugar factory. It was in a separate zone – the *zone interdite*. Because the far north of France was a rich, industrial area, the Germans had decided to annex it. My mother, who was in Paris with us, needed a special permit to go and visit my father in Thumeries. It got a little easier from 1942 – I remember spending my first holiday in Thumeries that year. Before then, we couldn't go there.

The fact that during those four years my father was not around was enormously important in my life, and in my brothers' lives as well. Today it's a two-hour drive on the motorway, but then it was a real adventure. And we had a sense of great freedom because we were pretty unrestricted. When I was at the Jesuit school – I was nine, ten, something like that – they would let us out in the afternoon to sell postcards of Marshal Pétain, in shops or to people in the streets, to raise money for the Red Cross or whatever. I did a little quote on that at the beginning of *Le Souffle au coeur*. I remember enjoying doing that, because they would just let us go at three in the afternoon.

PF: *After the war you went on to university and then to IDHEC; which was more important, the studies at the Sorbonne or at film school?*

LM: Because my parents were so adamantly opposed to my vocation, we went through a series of compromises. I finished my baccalauréat one year earlier than children normally do – I was not quite seventeen. They enrolled me in a course to prepare for one of the prestigious schools in France – the '*grandes écoles*'. If you get into one of those schools you're safe for the rest of your life, because you're part of the Establishment. I made sure I would fail. In one exam I left blank pages because I was terrified I would be accepted against my will. I managed to enter the Institut d'Études Politiques, which I wanted to go to because I was interested in history and in politics. At the end of my first year there I got a place at IDHEC – I don't know why, I had a knack of being accepted everywhere without really deserving it. I told my parents, 'This is serious, it's part of the Université de Paris. If you let me, I'll finish the Institut d'Études Politiques, and at the same time I'll go to the film school.' And they said yes. I did my second year at the Institut, then I gave it up. But after one year at IDHEC I realized I was not going to learn anything. I did half of my second year, and then I was hired by Cousteau.[4] I was twenty.

PF: *What was it about the teaching at IDHEC that you objected to? Was it too theoretical?*

LM: It was very theoretical, which was the problem with most film schools. For me, a film school is good for only two things. The first is: see as many films as possible, try to understand the history of cinema, try to understand the creative processes of people you admire, and examine their work. The second is practical study, which means having a chance to work with a camera or to edit. The school was extremely broke. The history part was good, we were always at the Cinémathèque. But there was a lot of theory about film-making which was taught by mediocre teachers and which very quickly struck me as quite irrelevant. So I never finished the course at IDHEC.

PF: *You made a film there, though, didn't you?*
LM: Well, it was five minutes. Each student made a five-minute film. IDHEC had so little money that we shot in negative – then cut on negative – and eventually they would make a print once it was edited. So yes, I did this one film.

PF: *What was the subject?*
LM: It was very much influenced by the early works of Beckett and Ionesco. It was when the Theatre of the Absurd was taking shape in Paris, but it was not yet recognized or successful. I was at IDHEC when the first production of *Waiting for Godot* opened at a little theatre on the Left Bank; it was not very well reviewed. And I remember the remarkable early work of Ionesco – *The Lesson* and those other one-act plays. I was very close to the actors and the directors working with him. I did my film with two of the actors from the cast of *La Cantatrice chauve* (*The Bald-Headed Prima Donna*). It was about people in a room waiting for somebody to arrive who didn't come. I think this film was made two or three months before *Waiting for Godot* was actually put on stage. So it was very much in the mood of that time.

PF: *A number of your contemporaries came together as critics working on film magazines. Did you form any lasting friendships with your contemporaries at IDHEC?*
LM: Well, there was a lot going on in my generation in those years, although *Cahiers du Cinéma* had just started and people like Truffaut or Rivette hardly even existed. I remember meeting Claude Chabrol, when he was working in the press office at Paramount. But in my class at IDHEC there was Alain Cavalier,[5] also Michel Mitrani,[6] and Pierre Geoffroy, who became a great designer. Most of my fellow-students ended up directing for television. I used to see Jacques Démy, who was making short films – he'd been rejected by IDHEC.

PF: *So what were the qualifications you put forward to persuade Cous-teau to engage you to work on the* Calypso?
LM: Because I could swim! It was very basic. Cousteau had a one-man film crew, Jacques Ertaud; later on I recommended him to Bresson for a

part in *Un Condamné à mort s'est échappé*. He was getting married, so Cousteau was nervous. He tried two other cameramen on the *Calypso* but I don't think he trusted them too much. I never understood why, but he went to IDHEC and talked to the Director and said, 'Do you have a student who'd be interested in working during the summer?' For some reason, they'd named me President of the class, so I was the first one to know about it and I said, 'I'll go.' Then, to be above-board, I checked with my fellow-students, but they were not so interested in documentaries. They wanted to work with Renoir, Bresson and eventually Jacques Becker.[7] So I came back to the Director and said, 'Well, I think I am the only one.' I pushed my luck a little bit. Then I met Cousteau. I'd absolutely no background, but I pretended that I had some knowledge of editing and photography – which I had actually, because I'd made lots of films with my father's 8mm camera. So I had more practical experience than my friends at IDHEC. They wanted to be directors and that alone; they were not interested in camera or technique. Their approach was very intellectual.

So I went to Marseilles to the *Calypso*, and learnt how to dive and to use a camera under water. And at the end of the summer Cousteau, realizing that his main man was really getting married and the others were not very competent, asked me to stay. I was approaching twenty-one, and it was a big decision, because I was supposed to go back to IDHEC. But I said, 'Sure.' And then he said, 'Well, you're in charge, direction and photography, editing'. I knew nothing: well, a little bit, but very little. It was an enormous responsibility. Fortunately, during the first year I had time to adjust doing routine work. Then we started working on *Le Monde du silence*. I must say, the moment I set foot on the *Calypso* and we went to Greece, I really wanted to stay. First, because I thought it was a wonderful introduction to film-making – just doing it. And, second, I was genuinely interested in this kind of life, in this kind of film-making.

PF: *Did the experience of observing the beds of the Indian Ocean, the Mediterranean and the Red Sea in any sense change your view about life, the universe, ways of looking? When* Le Monde du silence *came out, considerable claims were made for it on ontological grounds by Eric Rohmer and André Bazin, who said it opened up new vistas of experience. Did that strike you while you were working on it?*

LM: It was an extraordinary experience. I was amazed and proud to be part of it. It felt very close to what the first astronauts must have felt. But,

1 *Le Monde du silence:* Captain Cousteau (right)
prepares to descend
2 *Le Monde du silence:* diver inspects denizen of the deep

much as I admired him for inventing technologies and bringing this new world to cinema audiences, and the fact that he was extremely smart and creative and had a good sense of humour – I mean, I really admired him – at the same time, we disagreed about a lot of things. When you're very young you're very rigid about what you think is right, and I was – and I suppose I still am – very influenced by Bresson. I remember having a discussion about music with Cousteau during editing. And I said, 'What you're trying to do, this is not documentary, this is show business. It is not what it should be, it is becoming like Walt Disney.' Walt Disney was making those 'True-Life Adventure' documentaries in those years, very closely edited to music, trying to please the crowds. It would make me laugh now if I could listen to myself being so rigid.

But I was very much aware of the fact that there was something unique about what we were doing. In a way, you're always somehow the first spectator of your films and I was in a state of wonderment about what we were filming. We had to invent the rules – there were no references; it was too new. The camera by definition – because we were underwater – had a mobility and fluidity; we could do incredibly complicated equivalents of what, on land, would be a combination of crane movements plus enormous tracking shots – and we would do it just like breathing because it was part of the movement of the diver. What I disapproved of about Cousteau, outside the water, was that his reflexes were more for conventional spectacle. I would have liked to have kept it more of a unique and different experience.

PF: *You're talking about the differences you had with Cousteau – were you unhappy about what now dates the project: the false dramatic shaping of the film and the staging of dialogues, which may have fitted in with probably authentic material, but which brings into question the visual experience we are given?*
LM: Exactly.

PF: *For example, there's a scene where a diver is in great danger, and you cut from this to what's going on on deck. Clearly this never could have been an authentic montage.*
LM: Cousteau had made beautiful underwater shorts, which had won all kinds of prizes in festivals. They were just wonderful *reportage* of underwater life around a coral reef. But this one was much more ambitious. It seemed to me that it needed to stay absolutely pure without resorting to the techniques of what would be called today docu-drama. I remember

filming the scene where the diver suffers from *ivresse des profondeurs*, passes out under water. When we got into the cutting room, Cousteau needed to beef it up and, also, he wanted to explain. It was very didactic in a way. I would give my opinion, but it was always absolutely clear to me that this was Cousteau's film.

PF: *The line in the commentary – 'A motion-picture theatre, a thousand feet below the sea' – is that your line or Cousteau's?*
LM: I don't remember. I really don't. The astonishing thing about Cousteau, as I realized almost forty years ago, is that he's always been tempted by fiction. I had this argument with him last summer about something that we were thinking of doing together. His view was that we should do fiction; he said, 'All these years you've worked with fiction, you can help me.' And I said, 'But I'm not interested in working on fiction with you.' I had this same argument with him at the time, because he was interested in finding ways to go beyond documentaries. When I made my own documentaries, I think they were the extreme of documentaries, the extreme of *cinéma direct*, whereas Cousteau has always been tempted towards fiction – even his television films contain fabulous images, but I don't like the way they are dramatized.

PF: *There's a scene in the film where a dog barks at a live lobster on the deck, which some might think is an image characteristic of your humour. Was that something you saw and wanted to keep in?*
LM: I don't think it's mine at all. In those days my view of film-making was very Bressonian and austere and I was quite pompous about it. But Cousteau was always looking for the human touch. He was financed then by the National Geographic Society, and both in their magazine and in the films they were making they always went for 'human interest'. I remember the scene where the crew started killing sharks after the meeting with the whales. The baby whale was wounded – it was in the middle of the Indian Ocean – and out of the blue those huge sharks came and started eating that baby whale. This was the atavistic reaction of sailors against sharks – sailors hate sharks. In the film it became a little cute.

PF: *In 1956 you went to Cannes with* Le Monde du silence, *you had a co-direction credit with this national hero, the film was in competition. That must have been quite an extraordinary experience?*
LM: I was twenty-three, and here I was at Cannes. Cousteau came for a few days and said, 'Why don't you stay and watch what's going on?' It

was, of course, great fun for me to discover the world of cinema, because
I'd been this underwater cameraman for years, and when I was in Paris I
was editing. So suddenly I was exposed to producers, actors. I stayed ten
days, then went back to Paris, because Jacques Tati asked me if I would
be a second-unit cameraman for *Mon oncle*. It didn't happen, and
although it is often mentioned in my curriculum vitae that I was a
cameraman for Tati, I never was. So I went back to Paris, and to my
stupefaction I got a call from Cannes, and they said, 'You won the Palme
d'Or and there's nobody from the film to pick up the prize.' It was a total
surprise. It was in the afternoon, but planes were not as convenient as
they are today. So I don't even remember who eventually went on stage
to receive the prize. We discovered afterwards that there had been a fight
among the jury, and they couldn't come to a decision. One of the great
early Bergman films, *Smiles of a Summer Night*, should have won.
Eventually, as a compromise, they gave the prize to *Le Monde du silence*.
So, of course, we got a lot of attention, and the film was doing extremely
well at the box-office.

I was not really concerned about that, because right after Cannes I
started working with Bresson. And then I was asked to go to the States,
which was my first visit there, to film an Italian transatlantic liner, the
Andrea Doria,[8] which had just sunk off Nantucket. So I had a very busy
summer. But already I was thinking of using the lucky break that I had
had with *Le Monde du silence* to try to make my first feature film. That
autumn and winter of 1956 I wrote one of those autobiographical
screenplays – a love story set in the Sorbonne. I did a treatment, took it
around to producers and was turned down everywhere – this was before
the New Wave. Two years later they would have taken it immediately
because it was fashionable, but in those years somebody who had never
directed fiction and wanted to do a personal film had no chance of getting
finance.

Then, in the spring of 1957, my friend Alain Cavalier bought a book
called *Ascenseur pour l'échafaud* from a station newsstand. He read it
and said to me, 'You know, the plot is really interesting. It could be the
starting-point for a *film noir*.' The *film policier* was a genre which had
always been popular in France. I went to see Jean Thuillier, who produced Bresson's film *Condamné à mort*, and said, 'Read this book.
Maybe I could adapt it.' There was something exciting about it – it was a
good thriller. And he said, 'Yes, if we can come up with a cast, and sell it
to a distributor.' I chose to collaborate with a writer whom I admired,
Roger Nimier,[9] a young novelist.

PF: *There was a novel of his published in English which I remember being impressed by,* Le Hussard bleu [The Blue Hussar], *but he was a writer of the political right, wasn't he?*

LM: Yes, but that became more obvious later on, especially at the time of the Algerian war, when intellectuals had to take sides. He was many different things, Nimier. He was a great stylist, a literary critic, a polemicist – and a very good one at that. He was reacting against the post-war left wing that had taken power in France – you know, the followers of Sartre and Camus. You could say his novels were more on the side of Stendhal, but lighter and funnier. I re-read *Le Hussard bleu* recently and it is an excellent book. Nimier was also very important at the publishers Gallimard. He had his office there, and was working as an editor. When he read *Ascenseur* he said, 'This book is stupid.' 'Yes, but the plot is good.' He said, 'All right, but let's start from scratch.' From the beginning, we literally invented what people remember of the film today – the character of Jeanne Moreau. It hardly existed in the book. When you think of it, she's not really necessary to the plot, she just floats around trying to find her lover in Paris. But we made her part of the plot at the end. Once we started working on the adaptation, things went very fast, and we signed Jeanne Moreau. Now people often say, 'You discovered Jeanne Moreau.' I didn't – she was already a star then, a B-movie star. Also, she was recognized as the prime stage actress of her generation. She had been at the Comédie Française; she had worked with Gérard Philipe. But in films she had never come through, except in those B-movie thrillers with Jean Gabin, where her roles were not terribly interesting. But she was a commercial plus. In fact, the distributor insisted that we cast Jeanne Moreau.

PF: *It is a film that helped shape the iconic character that she was to have in the 1960s – in* Jules et Jim *and* La Notte.

LM: Oh, absolutely. Suddenly they discovered that she was potentially a big film-star. Up until then people used to say that although she was a great actress, and very sexy, she was simply not photogenic. I had this great cameraman, Henri Decaë,[10] whom I knew from the early Melville[11] films, like *Bob le flambeur*. I, as well as those in the New Wave, admired Decaë tremendously. He started me, he started Chabrol, and then Truffaut, and then a number of others. But I was the first one of my generation to work with him. When we started shooting, the first scenes we did with Jeanne Moreau were in the streets, on the Champs Élysées. We had the camera in a pram, and she had no light – it was black and white of course; we were using this new fast film, the Tri-X, which serious film-makers thought too grainy. We did several long tracking shots of Jeanne Moreau, and, of course, when the film was finished there was the great music of Miles Davis,[12] plus her voice, her inner voice. She was lit only by the windows of the Champs Élysées. That had never been done. Cameramen would have forced her to wear a lot of make-up and they would put a lot of light on her because, supposedly, her face was not photogenic.

That first week there was a rebellion of the technicians at the lab after they had seen the dailies. They went to the producer and said, 'You must not let Malle and Decaë destroy Jeanne Moreau.' They were horrified. But when *Ascenseur pour l'échafaud* was released, suddenly something of Jeanne Moreau's essential qualities came out: she could be almost ugly and then ten seconds later she would turn her face and would be incredibly attractive. But she would be herself. And, of course, it was confirmed by *Les Amants*, which I did almost right after. So I contributed to making her into a star, but she had already made something like seven or eight films.

PF: *In addition to the innovatory photography, and the risks you took there, you took tremendous risks with the structure. It's as if in* Double Indemnity *Fred MacMurray and Barbara Stanwyck never met. The two lovers, we see them just before the murder is committed – and we think they're together. Then the camera pulls back and he's in his office and she's in the phone box. They never meet and they're never seen together until the very last second of the film, in the photograph which is the ultimate piece of evidence that will send them to gaol. Were you afraid that this might alienate audiences, or had you actually hoped to produce something that was so absolutely chilly in this way?*

LM: As I said, the Jeanne Moreau character was not important in the book, she was just the wife of the man killed in the opening scene. The book – and the film – is about a man who commits the perfect murder, stupidly gets stuck in the elevator of the building, and two kids steal his car, go to a motel outside Paris and commit a murder – all the evidence is that he committed that second murder when actually he . . . well, that was the trick, the gimmick of the book. In the screenplay we extended the plot to his love affair. We didn't want it just to be about the two crimes. As well as somebody else committing a murder with his car and his gun, we thought it would be much more interesting if he was supposed to meet a woman immediately after he commits the first murder, she looks for

3 *Ascenseur pour l'échafaud*: Maurice Ronet dials M for Murder . . .
4 *Ascenseur pour l'échafaud*: . . . Jeanne Moreau answers
5 *Ascenseur pour l'échafaud*: a murderer fakes a suicide

him all over the place, but they never meet. We never thought that it was daring, frankly.

We hesitated a lot, I remember, while we were working on the screenplay, wondering if we should have them meet at some point. We decided not to, except that at the very end there's the scene, one of the best in the film, when she's finally arrested. The photographer is developing the photos and she sees the two of them in love, in the big enlargements in the water, and so they are reunited. But they're never together. For us, that seemed very romantic.

PF: *Quite a number of the themes, situations and characters in your later films are to be found here. The use of jazz music, the random accidental violence (the killings at the motel actually look forward to* Atlantic City*), the fate to which people are subjected, the way in which you use the political background (behind it is the Algerian war), the preoccupied lives of the people involved, suicide, and so on. Do you see all this yourself? Are you surprised to see something so characteristic, when you actually set out to make this cold, detached thriller?*

LM: When I did *Ascenseur pour l'échafaud* I consciously chose to start from this book, which was a thriller, aware that I would have to make something that could be sold to people in the industry as a B-movie. Of course, I was very ambitious, and the fact that I worked with Roger Nimier instead of with the screenwriters that were recommended to me, the fact that I took somebody who was a very respected writer at the time, indicated that I had great ambitions for the project. But if I had had my way, I would have preferred – and if I'd made my first feature three years later I would probably have been able to do so – to have done something more autobiographical. I realize now when I look at *Ascenseur pour l'échafaud* that I managed to inject – because we had the plot, but the plot was like a skeleton – a number of themes that were, probably unconsciously, close enough to me that they would reappear in my work. But I also wanted to make a good thriller. The irony is, I was really split between my tremendous admiration for Bresson and the temptation to make a Hitchcock-like film. So there's something about *Ascenseur* that goes from one to the other. In a lot of scenes, especially inside the elevator, I was trying to emulate Bresson.

PF: *Escaping from the lift is like escaping from prison in* Condamné à mort.
LM: Yes, absolutely. But that was very conscious. At the same time I was

6 *Ascenseur pour l'échafaud:* a confined man fails to escape from his lift
to the scaffold . . .

7 *Ascenseur pour l'échafaud:* . . . meanwhile his lover wanders
the night streets

emulating Hitchcock in trying to do, even if slightly ironically, a thriller that works. The suspense, the surprises. And of course, stylistically, apart from the fact that it was my first film and as such full of clumsy things, I was closer to Bresson. So I was split. On top of that, I was trying to portray a new generation through the characters of the children (in those days they were called *blousons noirs* because they all wore black leather, those kids from the suburbs) – a description of the new Paris. Traditionally, it was always the René Clair Paris that French films presented, and I took care to show one of the first modern buildings in Paris. I invented a motel – there was only one motel in France and it was not near Paris, so we had to shoot it in Normandy. I showed a Paris, not of the future, but at least a modern city, a world already somewhat dehumanized. I was not aware, making *Ascenseur pour l'échafaud*, that I was doing something personal; I saw it almost like an exercise. I did the same thing with *Zazie*. I don't think I realized at the time that there was something in the theme of *Zazie* that was certainly going to be crucial to my later work: the revealing of corruption to a child by discovering the world of adults. Of course, that was Queneau's world and I took it; I didn't know it was mine too.

PF: *I'd like to backtrack to Robert Bresson. What was it you wanted – you felt that you had served half an apprenticeship making documentaries, and you wanted to work with a feature-film director?*
LM: I never really wanted to be an assistant director. With Cousteau I'd started as a technician, a cameraman, an editor, a sound man. I was not really tempted to come back to Paris and pursue a career as an assistant director. The only reason I worked with Bresson was because I admired him. I put him on a pedestal, much higher than any other French director. I had great admiration for Renoir, but Renoir was not working in France at that time. I was lucky enough to meet Bresson through a friend. He liked *Le Monde du silence* and was intrigued by this very young man, so he said, 'Why don't you come and work with me?' which was great. I don't think I would have worked with René Clément[13] – I'm not passing judgement, it's just that I admired Bresson and was convinced that Bresson's was the only way of making films. I've changed my mind about that, but in those years I was pretty rigid about it.

PF: *What was your role on* Un Condamné à mort?
LM: I suppose Bresson found me interesting because I came from a completely different background, a background in documentaries. When

I started working with him he was finishing the revisions of the screen-play and he was seeing people for the cast, so I worked with him on that. Early on he put me in touch with the man on whose wartime experiences the film was based. His name was Devigny. He was a Resistance hero, an officer. Bresson said, 'You're going to work with Devigny, and you're going to prepare all the props and all the details. I want everything to be absolutely authentic; it's going to help me tremendously.' It was shot in the studio, *Condamné*, except for a couple of weeks on location in Lyons for the outside of the prison. But everything else – the cell, the corridors – was a set. I was in charge of the authenticity of the physical appearance of the shooting. I worked on that in pre-production and the first few weeks of shooting, which took place in the cell.

Then Cousteau asked me to go to America for a film about the *Andrea Doria*, so I told Bresson, 'I think I'm going to go because Cousteau needs me and also, frankly, because it's exciting.' It seemed to me that before the shooting started I was useful to Bresson, and his methods of prepara-tion and casting were fascinating and taught me a lot. When he was shooting, I noticed – that's why I never wanted to be an assistant director – that you don't really learn much from a director. The process of making a film, especially for somebody like Bresson, is so mysterious. He was so secretive about his approach. We would do twenty-five takes, and at some point I could see that he was satisfied, but it was hard for me to understand *why* he was satisfied. And so I told him I was going to leave, and he said, 'Well, I'm not going to keep you, I think you're right. I never was an assistant director, I don't think you learn anything from being assistant director, so you must go your own way.' But I kept on good terms with him.

Un Condamné à mort was the beginning of his greatest period. He then did *Pickpocket, Balthazar, Mouchette* and all those great films over the next decade. When I met him he had done only – well, they were great films – *Les Anges du péché, Diary of a Country Priest* and *Les Dames du Bois de Boulogne*. For me he was the ultimate.

PF: *This was the first film,* Un Condamné à mort, *where he used an entirely non-professional cast. Did this encourage you later on to use non-professionals in key roles, and did you learn from him how to handle such actors?*

LM: When I started my first feature, *Ascenseur*, I felt I was pretty much prepared technically, but I had this huge hole in my apprenticeship – dealing with actors. I'd no experience of that: I'd been filming fish for four years! I didn't feel I should take any risks, so the cast of *Ascenseur* was – with the exception of the young girl – entirely professional. I continued that with *Les Amants*. *Zazie* was the first film where I had the central character played by a child. Obviously, I was not going to use an actress. But I was always impressed by Bresson's theories about not using professional actors, although I have never been as extreme about it as he was. I realized fairly quickly, with *Zazie*, that it was great to mix professionals and non-professionals. And I've been doing that more or less ever since.

When I did *Ascenseur* I was scared to death of actors, just because I had no experience of dealing with them. And if it had not been for Jeanne Moreau, who was incredibly helpful in the first two films I did with her – well, I was such a novice, I knew so little about it; in those situations because you're scared – and young! – you tend to be very bossy. You just don't want them to take the upper hand, I suppose. And when I look at my early films I see that I made some gross mistakes, not only in terms of directing them, but sometimes in casting them. But this is part of your education. From my very first film I realized I was probably, of all the directors of my generation – apart from Alain Resnais – the one who was technically the best prepared, but at the same time I had to learn everything else, which in a way was more important, especially the human element. It took me several films to learn. I got more and more interested in this aspect of directing, and as long as all my collaborators knew that I was on top of it technically, I could concentrate on directing the people in front of the camera.

PF: *A final, important point on* Ascenseur pour l'échafaud: *Miles Davis's music. Now it became very common in the late 1950s to have jazz scores – Duke Ellington music for Preminger's* Anatomy of a Murder, *for instance, and the Modern Jazz Quartet did the music for Robert Wise's* Odds against Tomorrow – *but it was uncommon in 1957; in fact I can't think of a film that used jazz in precisely this way. Where did the idea come from, and at what stage? And how did you get Miles Davis to collaborate?*

LM: Well, that was another encounter in my early career. The first one was Cousteau. The second one was Miles Davis. As I told you, I was crazy about jazz, and at the time I was listening a lot to Miles Davis – he was at his most creative. When I was shooting the film it seemed inconceivable to me that I could have a score by Miles Davis, but in the room of the teenage girl, by her bed, there was the sleeve of a Miles Davis album very much in evidence. Then by a bizarre coincidence, when I was editing and was about to make the choice of music, Miles Davis came to Paris. He came on his own, without his usual musicians, to play in a club for something like three weeks. And I literally jumped on him. I got a lot of help from a writer called Boris Vian,[14] whom I knew and who was also a trumpet-player.

PF: *And also the pseudonymous author of a book which the hero of* Le Souffle au coeur *is caught reading –* J'irai cracher sur vos tombes (I'll Spit on Your Graves).

LM: Yes. I owe a lot to Boris Vian. He was the director of the jazz department at the Phillips record company, and Miles Davis was under contract to them in Europe. I called Boris and he arranged a meeting. Miles Davis was reluctant because he didn't have his musicians. He was playing with good musicians in Paris, but not the people with whom he was used to recording. I managed to convince him. I showed him the film twice, only twice. We agreed on the parts where we felt music was needed. And we took advantage of the one night off he had from the club. We rented a sound studio in Paris on the Champs Élysées, and started working, as jazz musicians do, very slowly. We worked from something like ten or eleven that night until five in the morning. In that one night, the whole score was recorded – I think that makes the score of *Ascenseur* unique. It's one of the very few film scores which are completely improvised; I don't think Miles Davis had had time to prepare anything. We would run those segments that we had chosen for music, and he would start rehearsing with his musicians.

The music is ever present in *Ascenseur*, but if you add up how many minutes, it's something like eighteen maximum; it's not that much. What he did was remarkable. It transformed the film. I remember very well how it was without the music, but when we got to the final mix and added the music, it seemed like the film suddenly took off. It was not like a lot of film music, emphasizing or trying to add to the emotion that is implicit in the images and the rest of the soundtrack. It was a counterpoint, it was elegiac – and it was somewhat detached. But also it created a certain mood for the film. I remember the opening scene; the Miles Davis trumpet gave it a tone which added tremendously to the first images. I strongly believe that without Miles Davis's score the film would not have had the critical and public response that it had. I tried in the following years to work with him again, but he had become very difficult and wanted to do it with a whole orchestra, twenty musicians, with arrangements. It could have been very interesting, but it would have meant doing it in New York, and that was beyond the possibilities of a French budget at that time.

PF: *Going on to* Les Amants, *it's almost as if you tried to reverse everything in* Ascenseur. *Stylistically, it is lit in a classical way: there are long takes, elaborate compositions, but done by the same cameraman. You've moved from jazz to Brahms, the Sextet No. 1. You also reversed the situation of the heroine: the Jeanne Moreau character does very similar things, commits adultery, leaves her husband, but she is rewarded by the prospect of happiness. It's also a very warm film, a sensuous, erotic film, whereas the other was very chilly.*

LM: It has to do with the fact that *Ascenseur* was so well received – for instance, the French critics gave me the Prix Louis Delluc, which was a complete surprise – and a commercial success. I could, as the Americans would say, write my own ticket. So I decided to do something more personal, something closer to me. I also wanted to keep working with Jeanne Moreau. I had found an eighteenth-century short story by Vivant Denon,[15] a contemporary of Choderlos de Laclos, someone who was a writer by accident. Later on he went to Egypt with Bonaparte and was one of the founders of the French school of Egyptology. It is one of the many '*contes libertins*' written before the French Revolution, though with a difference. It's about a married woman, a countess who lives a rather boring and cynical life in the country in a castle. And one night, she experiences love at first sight. It's very romantic, ahead of its time. It was called 'Point de lendemain' – 'No Tomorrow'.

I brought this text, which was something like thirty pages, to Louise de Vilmorin.[16] I was interested in working with her because I liked her novels and also because I thought *Madame de . . .*, which Max Ophuls directed from her novel, was marvellous. It was the opening night of *Ascenseur*. I gave her the book, which was in a beautiful little edition of the period that my brother had given me. I said, 'Please read it and call me and tell me if you think it would be interesting to do a modern adaptation.'

PF: *She was a very distinguished, rather grand lady, was she not? So your approaching her as a very young director was rather like your approaching Miles Davis.*

LM: Well, yes. Except that I knew Louise de Vilmorin through Jeanne Moreau. We started working together, incredibly quickly, around the end of January, and I started shooting in May. Today, it seems impossible. But I was very anxious to prove myself, on my own turf. Another reason why I was so interested in this story was because it had similarities with a scandal that had happened in my family. Somebody close to me had left her husband and children for a young man she had met just like that. An instant passion, but as it turned out the ending was not very happy. I cannot say it was autobiographical, but somehow I felt involved in that story. Of course, what I had in mind was a denunciation of the hypocrisy of the ruling class and the way women were supposed to be good wives and mothers and stick to that.

I worked with Louise, pushing her into writing things that I'm not sure she really wanted to write. I didn't intend to make a film that would be considered erotic or scandalous. Eventually it was. But it seemed crucial to understand why this woman decides to change her life completely, how she discovers in this one night something she had no idea even existed: the physical aspect of love, sex. And it happens by accident. As often in my early work, the stylistic approach was almost defined by opposition to the previous film. I was not totally pleased with *Ascenseur* and, in a way, when I was making *Les Amants*, I felt I was much more myself. I chose a way of telling the story with those long takes. There's very little editing. It was also fashionable at the time: Hitchcock had made *Rope* in a sequence of ten-minute takes and we had been greatly impressed. It was also the time when Alexandre Astruc[17] was talking about the *caméra-stylo*. I was trying to find my own style, if you like.

So that's the way I made *Les Amants*. However, I realized later that, weirdly enough, *Ascenseur* was perhaps closer to me than *Les Amants*. *Les Amants* was terribly sincere. I was sincere in the choice of subject and the way I was attacking my own milieu; I felt strongly about the theme and the characters, but I managed to express myself in a style that I don't think was really close to me. I realized that when I was editing it. There's something about those long takes – when you are running the scene back and forth in the editing room you realize you'd like to take out ten seconds here, add fifteen seconds there. You're not master of the rhythm. I've ended up with a sort of *écriture*, a way of writing films with my camera, which I think is much more subtle and supple and much less schematic. I still do some very long takes, but they're mixed with a series of fast cuts.

When *Les Amants* was finished, we went to Venice, and immediately it became this huge international hit, but also a big scandal. I felt at the

time that it was successful for all the wrong reasons. Yet it was an
important film in terms of my career. *Ascenseur* was very well received,
but *Les Amants* was a phenomenon. All over the world the film was
shown, and thought scandalous; in America it was banned in several
states and went all the way to the Supreme Court. So at the age of just
twenty-six I was an international director, suddenly appearing on the
scene. I don't think I've ever been more successful since. It took me
completely by surprise. I had a tough time recovering from it. I was
suspicious sometimes that the success of *Les Amants* was not deserved.
I knew that I could keep making this kind of film for ever and be very
successful, but it was not really what I was looking for. For six months
after the film was released, I went into hiding. I went scouting locations
for a film that I never shot. And when I was in Paris I stayed at home.
I've always been very critical of *Les Amants* and maybe unjustly so.
Today, I get all kinds of reactions to it: some people tell me it's the
most dated of my early films; others love it. If it holds together, it's
because of the sincerity I put into it.

PF: *It contains a fine and beautifully modulated performance by Jeanne
Moreau.*
LM: If only for her, it deserved to be made.

PF: *For the first hour or so it is a sort of social comedy, but then it takes
on a lyrical, romantic tone for more than a third of the film. Was that
always the intention, that it would take that amount of the time, or did
that come in the shooting and the cutting?*
LM: Well, it certainly came in the shooting, because Louise de Vilmorin
objected to that part of the film, so it ended up being vastly improvised;
it was not really written. I think it was literally a couple of pages in the
screenplay. There were two sides to the film, and I suppose if I were to
make it today I would be more capable of integrating the two sides. The
first half is a comedy of manners, a satire on the mores of the upper
class in France in the late 1950s; the second part is almost a homage to
the German romantic painter Caspar David Friedrich. I was very much
trying to make that kind of visual statement: very lyrical, very romantic.
Thanks to Brahms, it took off and became something completely different from the first part. The very end is something that I like because
she leaves with her new lover, they stop to have a morning coffee, and
there is something really pessimistic there. I think there was something
in the voice-over – she says that she's not sure it's going to work, but

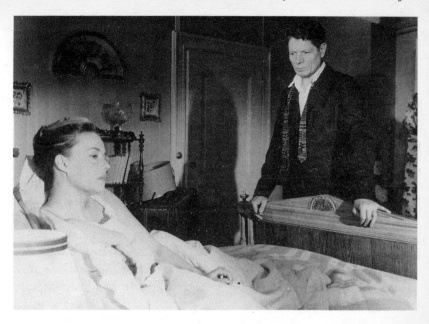

8 *Les Amants:* Jeanne Moreau cools towards her husband (Alain Cuny)
9 *Les Amants:* Jeanne Moreau warms towards her lover
(Jean-Marc Bory)

she's going to do it anyway. I think that was good, I liked that. It was pretty much my world. Today, I would feel close to that.

PF: *And she's still looking at herself, to check her appearance in the mirror, the way that she is in a crucial scene earlier when she nearly has a crash on the road while examining herself in the mirror. There are certain echoes of a film which you mentioned earlier,* La Règle du jeu, *and you cast Gaston Modot[18] in a similar role to the one he had in the Renoir film. In a sense, the boy gets away with what Renoir's young aviator doesn't; he does not play by 'the rules of the game', but he seems to win.*

LM: In those days I would not have even dared to emulate *La Règle du jeu.* I must say the casting of *Les Amants* was much better than *L'Ascenseur.* I'd already progressed. There were some supporting characters that were, I think, quite well cast, and Gaston Modot was wonderful; he was definitely there because of *La Règle du jeu.* For all of us, my generation of French film-makers, *La Règle du jeu* was the absolute masterpiece.

PF: *The painting behind the credits at the opening of the film, what is the significance of this?*

LM: It's something that is important in French literature, and I thought it would set the mood. It's called *La Carte du tendre.* There was a school of women writers in the first part of the seventeenth century, before Louis XIV became king. They were ridiculed by Molière in a play called *Les Précieuses ridicules.* The most famous is Madame de Scudéry, who had a salon. All their writing was about love: what precedes love, love itself, what follows love, all the variations. The first novel in French literature, *La Princesse de Clèves* by Madame de La Fayette, comes very much from that school. It's just a simple love story, but beautifully written. *La Carte du tendre* is like a map, but the names of the villages and towns are Passion, Remords, Jalousie, the rivers and roads go from Passion to Jalousie – it's very bizarre actually, it's a geographic representation of all the variations around the theme of love. So I thought it would be appropriate to have this *Carte du tendre* behind the credits.

PF: *After* Les Amants, *there was a radical change of gear –* Zazie dans le Métro. *What attracted you to the Raymond Queneau novel?[19]*

LM: Originally, it was the challenge. The book came out and I think it

10 *Les Amants:* Gaston Modot (left) turns the same cold eye on the haute bourgeoisie as he did as the gamekeeper in Renoir's *La Règle du jeu* (1939)

11 *Milou en mai:* Paulette Dubost, Modot's flighty wife in *La Règle du jeu*, still in the kitchen fifty years later

was the first and possibly the only book of Queneau's, a great writer, that became a bestseller. The book was extremely funny and it was *the* novel for the whole of that winter. A producer had optioned the book, it was to be directed by René Clément, but I suppose they realized fairly quickly that it was not feasible. Everybody kept telling me, 'Stay away from the book, you'll never make it into a film, it's impossible.' But I loved it.

PF: *It was thought impossible to translate satisfactorily into other languages, let alone make into a film.*

LM: Exactly. I remember saying at an interview at the time that it would take me a good ten years to become a decent director. After my first two feature films I realized that film-making was more complicated than people think, including myself. So I was in a very experimental mood. I thought the challenge of adapting *Zazie* to the screen would give me a chance to explore cinematic language. What was brilliant in the book was an inventory of all the different literary techniques and also, of course, a lot of pastiche. It was playing with literature and I thought it would be just as interesting to try to do the same with cinematic language. I asked my friend Jean-Paul Rappeneau[20] to help me with the adaptation, my production company acquired the rights, and we started working on the screenplay. It took a lot more time than I expected. I used to work very fast in those days.

But *Zazie* was difficult because we were always trying to find some equivalent to what Queneau was doing with literature. I pushed it to the point where a lot of things in *Zazie* are hardly visible; they are so, in a way, Byzantine. A lot of scenes are shot with the camera at the speed of eight frames or sometimes twelve frames per second, but it does not show because the actors play in slow motion. It was easy for Philippe Noiret, a wonderful actor – it was more or less his début on film (he'd just made a film with Agnès Varda) – but it was more difficult for the little girl, who had never appeared in front of a camera before. The result, when it works – and it doesn't always work – seems to function at a fairly normal speed, but things happen in the background three times faster than they're supposed to do. It's exhilarating.

I also attempted things that nobody really ever noticed. For instance, in the scene where the little girl and Trouscaillon are sitting at a table eating mussels, the shot on her and the reverse shot on him have the same background. It was incredibly complicated technically, and when edited it seemed almost normal, except for this anomaly of always

12 *Zazie dans le Métro:* Parisian Uncle Gabriel (Philippe Noiret) picks
up his bundle of provincial trouble (Catherine Demongeot)

having the same background. I thought people would notice and would
laugh. But nobody did. Of course, nobody looks at the background.
What was going on between these two was funny enough to hold the
attention of the spectator. But I realized that it worked extremely well, so
well that I've done it a few other times, when I was in situations where I
thought the background was not interesting. One of Queneau's early

works was called *Exercices de style* – that was what it was for me, an exercise in style, to deepen my knowledge of the medium.

But of course, I was much more involved than that. I suppose with *Zazie* I discovered what has possibly been my main theme in films like *Lacombe, Lucien*, *Le Souffle au coeur*, *Au revoir les enfants*, and certainly *Pretty Baby* too – at the centre of the film is a child, an adolescent, who is exposed to the hypocrisy and corruption of the world of grown-ups. It's very obvious to me now, but I'm not sure I knew it at the time. The end of the film is exactly like the end of the book. From the beginning, when she arrives in Paris, she wants to see the subway – 'Le Métro, le Métro' – but the subway is on strike. Finally, that morning the Métro is no longer on strike, but she is asleep when she goes to the railway station to meet her mother, who's spent the whole forty-eight hours with her lover. They leave, she is at the window of the train, and her mother asks, 'Well, Zazie, what have you done these past two days?' and she says (untranslatable in English, actually), '*J'ai vieilli*,' which means 'I've grown older' or 'I aged.' That is the last line of the book. I used that line in *Milou*, as a matter of fact, for the little girl – a sort of quotation for myself!

PF: *There's never any sense of her as an object of sexual interest, except perhaps to Trouscaillon. Is it that times have changed? You were able to present her in those days as a kind of dangerous Shirley Temple – Shirley Temple as a Puck figure really.*

LM: Well, you could also say she was a sort of anti-Shirley Temple. I've seen a few Shirley Temple films recently because my six-year-old daughter is crazy about Shirley Temple. She's so impossibly cute, whereas Zazie is really this tough-talking, restless little girl who objects to everything she's ordered to do. She terrorizes the adults, which is very funny. But the world she discovers is so chaotic, there's no sense of order or meaning, every character is going through changes. So each time she thinks she understands what's going on, something happens and she realizes it's become something else. And of course, this is pretty close to my own experience. It's something which I've observed over all these years: the world I'm looking at is never quite what it's supposed to be. What was absolutely central to *Zazie*, something that I keep discovering and put into my films more and more, is the fact that people – adults especially – constantly say one thing and do the opposite. The basic lies of our lives. This was, of course, pure comedy in *Zazie*; it was what kept the plot going – she was always lied to by her uncle, by everybody. She could never get a straight answer.

In a way, this film that I took from a book and intended as an exercise ended up being incredibly personal. I found what were to be my themes and obsessions in the future. Of course, the form of *Zazie* is very extreme. I really pushed my luck quite a bit! The last third of the film is not up to the rest because at some point it goes overboard. Even for people who love the film, there is a moment where it becomes repetitious. It works well for one hour, and then it becomes confused. That, I think, is the main weakness of the film. At the same time, I'm happy I had the courage to do it. It was a tremendous flop, you know. People don't remember that, because it became a sort of cult film. Of all my films of that period, it's the one that's constantly playing in Paris somewhere, and for some people now it's become a key film. I got amazingly good reviews at the time. The launching was a big event; the first week we broke records in the theatre. And then it literally died. Audiences were disconcerted and they didn't know how to handle it. Outside Paris it was a disaster. And almost everywhere else.

PF: *It seems it's the only time you deal with a particular traditional milieu of French cinema: René Clair's Paris. It also had an enormous influence, one can see now. It's made in a manner that was later to be called, in the mid-1960s, the 'Swinging London' style, and that's where I think the film may have had a bad influence, on people like Dick Lester[21] or even Karel Reisz in* Morgan. *The New Wave's jokey playing around with jump cuts and speeded-up film became a style that could be applied to anything to give a sort of spurious energy. It had nothing to do with a criticism of society, but became a celebration of consumer society.*

LM: I think it took two or three years before the influence was felt. I remember when I saw Dick Lester's first films, I assumed that he'd watched *Zazie*. Now, I'm not so sure. It's just a form that had become fashionable, and worked very well for young people. It was a very rebellious kind of film-making, anticipating the image of the early Beatles. A few years later young people became consumers, and started buying records, going to movies – 'La révolution de la jeunesse' that culminated in May 1968. So the style of film-making in *Zazie* became fashionable and seemed to correspond to the pop ethos. But, as I've said, in its time *Zazie* fell flat with the public – not with film buffs or critics, but with the public. It was too early. Even today it is very excessive. There were no precautions and I deliberately took big risks.

But I thought it was necessary, for my own sake, to go as far as possible in many different directions, and come back and try to get the best out of it for future films.

PF: *Did this seem to you the right point in your career to turn to colour – was this a subject that seemed to demand it?*

LM: From the beginning I wanted to work in colour. I found it more challenging than black and white, although these days I'm somewhat nostalgic because black and white is so beautiful and it has become almost impossible to work in black and white for commercial reasons. Actually, I wanted to do *Les Amants* in colour, but I didn't have enough money, and the distributor was adamantly against it. It was the very beginning of colour in France. So I gave up and shot it in black and white. That's another thing I want to say about *Les Amants*: I shot it in CinemaScope. It was a format, a size, but it was also a style; it was elegant, but very aesthetic in a sense that I didn't like. I never worked again in widescreen, except for *Viva Maria*. To come back to *Zazie*, it certainly was the opposite of *Les Amants* stylistically. I ended up having a lot more fun with *Zazie* than I had had with *Les Amants*. Although it's a unique film in my work because I never tried to repeat the extremes of *Zazie*, I think it's been very useful to me and it's a film that I cherish. There was something about it that was so adventurous and so wild and so young, and I think it's still a very challenging film to watch.

PF: *This stage we're talking about now, 1959–61, I wonder how conscious you were of being part of some larger movement? I was reading a 1960 interview with Truffaut in which he was talking about the journalistic backlash against the New Wave by the people who had created it, the journalists who had lumped you all together, and in talking about the movement's leaders he included himself, Chabrol, Godard and you. And yet there's a recent book by Claude Beylie,* Les Maîtres du cinéma français, *in which he puts you into a group that precedes the New Wave, a group which he calls 'La Transition', which includes Resnais, Astruc, Melville and a dozen others. How do you feel, looking back on it now?*

LM: It just happened that I was the first one of my generation to make feature films. Just before Chabrol, a year before Truffaut, and I think two years before Godard – but we followed in rapid succession. When I made *Ascenseur* at the end of 1957, there was no such thing as the New Wave, it was all the old structures of the French film industry, and it was very difficult for a young film-maker to break through. Then suddenly there were four, five, six first-time directors. The one thing people always forget to mention about the New Wave – the reason that the New Wave was taken so seriously – is that our first films (or even first two films) were very successful commercially. Suddenly producers discovered that these young men were making films for a quarter of the price of Clément and Becker, and that they were very successful at the box office. So overnight we became fashionable, and every producer in Paris wanted to make films with us. It didn't last very long, because we quickly had disasters at the box office, not so much Truffaut but Chabrol, Godard and me with, as you know, *Zazie*. Personally, as soon as I made *Les Amants* I started producing my own films. I felt it would give me more freedom, and I didn't like producers. So I had my own production company; Truffaut too. I stopped dealing with producers, except a couple of times like the film after *Zazie*, *Vie privée*, but that was more an accident than anything else.

I never was part of the *Cahiers du Cinéma* group; they were all very close, they were friends, they'd worked together as critics, they'd helped each other to make their shorts, then their first features – there was a real tight connection between them. I was never part of this, but I knew them. What we had in common was we loved films, we took film-making very seriously. We wanted to go against what we felt was becoming routine in the French cinema at that time, although some of us were very unfair about the cinema of the 1950s; there were great film-makers in France. I'm not even talking about Bresson – there was Becker; Clouzot was a brilliant director; Autant-Lara made great films. And the last two were really trashed by *Cahiers du Cinéma*. Some of us had to wait. Eric Rohmer made a film in those years which was a commercial disaster, *Le Signe du lion*, and it took him several more years before he filmed *La Collectionneuse* in 1967. Then he would make a film every year. But those of us who were successful at the box office pushed the older generation out, which was unfair. It was like a changing of the guard, in a way. I don't think it had ever happened before, or after, in the history of the cinema that a group of directors in their mid-twenties suddenly broke through and took over.

And it was strictly a director's movement, with a new sensibility. In a way, we were children of this new Kodak film, the Tri-X, because suddenly it was possible to shoot in the street, to shoot in real interiors, with very little light, which means a smaller crew, much smaller budgets, and it gave us the freedom to work infinitely closer to reality than the older generation. The New Wave was a return to what has always been dominant in the French cinema: realism. The paradox is that I worked a lot in the studio in those years. A lot of *Ascenseur*, *Les Amants* and *Zazie* was shot in the studio. But I was an exception among my contemporaries. Another difference is that the generation before us were people who often became film-makers by accident. René Clair had started as a writer and he kept writing all his life. Bresson was a painter and claimed he never watched films. We came to film-making because for us it was the one and only medium, and I think it made a big difference. Our reference was the great cinema of the past; we shared this admiration for Bresson and Renoir, and of course the great Hollywood directors of the 1930s, 1940s and 1950s – the classic period of Hollywood.

PF: *But although you were artistic radicals, with a sense of history, there was no great interest in politics. Indeed, there's been a great deal of misunderstanding about certain* cinéastes: *most people in Britain erroneously believe that Truffaut was a person of the left, which he was by no means. Likewise Rohmer.*

LM: Well, Truffaut might have been sentimentally on the left. But I think that of all of us he was the one who was not really interested in politics. I remember in May 1968 he refused to get involved. I was very interested in politics and I think some of my films took a critical view of contemporary French society – films as different as *Les Amants* and *Zazie*. But I never made a so-called political film. From the time when the Algerian war came to a climax at the end of the 1950s till the French left Algeria in 1962, I was very much against the war and was involved, but I didn't try to translate it into my work. I've always been convinced that militant cinema is almost by definition bound to be mediocre. There are some glorious exceptions – you could mention Eisenstein – and there have been moments in history when film-makers were very much in line with a revolutionary movement. It seems to me that the moment you try to convince or demonstrate, you're bound to do something artistically simplistic. In my work in the following years, if I was involved in political themes as with *Lacombe, Lucien*, I was always interested in exposing the contradictions and complexities – the opacity – of a political situation, rather than taking sides and simplifying in order to demonstrate.

PF: Vie privée – *we know where it comes in the chronology of your work, but how did the film come about? It is partly a biographical film about Bardot, but there was a suggestion that it might also contain some part of your own biography in a way.*

LM: No. I never felt a strong relationship to it. *Vie privée* is one of the two 'accidents' of my film career (the other one being *Crackers*, which I did in the 1980s in Los Angeles). They were, I think, the only two films that I didn't generate. *Zazie* is taken from a book, but it was my own choice to make it into a film; I felt a very strong impulse and some deep connection with the book. I could say the same about *Feu follet*. In the case of *Vie privée*, it was a film project that came to me from the outside.

Zazie had been released for about two months and it was a big flop. It's not that it made me nervous, because I was expecting it. And I was invited by a producer, Christine Gouze-Rénal, to make a film with Bardot, or rather, for Bardot. What they had in mind was a remake of Noël Coward's *Private Lives*, with a screenplay by Henri Jeanson,[22] who had written, for instance, *Hôtel du Nord*. He had been a very good writer, but I didn't feel we were on the same wavelength and I didn't want to work with him. I also suggested we forget about Noël Coward. I thought it might be interesting to try to re-create in the film the strange social phenomenon that Brigitte Bardot had become, the sex object who had become an object of scandal. In her way she was a pioneer of the feminist movement. She was not political, but she had decided to live her life as a man might; to be the equal of men on every level.

PF: *Did you know her at the time?*

LM: I knew her. Of course, every one of my friends told me, 'Stay away from Bardot. Don't make a film with Bardot, you're heading for trouble.' She was said to be very difficult; she had this infamous reputation; she was in the scandal sheets every week; she was like an obsession with the French of both sexes. A lot of women hated her, a lot of men had contempt for her – of course, they were full of lust.

PF: *Simone de Beauvoir wrote a book about her image.*

LM: Yes, it's a very interesting piece. She didn't know her and she made up a feminist heroine. She put Bardot on a pedestal as the symbol of the female revolution. It was never translated into French, because Beauvoir had written it for *Playboy* for a lot of money, and I think she was a bit nervous about the piece, so she wouldn't allow it to be published in French.

PF: *It was called in English* Brigitte Bardot and the Lolita Syndrome.
LM: I remember translating paragraphs of it to Bardot. She laughed and laughed, and said, 'It's nothing to do with me!' But actually it was pretty accurate in describing what Bardot represented at the time – this object of scandal and controversy; Joan of Arc for some, a slut for most. Before we wrote the script we talked to her a lot and used bits and pieces from her life, so it was pretty close to her. We gave her a slightly different background. The screenplay turned out to be a lot more difficult than I expected. But we had a starting date, a deadline, because Bardot was doing something afterwards. So when we started shooting we were not really ready, and the script was not even finished. I was working at night on the ending with Jean-Paul Rappeneau. Since we shot more or less in sequence we could do that, but it was very dangerous. I had almost no time for the casting, so the supporting cast ended up being quite weak.

I was so desperate about the film, so unhappy. Bardot was difficult. I agreed to cast Marcello Mastroianni, who I thought was not the right choice. Marcello is a great actor, but it was not a good part for him, and he knew it. He tried to pull out one week before we started. Then I tried to pull out! He and Bardot didn't get along at all. The film was supposed to have lyrical love scenes between two actors who hardly spoke to each other and behaved like strangers on the set. I remember saying at the time, 'I don't think I'm a good enough director to make it work, to make believe on the screen that people are madly in love with each other when they actually hate each other in real life.' I suppose I might have pulled it off now, though I would probably have fired one of them!

And then we all went to Italy, to Spoleto, for the last part of the shooting, and I said, 'Oh, what the hell, let's have a good time.' And that's when everybody began to relax. The last part is partly improvised, and I started working much more loosely. Because I was a beginner and not completely at ease with the medium, it was the first time I filmed without being tense. I felt I had nothing to lose, it was too late anyway. And that's when things started to happen; my shots suddenly became organic, sensual. I felt suddenly better and the script worked better. It was an important step for me. Many times I've remembered the end of the shooting of *Vie privée* and tried to arrive at this state of grace. Of course, it came from the fact that I had written off the film. When you look at the film today, the very beginning is good, I suppose; it holds together until she becomes a star, and then the end in Spoleto. Somebody told me the other day that it has a Douglas Sirk quality. It functions on a

13 *Vie privée:* Brigitte Bardot commands the attention of Marcello
Mastroianni and Louis Malle
14 *Vie privée:* Malle calls the shots on location in Spoleto

level where lyricism has little to do with reality. I don't know. I really don't know.

PF: *It hasn't been around for a very long time, it's very difficult to get to see it. It is bad that somebody should have the power, or be so indifferent, that they can prevent a work of yours being readily available.*
LM: Well, it was 100 per cent financed by a Hollywood studio, by MGM; they own the copyright. So it goes into a sort of graveyard. I suppose the film is not considered commercial enough to be revived. I have no say about it. I don't think it has ever been put on video. When it opened in the United States MGM thought it was much too slow for the American market and so they cut twenty minutes out of it – the best twenty minutes, of course; those at the end. I was so furious that I considered suing them, but then I gave up because my lawyer told me it was a quixotic enterprise, it would take years and, anyway, American law gives all the rights to the owners and none to the authors.

PF: *It must have been a very happy moment when you put* Vie privée *behind you and moved on to* Le Feu follet, *which I think most people would say is one of your finest films, a film with few, if any, flaws. Is it a film that you take a great deal of pride in?*
LM: Absolutely. *Vie privée* was the first film of mine that got bad reviews – you never get unanimous praise, but *Ascenseur, Les Amants* and *Zazie* were extremely well received. *Vie privée* was blasted by many critics. I was disoriented, it had been an unhappy experience, so I decided to take a sabbatical year. I got involved in what was going on in Algeria; it was my first return to documentary. It was 1962, the year the French gave up Algeria. I went twice. Altogether I spent four months there. And I shot in 16mm. I was not pleased with what I'd shot and never edited it, but I felt the need to go back to the real world.

Also that year, I filmed the Tour de France, the bicycle race. I had a camera and, with two other cameramen, we followed the Tour, and came up with a lot of footage. And I left that alone for a while and went back to Algeria. And then I started thinking about *Feu follet*. Eventually, I think three years later, I decided to put the Tour footage together. I had a first cut of forty-five minutes; I thought it was too long and very difficult to release as such, and I ended up with a short. So that was also part of my 1962, my going back to documentary. *Vive le Tour* was a happy experience, I had a camera in my hands again, and I really enjoyed that.

15 Louis Malle (who gives his leisure interest as 'bicycle racing' in *International Who's Who*) on the road with Pierre Blaise during *Lacombe, Lucien*

16 *Milou en mai:* the gentle Milou (Michel Piccoli) bikes around his decaying estate

PF: *Do you find something exciting and liberating about bicycles and cycling? It does turn up in the background in* Le Souffle au coeur *and the lyrical openings of* Lacombe, Lucien *and* Milou *have central characters cycling, to jazz.*

LM: I do a lot of bicycling myself, I always have, and the Tour de France is really part of my childhood. In *Le Souffle au coeur* (and that's directly autobiographical), at the end, when Laurent's at the spa with his mother, he comes back in the room and listens to the Tour on the radio and falls asleep. The Tour's something that's always fascinated me. So I decided in 1962 just to follow it on a motorbike with a camera. It's a very strange event, not only as a sport but also as a social phenomenon. The whole of France stops for three weeks and now, especially with television, it has become huge. When I shot *Vive le Tour* what struck me was the violence, the suffering – it's probably the toughest sport that exists. So I filmed that: the accidents, the falls, the incredible effort when they climb mountains and how it's seen on their faces. And the circus atmosphere that surrounds the Tour de France, the commercial aspect, the crowds – it's unbelievable. I also dealt with the fact that racers were taking lots of drugs in those days – they still do of course, different ones. I am quite proud of this little film and many times since I've thought of revisiting the Tour de France.

In the autumn of 1962 I came back to Paris after Algeria, and I started writing a screenplay of my own about a young man committing suicide. That was the first step towards what became my next fiction film. The genesis of *Feu follet* is complicated, but interesting, because it says a lot about the way I work. I had read the book, many years before. It was in my parents' library, with other books of Drieu La Rochelle.[24] He had written *Feu follet* in the 1930s and during the war he was a collaborator. After the war when I was a student nobody was reading him. Much as I was interested in a fashionable communist like Aragon, I was also interested in Drieu, the fascist; actually they were close friends. Anyway, when I started my project I didn't think of Drieu and *Feu follet*. A friend of mine had actually committed suicide, and the circumstances were, in a way, very close to the book. Drieu's novel was written about one of his best friends, a Surrealist poet called Jacques Rigaut, who was always talking about committing suicide. The few poems he wrote were obsessed with suicide. As usual in those cases, eventually nobody believed him any more, until one day he killed himself. Drieu was overwhelmed with guilt because, when somebody close to you dies or commits suicide, you think you could have done something to prevent it. So he wrote that book, which is a pretty close description of the last days of Jacques Rigaut. And in 1945 Drieu La Rochelle committed suicide himself.

Now, as I said, one of my friends killed himself under similar circumstances: he told everybody that he was going on a trip (he was a journalist), he said goodbye to them, and then he was found in his room several days later – he'd shot himself. I started writing a variation on this theme, and it was the story of a long night in Paris. It took place in 1962, at the time of the OAS,[24] the extreme-right movement that started in Algeria. They were putting bombs everywhere in Paris. They almost killed André Malraux. So, that was the background to my screenplay. The central character had a drink problem, and eventually at dawn, at the end of a long night, he would kill himself. I came up with a long treatment, but I was not too pleased with it. A friend of mine mentioned *Feu follet*, which he had just read, and I said, 'Oh, *Feu follet*. Yes, I remember it.' So I reread it, and in a matter of days I realized, right or wrong, that I should give up on my own story and use Drieu La Rochelle's book.

Then things went very quickly. I adapted the book myself. It was the first time that I'd written a script completely on my own; up to then I had always worked in collaboration. I decided to do it with Maurice Ronet,[25] and I started shooting. In a way, I was trying to hide behind Drieu La Rochelle and behind Jacques Rigaut and this story which was not mine. But it was actually; I felt very much involved. Also, I'd just reached thirty – and that's always a difficult time. I thought I was not young any more – like Alain Leroy, the character in the book and the screenplay. I *was* Alain Leroy.

I wondered at first if I should do it in the period in which it was written, the 1930s, and then decided I would just set it in the present, in 1962. But my adaptation was fairly close to the book, because the novel seemed to contain everything I felt the urge to express at the time. I shot it in black and white. We had a very small budget.

PF: *Back to the high-contrast black and white of* Ascenseur.

LM: Yes. You know what happened? We actually started shooting in colour, but when I saw the first two days of rushes I was not pleased with them. I thought colour was very distracting for that particular story. So we decided overnight to switch to black and white. We reshot the first two days, and I was very happy, because it's always good to reshoot the first two days. And we continued in black and white. The shooting was a traumatic affair, because the subject matter was extremely depressing. I worked with a very small crew. Everything was shot at real locations. And the whole film was concentrated on the central character, Maurice Ronet.

I remember when I went to see Maurice Ronet, he was shooting a film in Madrid, and I told him, 'Maurice, I am going to give you this part.' He wanted it very much because it was a great part and he felt very close to the character for his own personal reasons. And I said, 'But you have two months to lose twenty kilos, because you're too fat. Somebody who comes out of detoxification doesn't look like you.' Maurice had a drink problem, just like the character, except that he didn't do too much about it. So I forced him to lose twenty kilos, which he did. I don't even know how. When we started shooting he had the perfect emaciated and exhausted face for the part. I think you can say without hesitation that it is the best performance of his entire career. There was a very deep connection between him and the character; he was incredibly moving in that part.

I was worried that Maurice would make the character too soft. I kept thinking about my friend, who was very abrupt and hated anything sentimental, and so was the original character of the novel, Jacques Rigaut. I wanted to give Maurice a hard edge. I kept struggling with him about hardening his performance. This was the first time that I was able really to control an actor's performance. I now knew how to do it during the shooting, and also in the editing, to fine-tune and master a perform-ance. In that sense, it's perhaps the first film where I was really in control. It took me four feature films to investigate and discover and learn. In terms of style, it was with *Feu follet* that I really found what seemed right for me, the best form to express what I had in mind. It's very austere and the camera is unobtrusive. I had a strong script. We were fully prepared, so I felt confident enough to experiment and improvise. The result is a film that, I think, has two qualities that were not in my previous films. First, it is completely personal, deliberately personal, incredibly close to me; second, I started really to control the medium. The film was very well received, and people who had been following my work realized that I'd reached a point where I was really myself. *Feu follet* was the first of my films that I was completely happy with.

PF: *There is in the film a sense of disgust with society, or a particular stratum of society, as well as a terrible self-disgust, which comes to see death as a cleansing process, or a form of salvation, in a way. And yet*

17 *Le Feu follet: soignée* society hostess (Alexandra Stewart) listens to Alain (Maurice Ronet)

18 *Le Feu follet:* back in his room at the clinic, Alain communes with himself

*that is in contradiction to the Catholic idea, which you must have had
implanted in you as a child, that suicide is a mortal sin.*

LM: Well, I remember when I passed my baccalauréat I had one of the
highest grades possible in philosophy. The subject that was proposed to
us was the opening line of one of Camus' most famous books, *Le Mythe
de Sisyphe*: 'Le seul problème philosophique vraiment sérieux est celui du
suicide.' That's how I passed my baccalauréat; I was crazy about that
book, so I knew it practically by heart. It seems to me that with *Feu follet*
I dealt with something that I had been avoiding for years: my background, and this very rigid Catholic education I was given. I was actually
kicked out of that boarding school of *Au revoir les enfants* two years
after because they found notes I'd written saying that I hated God. It was
very childish, but from the age of fourteen or fifteen I started rebelling,
and it seemed I would never stop rebelling. I suppose it was good, but I
had to overcome it and reach a point where I could say, 'This is done
now, I've got rid of it, let's move on.' For me *Feu follet* was very
cathartic.

At the same time, it doesn't really approach the problem of suicide in
terms of sin or guilt. It's an existential film because it just observes the
behaviour of somebody who, in a way, is close to some other characters
of my films – although he is almost thirty he is still very much an
adolescent. You could say that the main reason why he decides to kill
himself is because he just simply refuses to become an adult. For
instance, when he comes out of the clinic after a cure, he goes to visit
his friends in Paris, and eventually starts drinking again. He goes from
one to the next, and every one of them says, 'Look at me, I'm trying to
become an adult, those days are over, this perpetual adolescence, you
cannot live like that any more, you have to become serious, you have to
move on.' It's not that he cannot do it, it's just that he decides that he's
not even interested. So it's almost as if suicide is the only escape, the
only solution. And by doing so, by a strange twist, he knows his death
will be a terrible signal to all his friends that what they are trying to do
doesn't work.

It's a very pessimistic, very dark film, but I think for me it was
completely liberating. It gave me a chance to proceed to other things. At
the same time, as a film-maker, it was the moment where I felt I was
capable of expressing certain things that I had been trying to deal with
before, but not totally successfully. Because I had written the screenplay
myself, I felt that I was completely in charge, that it was all my own
work, that I owned everybody in this chain, going from Jacques Rigaut to

Drieu La Rochelle, to my friend, to me, to Maurice Ronet. I'd made it work as a film and I was not even interested in what audiences would think of it. I remember saying at the time that although the film had to be released, I could almost keep it and not release it, because I'd made it mostly for myself. The strength of the film, and a certain state of grace in the filming, both come from that. Also, this was my first collaboration with an editor called Suzanne Baron. I worked with her throughout the rest of the 1960s and 1970s, and through my American career. She helped me to discover the infinite possibilities of editing – how you can fine-tune the material which comes from the shooting in terms of rhythm, of bettering performance, of going to the essential. This was also something I discovered in *Feu follet*.

PF: *There's a photograph of you and Maurice Ronet attending the Venice film festival for* Feu follet, *and you look like brothers. Presumably, because of the physical resemblance, you almost identified with him in the movie.*

LM: Well, we were very close, extremely close. He played the lead in *Ascenseur pour l'échafaud*, and we'd stayed very good friends. It was a time in my life where I was living by night. I would write or edit until two or three in the morning, then I would go to a club. I was drinking. And that's the way Maurice lived for most of those years. My collaboration with him in the making of the film was far more intimate than I'd ever experienced with any other actor or actress before. There is a scene where he gets dressed in his room at the clinic and everything in the closet was mine. I'd put everything from my apartment in suitcases and taken them to the set. The shirts, the suits, the ties, everything. Even the gun was mine. I almost resented the fact that he was playing the part. But at the same time I knew he would do it well. I think I was very hard on him – he kept saying, 'Louis, let me play the part.' Yes, there was a strange osmosis between the two of us. And then we drifted apart for various reasons. But in those years we were incredibly close.

PF: *If one looks at the Paris films, particularly* Ascenseur, Les Amants *and* Feu follet, *there are some parallels with the work that Antonioni was doing at the same time. You used the word existential – you could also attach it to them. Jeanne Moreau went from your films to appear in* La Notte. *I was suddenly struck, seeing* Feu follet *again, that just as the girl in* L'Avventura *disappears on the island, almost certainly having committed suicide, leaving behind her a copy of Scott Fitzgerald's* Tender is the

19   Maurice Ronet and Louis Malle at the 1963 Venice Festival where
Le Feu follet won the Special Jury Prize

Night, *the last thing that Ronet is doing in* Feu follet *is reading Scott
Fitzgerald's* The Great Gatsby. *Looking back, do you see any way in
which Antonioni's project was similar to yours?*
LM: I remember meeting Antonioni in Paris, a few months after *Ascenseur*, and he said how he had been fascinated by the scenes where Jeanne
Moreau walks on the Champs Élysées, by the way she walks, the way she
moves her hips. He went on and on about that.

PF: *Anticipating the famous walk in the Antonioni films?*
LM: Exactly. Actually I think he had made *L'Avventura* by then.

PF: *No, that was several years later.* L'Avventura *comes in* 1960. *Three
years after* Ascenseur.
LM: That's even more interesting. I thought he had made *L'Avventura*
then. When we went to Venice with *Feu follet* the Italians were crazy
about it. We won the Special Jury Prize and the film was very much in
tune with the sensibility of many Italian film-makers of the time.
     Then, as usual, I went to the other extreme. The shooting of *Feu follet*
had been so depressing. Halfway through it, on a Sunday afternoon in

my apartment in Paris, I was alone and I said to myself, my next film will be a big spectacular. It will be an adventure, it'll be exotic, it'll be a comedy, in CinemaScope, in colour. And I wrote down two pages that are the premise of *Viva Maria*. I had the bizarre idea of putting together Brigitte Bardot and Jeanne Moreau. Little did I know what I was getting myself into.

Notes

1 Roger Leenhardt (1903–85): distinguished French critic and director of numerous short documentaries (mostly on artists and writers). His only two features are *Les Dernières Vacances* (1948) and *Le Rendez-vous de minuit* (1962). He appears in Jean-Luc Godard's *Une Femme mariée* (1964) and has been called (by Claude Beylie) 'the spiritual father of the Nouvelle Vague'.

2 *Monsieur Vincent* (1947): reverential cinebiography (co-scripted by Jean Anouilh, directed by Maurice Cloche) of the seventeenth-century French priest Saint Vincent de Paul starring Pierre Fresnay. Financed by money raised from parishes throughout France (no doubt Mme Malle contributed), it won an Oscar as best foreign-language film.

3 *The Adventures of Baron Münchhausen* (1943): Josef von Baky's fantasy movie (scripted under a pseudonym by Erich Kästner) was a personal project of Josef Goebbels to celebrate the twenty-fifth anniversary of Berlin's UFA studio; it was among the most expensive productions of Third Reich cinema.

4 Jacques-Yves Cousteau (b.1910): French naval officer and oceanographer. He developed such underwater apparatus as the aqualung and from 1951 he commanded the research ship *Calypso*, making documentaries and writing bestselling books.

5 Alain Cavalier (b.1931): French director. He was assistant to Malle, who produced his directorial début *Le Combat dans l'île* (1962). Has since made half-a-dozen features, winning the Jury Prize at Cannes in 1986 for *Thérèse*, co-scripted by his daughter Camille de Casabianca.

6 Michel Mitrani (b.1930): French director mainly for television. For the cinema he made *La Cavale* (1971) and *Les Guichets du Louvre* (1974).

7 Jacques Becker (1906–60): long-time assistant to Jean Renoir and among the few older French directors admired by the New Wave. He directed the first of his thirteen features during the Occupation and in the 1950s made *Casque d'or* and *Touchez pas au grisbi*. His son Jean has directed popular thrillers and another son, Étienne, was Malle's cameraman in India.

8 On 25 July 1956 the Italian liner *Andrea Doria*, on its maiden voyage, sank off Nantucket after a collision with the Swedish liner *Stockholm*. Fifty-one lives were lost, though the Hollywood star Ruth Roman survived.

9 Roger Nimier (1925–64): French novelist and right-wing polemical essayist, best known for his 1950 novel *Le Hussard bleu*, set towards the end of the Second World War. He died in a car crash.

10 Henri Decaë (1915–87): one of the greatest French cinematographers, who worked regularly with Melville and lit the débuts of Malle, Claude Chabrol and François Truffaut. Like the other key New Wave cameraman, Raoul Coûtard, he used lightweight cameras and fast film. After the 1960s he was involved with few films of importance.

11 Jean-Pierre Melville (1917–73): officer in the Free French Army and flamboyant

independent producer with his own studio and a penchant for Hollywood crime films. His movies, especially *Bob le flambeur*, prepared the way for the New Wave and he is the director interviewed by Jean Seberg in Godard's *À bout de souffle*.

12 Miles Davis (1926–91): illustrious, innovative, Illinois-born modern jazz trumpeter, who studied composition and piano at New York's Juilliard School of Music and made his name playing with Dizzy Gillespie and Charlie Parker. He wrote the music for the documentary *Jack Johnson* (1970), but *Ascenseur pour l'échafaud* was his only score for a feature film.

13 René Clément (b.1914): French director who began in documentaries and entered features with *La Bataille du rail* (1946) and *La Belle et la bête* (on which he assisted Cocteau), two of the first important films made in post-war France. His movies include *Forbidden Games* (1952) and the Anglo-French *Knave of Hearts* (1964).

14 Boris Vian (1920–59): French novelist, playwright, poet, translator (of Raymond Chandler, Strindberg, Brendan Behan) and jazz trumpeter. Trained as a civil engineer, he worked for the National Bureau of Standards and was a leading figure in Left Bank circles. A contributor to Sartre's *Les Temps modernes*, he satirized Sartre in his novel *L'Écume des jours* (1947) and is best known as author of the outrageous hard-boiled thriller *J'irai cracher sur vos tombes* (1947), published under the American pseudonym Vernon Sullivan. Like his teenage admirer Laurent in *Le Souffle au cœur*, Vian suffered from a heart murmur and he died of a heart attack in the cinema watching the unauthorized film version of *I Spit on Your Graves*.

15 Dominique Vivant, Baron de Denon (1747–1825): French diplomat, artist, writer and archaeologist. A favourite at the court of Louis XV and Louis XVI, he served abroad in Sweden and Italy and worked as a painter and engraver. His property was confiscated after the Revolution, but his life was saved during the Terror by his friend Jacques-Louis David. He subsequently accompanied another friend, Napoleon Bonaparte, on the expedition to Egypt and on his return became director-general of museums. *Point de lendemain* (1777) is his only work of fiction.

16 Louise de Vilmorin (1902–69): French novelist and poet, noted for her witty, elegant style, skilful plotting and knowledge of upper-class life (her second husband was Count Paul Palffy). Several of her books were filmed, most notably *Madame de . . .* by Max Ophuls in 1953.

17 Alexandre Astruc (b.1923): Influential French critic, documentarist and independent film-maker with a small *oeuvre*. *Best known for a 1948 essay in L'Écran français* in which he coined the term '*caméra-stylo*' ('camera-pen') to advance the idea of a cinema that would 'become a means of writing just as flexible as written language'.

18 Gaston Modot (1887–1970): French actor, painter, friend of Picasso and Modigliani, his remarkable fifty-year career in the movies included appearances in Buñuel's *L'Age d'or* (1930) and Renoir's *La Règle du jeu* (1939) as the gamekeeper. The gamekeeper's flighty wife was played by Paulette Dubost, who appears as Milou's mother in *Milou en mai*.

19 Raymond Queneau (1903–76): avant-garde novelist, mathematician, philosopher and editor of the Pléiade encyclopaedia. An early associate of the Surrealists, he carried on the tradition of Alfred Jarry as a creator of the College of Pataphysicians, into which Boris Vian and Louis Malle were inducted. His fiction involved linguistic invention and verbal games of a Joycean kind – the opening of *Zazie dans le Métro* (1959), his most popular book, makes sense only when read aloud. He worked on the screenplays of two remarkable movies, Clément's *Knave of Hearts* and Nicholas Ray's *Bitter Victory* (1957), and appeared as Clemenceau in Chabrol's *Landru* (1963).

20 Jean-Paul Rappeneau (b.1932): a screenwriter and collaborator with Malle, he has directed only four films since his striking 1966 début, *La Vie du château*, a daring comedy set in Occupied France. His epic *Cyrano de Bergerac* (1990) elevated him into the forefront of French film-makers.

21 Richard Lester (b.1932, Philadelphia): in London after extensive American TV experience, he worked with the Goons (directing *The Running, Jumping and Standing Still Film*) and helped create the 'Swinging London' cinema with the Beatles' films *A Hard Day's Night* (1964) and *Help* (1965). Since then he has alternated between quirky small-scale pictures, such as *Petulia* (1968), and anonymous blockbusters like the *Superman* series.

22 Henri Jeanson (1900–70): this one-time actor and film-critic was among France's most prolific screenwriters, working with most of the leading directors of the classic era, including Julien Duvivier on *Pépé le Moko* (1936) and Marcel Carné on *Hôtel du Nord* (1938). He directed one film, *Paname* (1950). As a critic he was among the first antagonists of the *Cahiers du Cinéma* branch of the New Wave.

23 Pierre-Eugène Drieu La Rochelle (1893–1945): a native of Paris, he survived the trenches of the First World War in a state of shock, and his subsequent career as novelist, short-story writer, poet and essayist reflected his inter-war engagement with Catholicism, pacifism, Communism and Fascism, coupled with recurrent doubts about his own sexuality. During the Second World War, as an ambivalent Nazi-sympathizer, he edited the *Nouvelle Revue Française*, all the time attempting to intervene on behalf of the racially and politically persecuted. In 1944 he went into hiding and committed suicide in April 1945. *Feu follet* was published in 1931.

24 OAS: initials of the Organisation de l'armée secrète, founded in 1961 following the failure of the Generals' Revolt against de Gaulle to establish an Algérie Française. Violently active in France and North Africa for some eighteen months, it died out after Algeria received its independence.

25 Maurice Ronet (1927–83): this handsome son of an actor and actress had established himself as a romantic leading man of the stage and screen before appearing in Malle's *Ascenseur pour l'échafaud*. Like the character he played in *Feu follet*, his finest film, he had a drink problem. He became, for a while, a star of international co-productions, and directed two feature films, *Le Voleur de Tibidabo* (1965) and *Bartleby* (1978). His last major appearance was as the gang boss in Bob Swaim's *La Balance* (1982).

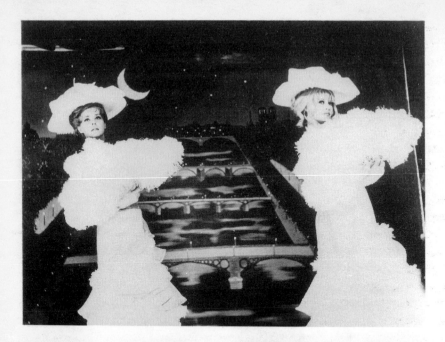

20 *Viva Maria:* Brigitte Bardot and Jeanne Moreau bring down
the house
21 *Viva Maria:* Jeanne Moreau and Brigitte Bardot
mow down the enemy

CHAPTER 2

Time Past, Time Present

PF: *Was* Viva Maria *as much fun to make as most people think it is to see?*

LM: No, it was not. It was so hyped by the French media. I've always shot my films in complete isolation. There isn't usually even a press release. I try not to talk to anybody until the film is finished. When I got on the set on the first day of shooting there were something like seventy journalists. Not only the French press, but the American press, the Italian press – it was ridiculous. In the months before we started they'd built up this rivalry between Moreau and Bardot; there were rumours in the press that they hated each other, which was completely untrue. They presented it as a duel between the two – 'Who was going to win?' – which of course was not what the film was about at all. It was about friendship – a kind of rivalry, but based on friendship. So, it created an almost unbearable atmosphere, and shooting was very hard. Something I've experienced a few times is that when you have a big budget, you have less freedom because, eventually, you find out that big as the budget is, it's not enough. It didn't matter if a film like *Feu follet* went over schedule because it was not expensive. But when I was shooting *Viva Maria* we had so many different locations all over Mexico, we had a huge crew, the logistics were impossible. Jeanne and Brigitte would take turns getting sick. We had to reschedule constantly. But writing the screenplay with Jean-Claude Carrière[1] was great fun.

PF: *How did you come into contact with him? He wasn't particularly well known in those days.*

LM: He had worked with Pierre Étaix[2] and he had just co-written *The Diary of a Chambermaid* with Buñuel. Well, Buñuel had become one of my great favourites, too, and I got to know him when I was scouting locations in Mexico. And because I'd liked the script of *The Diary of a Chambermaid* I met Carrière and invited him to help develop my synopsis. But I didn't go into *Viva Maria* right after *Feu follet*; I needed a breathing space. So I approached the producer of *Cinq Colonnes à la Une*, a very good monthly news magazine on French television – the producer was a famous French journalist called Pierre Lazareff, who was also the director of *France Soir* and an important character in the history of the French press. I went to see him, and said, 'I want to do something for you.' He said, 'All right.' This is also typical of the bizarre way in which I work – I said, 'I'm going to go to Vietnam.' It was when the American Vietnam war was getting very serious, and it just happened, by coincidence, that I arrived two days after Prime Minister Diem was assassinated. Immediately it was as if there was one camera per square foot; the whole of the world's press converged on Saigon.

I stayed one week with my television crew, and I realized that I was not a news journalist. So I took everybody next door to Thailand where nothing was happening, except that it was the backstage of the Vietnam war. And I decided to do this little twenty-minute film about a country where nothing was happening and which was not in the news. I just completely improvised, and tried to capture certain aspects of Thailand. Though journalistically it was utterly uninteresting, I wanted to show that everything is interesting. So it was partly a demonstration, and partly a personal quest, which eventually helped me when I went to India years later.

Then I had agreed to stage an opera for Gian Carlo Menotti at the Spoleto Festival. Because I'd shot *Vie privée* at Spoleto I had got to know Menotti, and he said, 'You've got to come back and do something for us.' I said, 'Why not?' because I like music. He said, 'Would you like to do the *Rosenkavalier*?' So I went to Spoleto for something like two months, and I directed *Rosenkavalier*. My assistant was Volker Schlöndorff,[3] which was very helpful because the opera is in German and my German is practically non-existent. And I had Jean-Claude Carrière with me, so I was rehearsing with the singers and I was working on the script of *Viva Maria*, which might explain the somewhat theatrical side of *Viva Maria*.

PF: *It's interesting that it should have been started in Italy, because in some ways it anticipates a particular vogue of a couple of years later for Italian-made Westerns.*
LM: I didn't think of that, that's funny.

PF: *The plot of* Viva Maria *is very close to the one used some years later by Sergio Leone for his last western* Giù la testa![4] *about an IRA explosives expert politicizing a Mexican during the revolution. Which is rather*

like the Bardot figure with Jeanne Moreau. Was there any model? Did
you show Jean-Claude Carrière certain films? Some Westerns come to
mind, particularly George Cukor's Heller in Pink Tights,⁵ *which has*
something of the same visual quality and the idea of a theatrical company
travelling around the West.

LM: Like many others of my generation, I'd been a great fan of American
cinema of that period, the 1940s and 1950s. Of course, the Western was
a very cherished genre for us. My idea was to put two women in a
situation where in Hollywood films it's always two men, two buddies – I
think the best example was *Vera Cruz*.⁶ And when I first discussed it with
Carrière, I said to him, 'You remember *Vera Cruz*?' and he said, 'Of
course.'

PF: *A favourite film of Sergio Leone, who was an assistant to Aldrich in*
1961, and they shared a credit on Sodom and Gomorrah.

LM: We thought it could be fun to put Bardot and Moreau in the same
situation as Cooper and Lancaster in *Vera Cruz* and to do a pastiche of
those buddy films. We started from that. Both of us realized that a very
important part of our childhood had been those turn-of-the-century
magazines published in books, like *Le Monde illustré* and *Le Journal des*
voyages. They were in my family's attic, dozens of them. I still have some
of them, as a matter of fact. And they had these beautiful engravings. For
instance, there were stories of adolescents lost in the Amazon, with great
illustrations of children in the jungle surrounded by all kinds of dangerous animals. These images had been the stuff of our childhood fantasies,
so we looked at these books again; took our inspiration from them.

   The problem I had with *Viva Maria* during the shooting stems directly
from that: trying to combine an evocation of childhood fantasies with a
pastiche of traditional adventure films. Not surprisingly, what happened
was it became a big Scope film. I was carried away, and this pastiche of
an adventure film eventually becomes *really* an adventure film, with an
enormous number of extras. And it lost a bit of its bite. Some of it is very
funny; in a way, it has certain aspects of *Zazie*, some of the absurd gags,
but it was never meant to be realistic – more a projection of the imagination. Ideally, I was hoping the spectator would see it with the wonderment of the child I was when I was looking at those books. But it turned
into something else; floating between genres, it was trying to do too
many different things. So when it came out, it got a lot of flak for that
reason. As I said, it was a big budget, a big French budget, and I think to
make those sorts of films you need more – more money, but essentially

more time. I ended up having to rush because the logistics were difficult, and we had all kinds of problems – not just with the stars, but with the Mexican government as well.

PF: *I think the musical numbers come off well. They do play together on stage extremely well, and it's often the case that music-hall duos hate each other off-stage. There are comic variations on two preoccupations of your more serious films, which is to say Bardot gets the job as Moreau's partner as the result of seeing the other half of the act commit suicide – you must have been worried about how people were going to take that. And the other is anti-clericalism, which is indeed what under-cuts what you might think the more serious part towards the end: anti-clerical jokes, for instance, when the dictator is reinstated as the result of Church intervention, partly because they can't stand competi-tion from women; opening up the old Inquisition dungeons and finding that the instruments of torture don't work any longer. I think probably that goes on too long, that torture sequence.*

LM: Yes, some of the gags were thin, but I saw it again recently, after all these years, and enjoyed it – more than I expected. It was very successful commercially, except in the US, where it flopped. In the socialist countries, the picture was incredibly well received. It was taken as a metaphor for Stalinism; Fassbinder explained to me once that at Berlin University they were fascinated by the film. It was at the time of those radical student movements, and they saw in the heroines the two different approaches to revolution. Bardot is action – 'Let's do it', armed struggle, terrorism. The other one, Moreau, tries to achieve her goals legally, to change society without violence. This was, of course, way beyond my expectations of how it would be perceived.

But in terms of the evolution of my work, it was a bit of a regression compared to *Feu follet*, because of all the unfavourable circumstances that I've told you about. I was not completely in control, and I had to finish a scene absolutely since the whole show was supposed to move to the next location. Every day Henri Decaë and I would be the first ones on the set, and we would look at the sky, which was desperately blue – the very hard light was a problem for the girls. Ideally, we should have been able to shoot early morning and late afternoon, but we always ended up shooting the main scene with the sun right at its zenith. I always had to adjust and compromise. Actually I had a better time with the screenplay than with the shooting of the film. When we were writing it, I had great ambitions. What I was trying to do was more complicated than it looked like when it was finished.

It's one of my films that I wish I could remake, because I know it could have worked much better. For instance, there was something that didn't work – partly to do with the script, partly to do with casting. I thought it was quite funny to make George Hamilton into Jesus Christ. But the irony was not perceived, and I don't blame the spectators. They took his character quite seriously. We were in a very dangerous area: it was comedy, but it was easy not to perceive it as comedy. For instance, there was a scene where Jeanne Moreau was declaiming (her character was such a ham) to the Mexican peasants that speech from *Julius Caesar* – 'Friends, Romans, countrymen'. The humour didn't come through. And I have to blame myself, because it was not quite clear what it was about. It was funnier in the script than it was in the film. The audience either didn't get it or took it seriously. That's the danger of pastiche. It's a very risky genre. Yet if you see it today, *Viva Maria* has great moments. It is funny and inventive and the two girls are excellent. I wish it could be re-released.

PF: *The humour is consistently ruthless and surreal. Presumably, you found that Carrière was on your own wavelength.*
LM: Oh yes, completely. You know, although it works better, I had a little bit of the same problem with *Milou*. A lot of people took *Milou* much more seriously than was intended; it was deliberately not realistic, with the appearances of the dead grandmother, for instance.

PF: *In* Viva Maria, *one recalls the suicide; the knife-thrower putting the knife through the boy; the bishop at the end having his head blown off, walking along holding it. This was deliberately provocative I suppose, and very black.*
LM: Not only did I see the film again, but I reread the screenplay, and if I was to do it again I'd have an even bigger budget or – much better – I would make it on a smaller scale, because of the humour and the ferocity of some of the jokes. At one point before the shooting, when both actresses and their agents were being very difficult, and I thought I was going to lose them, or one of them, I got fed up and suggested to United Artists, who were financing it, that we switch to the English language and do it with Julie Christie and Sarah Miles. They were really exciting young actresses, and not yet stars. I think it would have worked better but the UA executives didn't want to hear about it.

PF: *Did you supervise the American release version, or did you just leave it to someone else?*

LM: They thought that it was going to be a big commercial hit in America and they decided to go for dubbing. They opened it in English with very mediocre dubbing. I was supposed to supervise it, but I was very unhappy with the voices – especially the actress who dubbed Bardot – and I lost control.

It failed completely when it opened in America. They had Brigitte Bardot come over. She was very big then. I remember the opening night. They had publicized that she was going to be there, the sex symbol of the 1960s, and there was a near-riot outside the theatre. All this hoopla didn't help the picture. Fortunately, it worked very well in the rest of the world. When I look back on *Viva Maria*, I can see that, once more, I could not resist a challenge: I was the only one who could put Bardot and Moreau together in a film and make it work. I would never do it again, much as I like them. It transformed the film into something else.

PF: *Was it by accident that you moved on from* Viva Maria *to* Le Voleur *– is there a connection between the two films?*

LM: I had a two-picture deal with UA and I wanted to move on after *Viva Maria*. Because of all the nonsense that surrounded the film I wanted to do something else quickly. So, I took some time off in New York, toyed with an American subject for a while, then decided it was time to deal with an old project of mine – adapting *Le Voleur*, which had been published, completely unnoticed, at the beginning of the twentieth century. It was discovered by André Breton and the Surrealists in the 1920s, and republished in the 1950s. I'd read it at the time and was fascinated by it. I think the central character is very close to the author, Georges Darien, whose life is mysterious. He was close to the anarchist move- ment, which was so important in France at the turn of the century. They were determined to destabilize the bourgeois order through terrorist actions, like throwing a bomb into the Chambre des Députés. In order to raise money for the cause, many had become professional thieves, and it seems that Georges Darien was one of them. This would explain why the book is so well documented about the various techniques of burglary of that time – like the different ways of opening a safe. The hero of the book, Georges Randal, comes from a very well-off family. At the begin- ning of the story his parents are already dead so he is an orphan; he is raised by his uncle, along with his cousin, who turns into a very pretty girl; they're very much in love with each other. The uncle steals all of

Randal's money, inherited from his parents; by various devices, he manages to make all the money his. So, when Randal reaches twenty-one and asks for his money the uncle explains there is none left; he does it very cynically. Randal wants to marry his cousin, but he is turned down because he is poor. The cousin is engaged to some half-wit from the aristocracy – for the uncle it's social advancement. Randal steals all the jewels belonging to the fiancé's family. So, it's more or less an accident, out of a sense of justice and revenge, that he becomes a thief. I loved the way the character was set up, the irony of the early scenes of the book.

PF: *There are two classic themes here of nineteenth-century literature – the lost inheritance and the gentleman-thief.*
LM: The gentleman-thief – absolutely. And, actually, a lot of people think that this character and this book, although it got little attention when it was published, influenced people like Maurice Leblanc, who created Arsène Lupin, and Hornung, who invented A. J. Raffles. This young man, this dandy, becomes a professional thief. He has a lot of fun doing it, but then, little by little, he gets addicted. Both in the book and the film there is a classic confrontation with another famous thief who has just escaped from Devil's Island. In the film the character was played by Charles Denner, who tries to convince Randal to join their movement, to become political. But Randal refuses. It's a beautiful scene that comes directly from the book. Darien knew extremely well what he was talking about; it was certainly autobiographical. Randal explains that he is a thief for personal reasons. For him it is a sort of solitary pleasure, almost sexual. And like Don Juan, his life is a relentless, never-ending quest. He describes the moment when he breaks a safe as almost like an orgasm.

The book was huge, almost 500 pages, and we had some problems in getting a screenplay out of it. *Le Voleur* is the last book I adapted. Ever since, all my scripts have been original. Well, until the one I am doing now – until *Damage*. I felt comfortable working with Jean-Claude again; he has an impressive knowledge of the Surrealists and the nineteenth-century literature that precedes the Surrealists, and we had the same admiration for the book. Furthermore, I had my own personal reasons. When I reread the book I identified with Georges Randal. I had reached a certain point after ten years of directing and I thought I could use the book as a metaphor for what had happened to me. I could not help comparing Randal the thief to Malle the director. We both came from a conventional, affluent background and broke with it out of rebellion, anger, and the desire to take revenge and shatter it. Of course, then

22 *Le Voleur*: Jean-Paul Belmondo
23 *Le Voleur*: Louis Malle

follows an adventurous romantic life, lots of women, success, money. The society you rejected acclaims you, and you find yourself back where you started. The irony of the book is that at the very end Randal has *everything*. He's got his revenge. He's married to his cousin, he lives in his uncle's house, he has recovered the money that had been stolen from him, plus the money he stole from others. In one of the last scenes, his cousin tells him, 'But you don't have to steal any more,' and he says, 'You don't understand!' He has to keep doing it, knowing that at some point he'll be caught. In a pessimistic, desperate way, he's trying to be faithful to his youth, and also he is hooked, he is addicted, he has to do it.

We built the structure of the film as a huge flashback. In the opening scene we see Randal forcing the door of a big house. He starts breaking the glass cases and gathering *objets d'art* and, as he begins telling his story, he opens a beautiful eighteenth-century writing desk using a crow-bar. The first line of the narration came directly from the book: '*Je fais un sale métier mais j'ai une excuse, je le fais salement*' – My work is dirty work, but my excuse is I do it dirty. It was very strong, breaking this precious rosewood thing – rrrrrrgh – almost unbearable. I remember friends of mine said they had to close their eyes, as if they were watching somebody's throat being cut. It's a series of flashbacks, returning a few times to the present, to his systematic raping of the

24 *Le Voleur:* Louis Malle shooting with (right to left) Vincent Malle,
Elizabeth Rappeneau (Continuity), and Juan-Luis Buñuel
(First Assistant Director)
25 *Le Voleur:* the thief at work

house. It's like a night of love, of violent and debauched sex, as he fills
his bags with *objets* or rips out paintings just leaving the frame, cutting
with a razor, doing it in a dirty, brutal way. And at the very end you see
him at dawn in this little town outside Paris carrying what he's stolen,
and getting on to the train – there's something desperate about him.

PF: *Did that UA deal make it necessary to have an actor of international reputation, of Jean-Paul Belmondo's stature?*
LM: Well, it worked the other way. The moment I told them I would
cast Belmondo, I didn't hear from them until the film was finished.
Carrière and I thought it a perfect part for Belmondo, who was at his
peak then, the number-one French film-star. I was interested in
Belmondo playing against type, against that cinematic image derived
from *A bout de souffle* – that low-life, streetwise persona. Actually
Belmondo's father was an academic sculptor; he had a very bourgeois
education. So I said to him, 'Maybe it would be interesting for you at
this point to play something that you've never played, a dandy.' I don't
know if he ever read the book, but he liked the idea. So I came back to
UA and said, 'This is it. I'm going to film this exciting book called *Le
Voleur* and I'm going to make it with Belmondo.' Green light: they gave
us complete freedom.

We had a fairly big budget, and unlike *Viva Maria*, the money is all
on the screen. Of all my films, it's the most lavishly produced; for
instance, we had a vast number of sets because he was breaking into
numerous houses, and I wanted to establish that the bourgeoisie of the
period – not unlike during the 1980s – was showing off its wealth: the
walls were covered with paintings and the houses crammed with *objets*.
Visually, it was part of the metaphor that he was trying to destroy this
wealth, but in the process he was being reclaimed because he was
becoming wealthy himself. At the end, in this London house where he is
living before he comes back to his cousin, he has become a hostage to
his wealth.

PF: *Making it in period, this could mean that the middle-class audience
would feel less personally threatened than they would had Randal been
a contemporary burglar breaking into their own houses, threatening
their own property.*
LM: Yes, maybe. But the story was so much part of that period. There
were many political aspects in the book, and in the film. I remember we
had this corrupt politician who goes to his constituency in Normandy,

and delivers an aggressive, right-wing speech at a banquet. Many people felt the speech was over-written and too much of a caricature, when actually it was taken directly from a speech of a politician of that time – literally word for word. If I had made it contemporary, I would have lost the anarchist Charles Denner character, and the uncle's crazy declarations about wealth and money and ownership. There was this frightening line at the beginning when Randal is a little boy and he bites his nails, and the uncle tells him, 'Don't bite your nails. Your nail is your property, you must not touch your property. If you must bite nails, bite somebody else's nails.' Darien was so fierce and sharp.

The film was not very well received and even today people don't think of it as one of my important films – but for me it is not altogether different from *Feu follet*, and I always look at it as something very personal. But because it's a period film, maybe because it was so well produced, many critics thought of it as just a costume film. Maybe it had lost some of the bitterness, although it's very much there; for instance, in the uncle's death scene. As you said, because it was a period film, I don't think people felt as threatened as I wanted them to feel. One of the best French critics, who died a few years ago, Jean-Louis Bory, the critic of *L'Observateur* and somebody who liked my films, gave me a negative review. The headline of the review was 'Louis Malle has put a bowler hat on his camera.' I guess the timing of the film was off. It came out one year before May 1968. They wanted militant films. Everyone was a Maoist then.

I care deeply about *Le Voleur*. For me it was the end of this first period of my film career. What I did afterwards came out of my own confusion. I agreed to do an episode in a three-part film of Edgar Allan Poe stories, *Histoires extraordinaires*, with Fellini and Vadim. My private life was in a shambles then, and I wanted to get away from Paris. I was afraid that, like Randal, I was being reclaimed. I wanted to run away.

PF: *One last thing on* Le Voleur. *There is an anti-clerical element in it – was that in the novel?*
LM: Oh, yes, definitely. The novel was very anti-clerical. One of the crucial characters in the book is a priest, with a comic name, l'Abbé La Margelle. He is introduced as a friend of the family of the cousin's fiancé. Then little by little you understand that he is a thief himself, not only a thief but a fence. The thieves would bring him their loot and he would sell it. He is an extraordinary character, lucid, cynical, and

26 *Le Voleur:* Randal approaches the scene of the crime

27 *Le Voleur:* Randal (Jean-Paul Belmondo) with the extraordinary
fence, l'Abbé La Margelle (Julien Guiomar)

moving. In his last scene, he suggests that he is sending all this stolen
money to the missions in Africa and is thinking of retiring to a monas-
tery; he has this beautiful conversation with Randal in which they talk
about their dreams.

PF: *The way that you describe him, it's almost as if you warm to him,
admire him.*
LM: Oh, very much so. I love many of the characters in the book, not
only the central character, but the others. And, best of all, there was a
great collection of women. We had to reduce it, because the book is huge.
We ended up with six great women characters: thieves, *femmes du
monde*, women from bourgeois families who were helping thieves
because they needed money and their husbands would not give it to
them. Then there's the wife of a Belgian banker who falls in love with
Randal, tries to blackmail him, and ends up as a high-class prostitute.
The part was played by Marie Dubois who was just wonderful.
  In *Le Voleur*, one of the things I'm very proud of is that it's probably,

up to *Milou*, the best ensemble casting I ever put together. There was a series of great supporting characters. On that level the film is close to perfection. It's the first film where I spent most of my pre-production time in casting; I knew enough about actors and what I was looking for to make the right choices. It's one of the things that are most difficult for a director, and it takes you a long time to learn how to do it – not directing the actors but the actual choosing of them, which I think is at least 50 per cent of the final result. When you get your casting wrong, you're in serious trouble. But it's a great joy when you've made the right choice, when you see a group of actors working well together.

PF: *Is that because they know why they're cast? Bresson, as I understand it, does not explain to people why he has chosen them for a role – he has his personal reasons. They become, well, not dehumanized, but almost like objects in the way he directs them. Presumably, if you have the right actor in the right role, you can then let him or her take it over and make a contribution even to the script at certain stages.*

LM: Yes. I must say this is the point where I part company with Bresson or Hitchcock, my old masters. They are of the school of directors – and there are many of them much less talented than Bresson and Hitchcock – who see actors as objects. Actors or non-actors, for that matter. Bresson calls them his *sujets*, his 'models': take that position, move your right arm up. A little more. Good! Don't move now. I remember once having a discussion with him and saying, 'I don't think they're *sujets* for you, I think they're *objets*'. He protested, 'No, no, it's like painting, they're my *sujets*. They're what I film.' It made me think of Cocteau. They had a similar sensibility, in many ways. The same voice, too.

A couple of years ago on a music programme on French radio I heard a conversation with Darius Milhaud, going back to the 1950s, and I realized that the way Milhaud talked was very close to the way Bresson talks, to the way Bresson's characters talk. And it suddenly struck me that it was a certain intonation, or absence of intonation – a flat, very articulated, expressionless way of speaking the French language. I think it has a lot to do with the intellectuals and artists of the 1920s. Bresson must have kept that in his ear, as if that was the way normal people speak. At the end of shooting *Un Condamné à mort* he spent nights in a sound studio with François Leterrier, his main *sujet*. Bresson has always done a lot of post-synchronization, a lot of looping to get the perfect intonation, and in this case, he forced Leterrier to repeat the same line for something like three hours in front of the microphone. Bresson had him repeat and repeat and repeat it until he found the perfect pitch, *le ton juste*. For us, it was very mysterious, and somewhat nightmarish.

In my collaboration with actors and non-actors over the years I have tried to make them more and more a part of my work. I reached the conclusion with *Le Voleur* that, after all, my interpreters were in front of the camera and I was not. From the moment I say 'Roll' and 'Action', they are alone in front of the camera and all of us, the technicians, are on the other side in the dark. It's only fair to love them, to help them. I think film-acting is a very dangerous occupation; there's this moment of truth when they are in front of what is, strangely enough, called in French *l'objectif* – the lens, the glass eye. It's very scary. A couple of times I've been asked to act in films for friends of mine, and it's given me a chance to realize how scary it is and how lonely you are up there. So you have to choose them well, work with them, prepare them, help them as much as you can. You have to tell them what you want precisely, but at some point they have to take charge and take responsibility for their characters. And that's the way I've been working more and more. Although in the 1970s I started to make some of my films, *Lacombe, Lucien* for instance, with a cast most of whom had never seen a camera before, I still kept working that way. For me, the Bresson method is too autocratic. I am not the kind of director who imposes his vision tyrannically.

PF: *So the more confident you are, the less tyrannical and autocratic you are likely to be.*
LM: In my case, yes. As I told you about *Ascenseur*, or *Les Amants*, when I was not confident I would boss everyone about. But I realized very quickly that actors need all the help they can get. There is a scene in *Les Amants*, one of Jeanne Moreau's great moments in the film, where she starts laughing. She arrives late at her country house where both her husband and lover are waiting. It's a very embarrassing situation. And she starts laughing. She cannot stop laughing. She goes upstairs to her room to change and starts laughing again. That long take in her room where she had to laugh, then try to stop laughing, then start laughing again was, of course, very difficult for an actress to do. So we did it again and again. I was not happy. At some point in the middle of a take she stopped and she said, 'Well, do you think it's easy to laugh when I see the two of you behind the camera looking at me with this sinister expression?' – the two of us being Alain Cavalier and myself.

When I did *Le Voleur*, it was the first time I had an almost perfect cast, so I let them really take over their characters. I wanted them to be happy, to be responsible.

PF: *During the 1960s there was a great vogue in Europe for – they're mostly international co-productions – portmanteau films, three or four stories by different directors. Almost every major director was involved in one or more of these projects. You must have had offers to take part in such ventures from as far back as 1960. How did you come in 1967 to accept the invitation to take part in* Histoires extraordinaires?

LM: There were a lot of these in France and Italy. They call them *films à sketch*: that is, five or six directors each do a segment of fifteen or twenty minutes. I always turned them down, although I was tempted a couple of times. Because I'm fairly slow, it's hard for me to make more than one film every two years. I am happy to take time off between films. So it seemed to me if I was to get involved in one of those productions I would be very frustrated, because it would be only part of a film, which would not really be mine. I was under the impression, right or wrong, that it would take me just as much time as a full-length work, and so would not be worth it. Also you must understand that these segment films were a great producer's scam: you gather together a lot of famous directors; they bring stars; each works a week; it's very cheap. Of course, the producers would present them as a sort of *exercice*, and would ask you to do them for ridiculously small budgets. Godard and Truffaut made a few of them. But the way I work it seemed that it wouldn't be good for me.

But during *Le Voleur* I had a crisis in my personal life, and in my professional life as well. I remember we were shooting in the Saint-Maurice studio and I was setting up a tracking shot with Henri Decaë (that was my last work with him, and I must say Decaë's photography in *Le Voleur* is near perfection, one of his two or three great works) and I said to Henri, 'Do you remember, Henri, I don't know how many years back, something like eight years, in 1958, on the same sound stage, pretty much at the same place, we were putting down rails for a tracking shot for *Les Amants*?' And he said, 'God, you're right, it was this stage, yes.' I said, 'You see, all these years and we've come back to where we started.' It was something to think about. It scared me. I felt a lot like my character, Randal. I was beginning to repeat myself. And what did my future hold? Becoming one of the major French directors, making films one after the other.

I decided I had to shake everything up, question everything. I did not

28 *Le Voleur:* Randal becoming part of the Establishment
29 *Histoires extraordinaires:* William Wilson (Alain Delon), the man
split from himself

want to keep making a film every eighteen months or two years. I did not want my work to become routine. I over-reacted in a way, but I felt it very strongly then. And I still do today. So, when Alain Delon called me and said, 'Will you participate in this series of three films?' at first I refused. I knew that Vadim was going to make one with Jane Fonda. I was not too pleased about that; Vadim was not someone I greatly admired. But the third one was meant to be directed by Orson Welles. And I felt I had to leave Paris, quickly. So I agreed. I had *carte blanche* provided I used one of Edgar Allan Poe's short stories. I reread Poe, and I found the story of 'William Wilson'. The main producer was Italian, the main money was Italian. I suddenly said, 'Well, OK, I'll do "William Wilson", I'll do it with Alain Delon, but I want to do it in Italy.' And then things moved very quickly. I ended up spending half of 1967 in Italy. It was like *Vie privée* or *Crackers* – something that came to me, that was not mine, a producer's film – except that, in this case, it was one-third of a film.

PF: *It's a great story, though.*
LM: It's a great story. But I was in a strange mood: dark, very dark, suicidal. I had a terrible time with Delon, one of the most difficult actors I ever worked with – probably *the* most difficult actor I ever worked with.

PF: *What was the nature of the difficulties?*
LM: Well, he's always had this reputation. Delon, like a number of male actors, especially a number of American male stars, basically resents being directed. Very soon after that he became his own producer and started bossing everybody around. Also, I had great doubts about Delon's sincerity and talent. So we started having arguments and it became very difficult. I was irritable; I was basically very uncomfortable. I kept wondering, 'What am I doing here?' Of course, I should never have agreed to work under these conditions, although I liked the story of the double which is central to 'William Wilson'. When the film was released, a friend of mine, an analyst, told me, 'You are in a period of change, a period of doubt, you had great identity problems, so it's not surprising that you ended up dealing with a story of a man who has a double.' But I was certainly not consciously aware of that when I chose the story.

Basically, I didn't much enjoy doing it. I liked being in Italy. I got tremendous help from my Italian cameraman Tonino Delli Colli, who later worked with me on *Lacombe, Lucien* and was one of the cameramen, with Decaë, Sven Nykvist and recently Renato Berta, who have been really important in my work. He's a great, underrated cameraman.

PF: *You framed Poe's tale as a confession made to a Catholic priest by a Protestant. Was this a way of preserving a sense of the original English setting and the northern idea of the* Doppelgänger – *something we find especially in the literature of Scotland, Germany and Russia?*
LM: I did the adaptation with an American, Clement Biddle Wood, and a French novelist, Daniel Boulanger, and we tried to keep the character as someone who came from a Nordic country. For production reasons it had to be made in Italy and part of the original story does take place there. We made it in Bergamo, a most austere town in northern Italy, to keep it closer to the world of the original.

PF: *Presumably switching the crucial card game between Wilson and an English aristocrat to a game between Alain Delon and Brigitte Bardot came about as a result of the production package and to give the story a greater sexual edge?*
LM: Well, of course, we had to have stars, any stars! I wanted to cast Florinda Bolkan, who was very beautiful, very enigmatic and hadn't then worked in films. But she was unknown and the producers did not want her. After we'd started shooting they came to me and said, 'What about Bardot?' I'd heard that Bardot was away somewhere on a cruise and was so convinced that she wouldn't be available that I said, 'Sure, why not?' However, she'd had a row with her boyfriend and come back to Paris, and she said, 'Oh, I'd love to work again with Louis and with Alain Delon.' So I was stuck. I tried to do what I could – putting her in a dark wig and so on. But it was terrible casting, unforgivable. But somehow, the casting of Delon worked – because the anger he had against me served the character – and I made sure I kept him angry all the way through!

PF: *There is also in* William Wilson *one of your recurrent preoccupations – suicide. In this case as a philosophical proposition. One side of Wilson destroys the other, though you make this less ambiguous than it is in Poe's story.*
LM: The whole thing was far less ambiguous than I'd have liked it to be. The script was so-so and my direction was completely unfocused. Luckily, in addition to working with a superb cameraman I met a great Italian editor, Franco Arcalli, who collaborated with Bernardo Bertolucci (he

died just after editing *1900*). He was also a writer. I'd shot too much footage, as you do when you're not happy with what you're doing, and I had a difficult but very creative time editing with Arcalli. I learnt quite a lot from him. He understood that, given this forty-minute film and its subject, it had to be very unsettling and never at rest. We broke up the scenes and that's what I remember most from the film.

PF: *Anyone seeing* William Wilson *now will be struck by the treatment of Wilson at school – the way this early section anticipates the school sequences in* Le Souffle au coeur *and particularly* Au revoir les enfants *– the way children are paraded, their dress, their behaviour in the winter playground, the activities in the dormitory. You were drawing on your own experiences at school?*

LM: Definitely. This was the part of the shoot when I felt the most comfortable, on familiar ground. It was easy for me to imagine these scenes and I ad-libbed them, using my personal memories. The conflicts between the boys and the rough discipline – it was something I'd never dealt with before; it was the first time I dealt with my childhood. I recently saw the movie on late-night TV in America, where they show it from time to time. I turned on at one o'clock in the morning, just as the Vadim episode was ending and I watched mine and Fellini's, and realized that I'd put more of myself, on an unconscious level, into that film than I appreciated at the time. There is something about this character, Wilson, undergoing a deep crisis, that echoes the character in *Feu follet* – but in an overly operatic way, which was my mood at that time.

In the autumn of 1967 I was asked by the French Ministry of Foreign Affairs to present in India a series of eight French films, including *Feu follet* – films more or less representative of the new French cinema. And I said yes. So I went to Delhi and Calcutta and Madras and Bombay presenting those films. I was supposed to stay two weeks but I ended up staying almost two months. I was so amazed by India – it was my first trip, but I had always been interested in Indian religions. I knew India would be a shock, but it was much more so than I expected. After those two months I realized that although India was impossible to understand for a foreigner – it was so opaque – yet I was so completely fascinated by it that I would have to come back. So I returned to France at the end of 1967, and in a couple of weeks I raised the money I needed, which was almost nothing, and went back in early January with two friends of mine – a cameraman and a sound man. My proposition was that we would start in Calcutta, look around and eventually shoot. No plans, no script, no lighting equipment, no distribution commitments of any kind.

PF: *Had you done a great deal of preparation before you went, between the first visit to India presenting these films and going back with your crew? Had you made contacts there, had you read a lot, had you an idea of what might come out of the experience, or did you just lay yourself open to it with the camera? Presumably you had to get permission to shoot in many places – the Indians can be rather difficult, can't they?*

LM: The Indian bureaucracy has always been a nightmare, and they are very suspicious of foreigners. When I went the first time, it was on an official mission. I had a camera, but I hardly used it. I was looking, listening, smelling. Presenting those French films was the perfect pretext; it gave me a chance to meet people – for instance, spend a lot of time with Satyajit Ray. He took me to his studio in Calcutta and showed me several of his films that had not been released in France. I also met a number of westernized intellectuals and artists and, like a good Frenchman, I tried to understand Indian culture and Indian religions rationally. Of course, in a matter of days I realized how silly it was. Indians have such a completely different approach to everything – for instance, how they deal with death. The Indian way is the opposite of our Judaeo-Christian tradition. At this moment of crisis in my life, when I was trying to re-evaluate everything I had taken for granted so far, India was the perfect *tabula rasa*: it was just like starting from scratch.

So I decided to immerse myself in India, the real India, not the westernized one, and see what would happen – and do it with a camera. The result was like being brainwashed. When I came back, I said, 'After six months in India you're not even quite sure that two plus two is four.' Everything in India – their way of life, relationships, family structure, spiritual needs – is so opposed to what we in the West are used to and take for granted, that living there constantly provokes your mind, and your heart. So, instead of wasting my time trying to understand, I decided that we would just drift around India and let things happen. The climax of our trip was the two months we spent in south India. Nobody in Paris or Delhi knew where we were. We had a van and a driver who could speak the five languages that you have to speak in south India to find your way around. From Madras we started drifting from temple to temple, from village to village. Little by little, we acquired a different perception of time. For the first time in my life I found some kind of peace. I started letting go. I felt incredibly well in this environment, which was unknown to me and so different. There was something about the relationship of Indians to nature that I felt was so organic and so true. Of course, I knew there was no way one could become Indian or Hindu – that's ridiculous. A lot of Westerners were trying to do that in those years.

PF: *You're very sceptical about those Westerners who were trying to do that. Early on you meet two Frenchmen, and then later on you meet them again, and in a sense as a result of their naïvety they have become cynical wrecks. Later there are people who are not as severely affected; neverthe-less, they are presented in an objective but somewhat sceptical manner for the way they've embraced India at a rather comfortable ashram. They're not genuinely absorbed in the local culture. The earlier figures may be thought to have turned up much later in your work as the two flower children, survivors of the 1960s culture who come to Atlantic City.*

LM: Yes. Well, actually, that ironical evocation was John Guare's idea. He said, 'Let's have those characters as a sort of quotation from your cinematic past.' I never felt I would ever belong there, but as an observer I was fascinated. It was a permanent challenge to a lot of preconceived ideas that I had accumulated since childhood.

PF: *Also preconceived ideas you had about documentary. The major change from ten, twelve years before, between working with Cousteau on Le* Monde du silence *and this, is the change both of the available equipment and also of the perception of what a documentary is through* cinéma-vérité, *the way it is presented, the relationship between the film-maker and his subject matter and the people he observes. L'Inde fantôme begins the series with an essay, as it were, about documentary, or La Caméra* impossible.

LM: The first two months I was in India alone. I had a 16mm camera with me, but I shot very little. And I had no sound. I went back with the skeleton of a crew, three of us – the cameraman was Jacques Becker's son, Étienne, who was a specialist in this type of *cinéma direct*, and Jean-Claude Laureux, a young sound man who stayed with me and has worked with me ever since, including on *Damage*. He is also one of my best friends. During those four months of shooting I had not the faintest idea what I was going to do with the material. I thought vaguely that at best I could make a feature-length, hour-and-a-half documentary about 'my trip to India'. But very quickly I forgot about that; we just kept filming when it seemed necessary or pleasurable or interesting. When I was shooting I was never thinking, 'Well where is it going to come, how does it relate to something I did yesterday?' No, we were just shooting at random.

When I first discussed my plans with Étienne and Jean-Claude, I said, 'I just want to immerse myself in India, be there, and eventually shoot.' For about two weeks, before we went to Calcutta, we stayed in a village about 100 miles north of Delhi. I thought it was important to start in a village, because it is still the essential Indian social structure. After a couple of days, Étienne Becker rebelled. He said, 'I don't understand what you want, Louis. I cannot work that way. Tell me what you want.' I said, 'I don't know what I want.' And then we started shooting scenes in the village, around the wells. We found out that the wells defined the caste system, in the sense that women from the same caste or sub-caste always went to the same wells – I'd found the invisible borders of the Indian social system.

And Étienne said, 'But they're all looking at me, it's not right, tell them not to look.' I said, 'Why should I tell them not to look at us since we're intruders. First, I don't speak their language; just a few of them speak a little English. We're the intruders, disturbing them. They don't know what we're doing, so it's perfectly normal that they look at us. To tell them not to look at us, it's the beginning of *mise-en-scène*.' It's what I resent about so many documentaries where film-makers arrive from somewhere and start by telling the people, 'Pretend we are not here.' It is the basic lie of most documentaries, this naïve *mise-en-scène*, the beginning of distortion of the truth. Very quickly I realized that these looks at the camera were both disturbing and true, and we should never pretend we weren't intruders. So we kept working that way.

Then we went to Calcutta, and filming in Calcutta was very difficult. We were shooting in the streets, and sometimes twice a day we would be arrested because they would think we were Pakistani spies! There was a lot of tension in Calcutta about the neighbouring state, with what has become Bangladesh but then was Eastern Pakistan. Because there were border incidents, people were suspicious and so we always ran into trouble. Or else middle-class Indians would come to us and say, 'You're shooting in the street; of course you're Westerners and you want to shoot the poverty in India.' Well, if you shoot in the street in Calcutta, every morning you do find people lying on the ground and they're dead; they died during the night.

The first few days we were walking around with cameras it took us a while to find – I don't know – the innocence, I suppose; to deal with the reality as it was, and not try to distort it or interpret it, but just be there, and film it. Little by little it became a way of life. And my two friends started enjoying it. I'm not saying it became a method, because it never was in any way systematic. But we would go into temples and we would shoot or we would not shoot – sometimes they didn't want us to shoot and then we would not. Or we would be in a religious festival, and there was something about it that pushed us to film. Sometimes we would film a lot of footage in a matter of hours, and then we would not work for several days. It was completely improvised. We were sort of witnesses, but we never pretended that we were part of it or even understood it. Very quickly we felt very good about being there; we thought it was really doing something to us. We could have continued filming for ever. There was no reason to stop. It's just that at a certain point – it was the beginning of the hot season and we were physically exhausted – we decided to stop.

I was not sure I wanted to go back to France. I stayed one week after my two friends left, and I thought of going back to France to look at the footage, because I had not seen one foot of what we had shot, which was also part of the experience. We had shot something like thirty hours of film. I wanted to look at it, and then eventually return to India. What happened was, I came back and it was the beginning of May 1968. The whole of France was on strike, including the film labs, so I had to wait for weeks before I could start looking at the footage with Suzanne Baron, my editor. It took us through the month of July. And we didn't know what to do with it. Suzanne suggested that we start trying to put together all the Calcutta footage. We'd shot it in three weeks, and at least it was all Calcutta. So we edited Calcutta into a feature documentary. We'd shot in 16mm, we blew it up to 35mm, and it was released theatrically in 1969.

As far as the rest of the footage was concerned, my attitude was that if I wanted to be completely honest with the material, what I had shot had to be shown. If I cut out a lot of stuff for this reason or that reason in the editing process, I would be abiding by conventional rules, and trying to build an artificial rhythm that was not the rhythm of the experience we had in India. Of course, out of the thirty hours, ten to fifteen hours, say, were repetitious, or something that we'd started and given up on, or the material was really not interesting. So we selected and came up with about half of what I had shot, and we started from that. After we'd made *Calcutta*, which was an hour and forty minutes, we decided to do a series, which of course was meant for television, because it was too long for the cinema. And we tried vaguely to structure it as a series of six (which eventually became seven) films. I had made an agreement with French television, and the standard length in those days was a little under an hour – fifty-two minutes or something like that. So I ended up editing more than eight hours out of my thirty hours of rushes, so the ratio was about three to one, which is very unusual in documentaries; it's sometimes a hundred to one, or at best ten to one.

I thought it was also part of the experience that we would more or less follow our itinerary – not our geographic itinerary – it would have been a simple travelogue – but the itinerary of our emotions. In the narration I kept constantly coming back to the fact that I had not understood a thing about India. Each time I thought I'd understood something I was proved wrong. A good example was a religious ceremony in a little temple near a village, and after the ceremony the faithful were giving money and food to the beggars. But when I talked to them afterwards I realized those beggars were not really beggars, they were Brahmins. They were members of the higher caste, the priest caste, and were, by Indian standards, quite well off, but it was part of the ritual to give money and food to the Brahmins. We Westerners thought we were filming beggars and actually it was something else. It was typical of what always happened to us in India; we thought we were filming a reality and behind this reality there was another one. The truth was always more complicated and devious. So, I never pretended, 'This is eight hours of India, I am going to explain it to you' – I did exactly the opposite.

PF: *But two premises are established, one by implication, one directly, in the first film. First, you're not much concerned with the British legacy, though where that does come up, it's handled very critically. The other is that, after an opening montage of highly articulate Indian intellectuals, you reject the idea of India being mediated to you by westernized Indians. Were they conscious decisions, or was that something that came out in the way you presented the material?*

LM: It was a conscious decision because I realized very early that there were two vastly different Indias. There was this élite: Anglicized middle class by definition – people who would speak English, many of them would send their children to schools in England or to universities there. These Indians – although they came from different castes – were the ruling class, the politicians, the bureaucrats, the people on top of the economy. What these people had to say was very ambiguous and somewhat insincere because they were caught between two cultures. What I immediately noticed was that they were extremely uncomfortable. Many of them, not all of them fortunately, but many of them, were aggressive or very dubious and sometimes made fun of what we were trying to do: 'You're going to come up with these stereotypes again. It's always the same story when Westerners come to India, they just don't get it.' Which, of course, was true. But I realized that if I wanted to see the real India, then these people were not the people that I should be dealing with.

So my original statement at the very beginning of the series – the introduction to the first film, *La Caméra impossible* – was to say that 99 per cent of the Indian population don't speak English, but this 1 per cent is the people who always talk for the rest of the Indians: they rule India, and I would rather not deal with them. For instance, when I interviewed political leaders in Calcutta – whether they were Communists or right-wing – they had the same kind of double-talk, trying to accommodate both their Indian and Western backgrounds. This language was not the language of the truth. It's probably the reason why I got so much flak for those films, especially from Indians abroad – in England, America and France. The films were never shown in India. Many of the ruling-class, Anglicized, middle-class Indians resented my films – because they were about an India they knew nothing about. And by stating at the beginning that I was not interested in dealing with their kind, they were the ones who gave me a lot of trouble when the films were released.

The interesting aspect of those documentaries for me was that I took one month just to examine the material, and then stayed in the cutting room for a year, until the end of 1969 practically. I was in Paris, I was going to the editing room every day and it was as if I was still in India. It was the continuation of my trip. Just looking at my images and remembering what happened, I discovered certain contradictions that I had not even noticed. I had a couple of Indian friends in Paris and I would show them a scene and they would give me their explanation. Sometimes two different friends would give me two different explanations – India, it's so complicated! So I was deepening my experience of India by just watching what I had shot, and trying to make sense of it. I can almost say that I spent six months in India, plus one year in the cutting room, so it's like almost two years of my life, completely immersed in India. Plus the fact that after that I had to present the films and talk about them, and I was involved in this controversy. It's been like a big chunk of my life. It was enormously important for me, and I'm still trying to make sense of it today.

PF: *There were different levels of response. There are, for example, sections which I think may have proved later to be controversial politically – the authoritative account of the situation of the Untouchables; the sections about the problems of tribal minorities and their treatment. There is another area, entirely personal, examining your own reaction. But there was a third area, which is a great problem in this kind of film, where you find and present things which may or may not be metaphors or representative, but because of their great power they are often the most impressive parts of the film. In this latter category there's the unforgettable scene of a dead buffalo being picked over by dogs and vultures, and you say, 'We see this as a tragedy in a number of acts.' Now, when you filmed this – it seemed to have some meaning which you later came to understand or could have interpreted in quite different ways, but it must have been just visually very striking at the time.*

LM: This is a very good example of our *démarche*, of how we proceeded. In India you know they don't kill animals, cows or buffaloes, because they are sacred – well, it's more complicated than that. But, anyway, if you drive on Indian roads it's almost routine to see a dead cow or a dead buffalo on the side of the road and hundreds of vultures. I told my two friends, 'At some point we have to film it.' And it just happened that one day we stopped and we spent half an hour just filming what we'd seen many times before.

PF: *There's a savage beauty about it.*
LM: Of course, for us it was incredibly striking. My reaction was that what struck us would probably not strike Indians. It seems incredibly dramatic for us when for the Indians it is just the cycle of life and death – animals die and the vultures eat them. Everything is part of a whole. You see it in all aspects of life. So it's not so noticeable. But for us it was very striking because of the savage and dramatic beauty of it. Or was it our imagination? Was it the way we shot it? I don't know.

For me as a film-maker it was an extraordinarily liberating experience shooting these documentaries. *Le Monde du silence* was a very prepared kind of documentary. I don't want to say rehearsed, because there were real accidents like the death of the whale and the sharks, but essentially it was a reconstituted documentary. When I was shooting in India, what I

30 *L'Inde fantôme:* Louis Malle and his crew observe vultures at work
on a buffalo
31 *L'Inde fantôme:* Louis Malle observes a village artist at work

discovered was the incredible freedom of being there and finding myself in front of something happening that I was curious about and shooting it. And then we would try to understand what we had shot. We had no time to organize the shooting, or decide whether we would choose this angle rather than that, or how we were eventually going to structure the scene in the editing – this was a moment when I worked completely by instinct, by reflex. One of the interesting aspects of this editing period was for me to look at the material and say, 'Why did I shoot it that way?' The only thing I might do was to tell Étienne, 'To your left, the little girl to your left,' and he would pan to her – he's a remarkable cameraman.

I think this experience of relying on my instincts was quite decisive in my work. When I went back to fiction, I've always been unconsciously, and also very consciously, trying to reinvent those very privileged moments. I've always tried to rediscover the state of innocence that I found so extraordinary working in India. Of course, it doesn't always work that way, but since then I have made a number of films with children and adolescents, and have always tried to give them the freedom of expressing themselves, trying to let them loose, rather than trying to boss them around – seizing those moments when they were free, when they were themselves – for these privileged moments will always bring to the screen something completely different. I was able to accomplish that when I did documentaries in the following years. But even in my fiction work I think I've been enormously influenced by what I discovered in India.

PF: *When you put together* Calcutta *and the* L'Inde fantôme *series, although the films are critical, they are manifestly sympathetic and fair. Were you surprised by the hostility – the Indian reaction in the West, and the reaction of the government of India itself?*
LM: I have to tell you, it was unexpected. *Calcutta* was released in France and certain other European countries in cinemas – it even went to the Cannes Festival in 1969 – without any extreme reactions from the Indian community in France. There was criticism, but it was subdued. The trouble arose a couple of years after – I remember precisely because I was shooting *Le Souffle au coeur* when the series was broadcast by the BBC. I had been to London before I started *Souffle*. They put me on a sound stage in a BBC studio and they had me narrate the series in English. They gave me a hard time because they thought I had this frightful accent, a horrid combination of French and American intonations. I was more bossed about than I've ever dared do with an actor! It took a whole

week! Horrible! Anyway, we did that very carefully. In making the
English version I improved aspects of the films. We fine-tuned the editing.
We had had this contract with French television and were rushed by our
deadline. The English version is a little better: the sound is better; my
narration is better. I incorporated some changes as a result of the reactions I got when the films were shown on French TV. So, I was rather
pleased with myself.

They started running the series and opened with *Calcutta*. Immediately
there was a storm of protest from the Indian community in England. The
BBC received hundreds of letters. And then the Indian High Commis-
sioner moved in, I think only because of the violent reaction from Indians
in England. And it became a huge diplomatic affair. The Indian government officially asked the BBC to stop showing the films. The BBC
refused. Then they expelled the whole New Delhi BBC bureau, something like fifty people! There were also stormy debates in the Indian
parliament. Members of the Opposition seriously asked for the government to start proceedings for my extradition. It was grotesque. My films
made headlines in the Indian newspapers for weeks. But, as I said,
nobody had seen them in India.

PF: *It's almost like farce preceding tragedy, rather than the normal
Marxian way – like this farce preceding the tragedy of Salman Rushdie.*
LM: It was incredibly intolerant. When the BBC finished showing *Calcutta* and the seven films of the *L'Inde fantôme* series, they asked me to
come over. I flew to London late on a Saturday afternoon, leaving the set
of *Le Souffle au coeur*, completely exhausted. They took me from the
airport to the BBC studio, and here I was, live, after they had shown the
last one, in front of six Indians, who started attacking me fiercely. An
Indian friend of mine in Paris had called me and said, 'Among the people
that are going to be on this panel is a woman who is probably going to be
the toughest on you. I want you to know that she is the daughter of the
Prime Minister of Orissa, one of the Indian States, and this Prime
Minister has just been deposed and is going to be on trial for corruption.'
It was interesting that this woman should attack me for misrepresenting
India. It would have been a cheap shot to mention her father and answer
her on that level, which I didn't do, but it gave me confidence to know
that the whole thing was so biased. One of them was actually on my side,
saying that what was expressed in those films was an immense love of
India, a profound interest and a great deference.

I believe what you see first in those films is my admiration for Indian culture and religion – so different from ours – and my wondering if in many ways it is not better. Anglicized Indians would tell me, 'All you've been filming is beggars.' I said, 'Well, if you're filming in India, what do you do, chase away the beggars? They're all over the place.' I did only one sequence about beggars, and in that sequence, as I've said, I found out they were actually not beggars. Many beggars in India are just people at the end of their life who go on these big tours from temple to temple, and they expect to be fed; it's part of the social structure and religion. Somebody else told me, 'You've not been showing the great achievements of modern India like our nuclear plant outside Bombay.' I said, 'I was willing to film that' – actually I was very curious about the nuclear plant, but I never got permission because it was secret and I was turned down. 'Why didn't you shoot the Taj Mahal?' I said, 'Every tourist who goes to India shoots the Taj Mahal. It was not on my itinerary.' It was all like that.

Those films were eventually shown in the States and became cult films; they were shown on public television, and also in small cinemas in university towns. And many people told me that watching my films they got so curious about India that they went there. So I think I deserve a medal from the Indian Ministry of Tourism! Indira Gandhi was in charge then, and a friend of mine who had helped me in Calcutta, Vijaya Mulay, a remarkable woman, who is a specialist on education and was at some point in Indira Gandhi's inner circle, tried to organize for Indira Gandhi to see the films. She said, 'I'm sure she'll like them, she'll understand what they are about.' That was just when the war with Bangladesh started, and of course Mrs Gandhi had other things to do than watch eight hours of my films! So that was the end of it. They were never shown in India.

I went back to India in the early 1980s when Candice was playing the part of Margaret Bourke-White in *Gandhi*. The day after I arrived in Bombay, on the front page of one of the English-language papers, the *Indian Express*, there was a piece, 'Louis Malle is back' – it was like I was still Enemy No. 1! It became so bizarre, because journalists started coming to the set of *Gandhi*. So I had to talk to them and say, 'Look, no cameras. I just came to see my wife.' In the following years it became really difficult for foreign film-crews to work in India. Of course I've always felt bitter about the fact that those establishment Indians took my films so badly. It surprised me, but it could have been expected and I should have known better.

Notes

1   Jean-Claude Carrière (b.1931): one of the most accomplished and prolific screenwriters of the past thirty years, he worked with Buñuel on seven films as well as his auto-biography. His other scripts include *The Tin Drum, Swann in Love, The Unbearable Lightness of Being, The Mahabharata* (for Peter Brook) and *Cyrano de Bergerac*.

2   Pierre Étaix (b.1929): painter, actor and assistant to Jacques Tati on *Mon oncle*. He co-directed two shorts (*Rupture, Heureux Anniversaire*) with Jean-Claude Carrière, who also worked on the scripts of the feature-length films Étaix directed.

3   Volker Schlöndorff (b. Berlin 1939): after studying cinema in France he worked as an assistant to Malle on *Zazie, Vie privée, Feu follet* and *Viva Maria* before returning to Germany to make *Der junge Törless*, which Malle co-produced through his NEF company. He collaborated with his wife, Margaretha von Trotta, on several films and in 1978 won an Oscar for *The Tin Drum*.

4   *Giù la testa!* (1971): Sergio Leone's final spaghetti Western (a.k.a. *Duck You Sucker* and *A Fistful of Dynamite*). In 1914 in Mexico an Irish explosives expert (James Coburn) draws a local bandit (Rod Steiger) into the revolution.

5   *Heller in Pink Tights* (1960): light-hearted romantic western (the only essay in the genre by George Cukor) starring Anthony Quinn and Sophia Loren as the leaders of a troupe of travelling players on the American frontier in the 1880s.

6   *Vera Cruz* (1954): Robert Aldrich's widescreen western features Gary Cooper and Burt Lancaster as rival mercenaries in post-Civil War Mexico. It was much admired by Sergio Leone.

CHAPTER 3

Scenes from Provincial Life

PF: *After the Indian experience, you embarked in the 1970s on three films with adolescent heroes and heroines, living in provincial France, two set in the recent past, one a fantasy set in the near future. The first of these, possibly the most controversial film you've made, is* Le Souffle au coeur. *What was the initial impulse in setting it in 1954, the time of the fall of Dien Bien Phu,*[1] *and in choosing Dijon, which you had previously used in* Les Amants?

LM: Well, as usual the genesis of *Le Souffle au coeur* is a little mysterious to me. After I finished my Indian films I worked for some time with Pierre Kast,[2] on a project that was literally a Utopia. May 1968 was not really a revolution, but its most interesting aspect was Utopian. They were very young people, of course, they were students, and they were saying, 'We completely reject the society that we're about to enter, we want to start from scratch.' Their expectations and vision of an ideal world were frankly Utopian, in the best sense of the word. The best slogan of May 1968 was '*L'Imagination au Pouvoir*'. We saw on the walls of Paris in May 1968 a lot of slogans that came directly from the Surrealists; and the most interesting aspect of the Surrealist movement was this Utopian aspect – they were looking for a world that would be drastically different.

Kast and I started with premises that were not altogether different from *Lost Horizon*. It was about a small society in a remote valley in the Andes that had managed to combine the best of the culture of the Indians before Pizarro came with the culture of the people who had come from Europe because they were persecuted for religious reasons. The meeting of these two groups: Incas running away from the Spaniards, and Europeans who drifted down south and may well have been Huguenots – anyway, the idea was to define and describe an ideal society where money was nonexistent. The whole project was Utopian. It was dramatically quite weak, because by definition in an ideal society there is very little tension. I thought about it for a while and I did a lot of interesting research about how you would, in today's terms, define what had gone wrong with our society and how it could have been different. And I remember going to seminars with people ranging from Margaret Mead to Bruno Bettelheim and many others.

With the combination of my Indian experience and May 1968, I found myself in a strange spot. What was I going to do next? My Indian work had been well received and I realized I'd become somebody else, somehow. I was reluctant to go back to making normal fiction films – find a story, write it, shoot it. So for a while I worked on this project about an ideal society. It was like a continuation of my search. Then I realized the project was never going to work; the reconstitution of such a perfect society would be in a way very naïve, and probably quite dull. And then, because of all that had happened to me, elements of my childhood came back to me with a vengeance. During my early years as an adult – not that I had been an unhappy child, actually I had a happy childhood – I rebelled violently against my background and education. I suppressed my childhood and didn't want to deal with it, which perhaps explains why my early films were not about my childhood the way most first films are. But, after India, it came back. I had reached a point where I was beyond rebellion and I was trying to understand what had happened to me and how I'd become who I was. It's not that I consciously went back to my childhood; my childhood came back to me.

I remember how I got to do Le Souffle au coeur – this is something I have never mentioned before as a matter of fact – I worked for a while on a book of Georges Bataille called Ma Mère, which is a very dark and tragic story of incest; very beautiful, but very desperate. I wrote an adaptation here, working for something like a month in 1970. At some point I realized: this is not my voice, this is not my tone. But I don't think it was an accident that I became so fascinated by this particular book. There was something about it that had to do with my own experience as a child. I put aside Ma Mère – I'd written fifty pages, something like that – and I started making notes about what had happened to me when I had a heart murmur. I suddenly admitted to myself, maybe for the first time, that I'd had this strange and very passionate relationship with my mother. And then I wrote a long treatment, eighty pages or something, literally in one week, for what became Le Souffle au cœur. I reread it last summer and it's very close to the finished film. It came like what the Surrealists call 'automatic writing'.

Of course, my imagination took off in the sense that, maybe unfortunately, things didn't happen to me the way they happened in the film.

The accidental incest as described in the film never happened in real life. But the beginning of the film was pretty close to where I was at that age: my passion for jazz, my curiosity about literature, the tyranny of my two elder brothers, how they introduced me to sex – this is pretty close to home. And when I got this heart murmur, the doctors said to my mother, 'You have to take him to that spa, that's the best thing you can do.' So my mother took me, and for bizarre reasons we shared the same room. My mother was a very religious woman, and she would see no sin. I don't think it ever crossed her mind that it was strange to share the same room with your son, who a is thirteen-year-old.

So the premises of what happens in the second half of the film are close to my own experience; I took off from that and started fantasizing. It's partly autobiographical, and partly my imagination. I had suppressed it for many years, but it occurred to me that I must have been very disturbed emotionally by sharing my mother's room during those three or four weeks. The script came all at once. In the very first version I still had those conventional reflexes about incest being such a taboo, something that has to be condemned and suppressed. So I injected some guilt. Typically, there was a scene – I even shot it and I cut it in the editing room – where, after the incest is consummated, the boy wakes up and the mother is asleep, so he goes into the bathroom, and is considering suicide. That's where I stopped my first script. I didn't know where to go from there.

Jean-Claude Carrière was here in the house at the time. He'd come to revise a play that he'd written. So the night after I'd finished, I read it to him. He said, 'But Louis, it's great, you must do it.' I was scared of it. I thought it was a little too close, too personal, too intimate. But the way I had dealt with it, which was already strongly indicated in the first text, was very much on a comedy level, which I liked very much. The way the mother and son ended up in the incest scene, it was described as almost inevitable; when it took place it was an accident more than anything else. Actually, there was no guilt involved. I realized reading it to Jean-Claude and discussing it with him that there was something that was completely natural about it. Maybe that's why incest is so scary, why there is such a taboo about it, because it's so natural for maternal love to turn into something else. I realized that if I wanted to be honest with what I had written, I should go all the way. I came up with the idea that the boy would wake up, and obviously would be very disturbed, but the way he handled it was to go downstairs and sleep with the little girl he was flirting with in the scenes before. It was actually during the shooting that the last scene came to me. The scenes at the spa were shot at the end, and even during the shooting I was wondering, 'How can I end this story?' Then I thought: it must end with a laugh, with the surprise of the whole family being there when he comes back holding his shoes. He would look so bizarre and funny having just come out of the little girl's bed; everybody would be in the room, his brothers would start laughing and it would end up with the whole family laughing. It was very provocative, but I think a great way of ending the story – like a suspended ending, yet giving a clue to how they could handle what had happened. When I reworked the first treatment, I made sure that when the mother wakes up, she talks to him and tries to explain all this to him: 'This is going to be our secret; this has happened because we love each other very much. I don't want you to feel guilty. I don't want you to forget it, but just to keep it to yourself.' She was trying to make him understand that it was not necessarily a trauma, it was just an excess of love. It would not happen again, but it was something that they would remember and cherish. This speech of the mother's was a key moment. There was something deeply true about it, deeply sincere and honest.

PF: *The mother is more, you might say, a figure of the late 1960s, rather than the repressed post-war decades. She is also an Italian. Her relations are quite cool with the father, who's some years older than her; she is a young woman and has an immense sensuous warmth as played by Léa Massari. Was the casting important?*

LM: The casting was very important, since from that early treatment, instead of describing my own mother, I created somebody else. The mother in *Souffle* is not my mother. I modelled her on a friend of mine, somebody I'd been very close to in the 1960s, who was South American. She'd married into a conventional French family; her husband was great, but the family was the extreme of conventional bourgeoisie. She had always rebelled, she had this Latin temperament, and she once told me that she'd had an incredibly passionate relationship with her son. So I took my inspiration from her, changed a few details, and made the character an Italian. It was essential that this woman should be a rebel, somebody who had never accepted the values of the milieu into which she had married. She had a lover and a very intimate, physical relationship with her sons – especially the third one. I got some stupid comments. People told me, 'Of course you made the mother an Italian and not French because she is scandalous.' It didn't make any sense. If she'd been a French bourgeoise, the whole story would have been absurd. She had to

32 *Le Souffle au coeur:* the taboo (Benoît Ferreux and Léa Massari)
33 *Le Souffle au coeur:* the taboo resolved in laughter

be an outsider, someone with a completely different system of values.

If the film works, I think it's for two reasons. Because I dealt with the subject somewhat on a comedy level; and, secondly, because the incest comes immediately after the Fourteenth of July Ball; everybody dances and drinks, including the mother. I wanted to make sure that it would very obviously be an accident. The boy helps his mother to undress, and so it happens – the accidental climax of their passionate relationship.

When the picture was released, I was standing outside a theatre on the Champs Élysées listening to people's reactions as they came out. I remember two women, obviously members of the bourgeoisie, coming out of the film. They had wonderful smiles and really seemed very happy. Suddenly one of them said, 'It was horrible what we just saw.' Then they started arguing. One said, 'I thought it was funny and touching.' Then, 'No, no, it's terrible.' And she suddenly became very pompous. I tried to follow them on the Champs Élysées, but at some point they noticed that I was listening. I think it was a case of double-take for many people; they enjoyed the film tremendously, and then when they thought about it, they said, 'Hey, this is a very scandalous proposition.' I really liked that. It's one of the things I've always liked to do, forcing people to reconsider preconceived ideas.

Mother–son incest is the ultimate taboo; nobody wants to talk about it. People find it easier to deal with the other one – fathers raping their children, which is present in most societies, almost accepted by some. Having made *Le Souffle au coeur* made me an expert on incest – whether I liked it or not. In the following years, because of the film, I received a number of confidences from women who told me what had happened between them and their sons, how it happened in a way that was close to the film. I had started fantasizing about my own memories as a child and ended up with something that was quite a shocker. But probably in a good sense.

In those years of sexual liberation, the early 1970s, when there were no more taboos about anything, incest was still one. I ran into a lot of trouble. I did the picture with very little money, hoping to get an advance from the government, what we call *avance sur recette*. I presented my screenplay and they pledged it to me. But I didn't get the money because in those days we had pre-censorship, we had to show the screenplays for approval. They didn't forbid me to shoot it because they couldn't do that, but they warned me that the finished picture would be banned. Because of that letter from the Censorship Board, I couldn't get the money from the government and I had a terrible time finding a distributor. Of course I was never worried by the threat of a ban because I knew that the way I was going to handle the sex scene would in no way be pornographic. The film was not banned, and turned out to be very successful.

PF: *But what the conventional moralists and censors would have preferred, I suppose, would have been a tragic ending in which the mother rejected the son and he committed suicide. That would have been very acceptable for many people, and they would have gone out of the cinema feeling happy.*

LM: Yes, but it would have been out of context with what the film was about. I was aware of the fact that for a child to end up in a situation like that was traumatic, but I thought it was truer to present a particular example where what happened did not have a terribly destructive effect on the child. One of the qualities of the film, and it has a lot to do with Léa Massari and Benoît Ferreux, the boy, is that they express such a generous love, so much understanding. For instance, take the scenes preceding the incest where the boy is devastated because his mother leaves him to spend a night with her lover. When she comes back, she has broken with her lover, and she is distraught. At first, the boy is really furious with her, then he understands she's in pain; he shows understanding and compassion, he becomes a grown-up friend to his mother. It's not only love but the best side of love, love which is giving, which is generous, on both sides. That's really the key. If it was not for that, the film could have been hard to take.

PF: *In addition to incest, there is a strongly anti-clerical view of this harsh Catholic school the hero attends. There is the depiction of the most sympathetic Catholic teacher, the homosexual priest played with wonderful subtlety by Michel Lonsdale.*

LM: I didn't want to make him openly homosexual – but think of those Catholic priests, unmarried, sworn to chastity and constantly exposed to this young flesh. I remember having to confess to a priest, in his room, on my knees, just the two of us. But the priest in the film saying, 'Let me see, you have all these muscles now. I bet I can't put my hands around your thigh any more' – that came from Jean-Claude Carrière. That was a story from his Catholic boarding school.

Now you asked me why I set it in 1954. I had this heart murmur in, I think, 1946, and I went to that spa with my mother when I was thirteen and a half. I moved it into the 1950s, I suppose, because I didn't want to

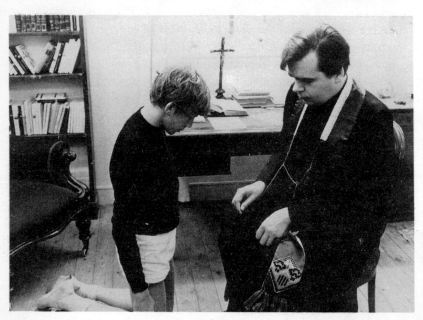

34 *Le Souffle au coeur:* Benoît rehearses with a cigar under the critical
eye of his director
35 *Le Souffle au coeur:* Laurent (Benoît Ferreux) confesses his sins under
the concupiscent gaze of his teacher (Michel Lonsdale)

deal directly with my own past. Mine was also a bourgeois background, but it was something else. Because the character of the mother was completely different from my own mother I naturally changed the milieu and eventually changed the period by seven years. I thought it was interesting to put it right in the middle of the French Indo–China war, at the moment of Dien Bien Phu. It would provide a counterpoint and would put my character, Laurent, in a political environment; for instance, the demonstration by the extreme right at the beginning. As I told you, when I was a child during the war, they sent us out to sell postcards of Marshal Pétain; in the same way, in the opening scene of the film the boy and one of his friends are asking passers-by for money for military hospitals for the wounded in Indo–China. Those discussions in the family, the brothers being very aggressive and contradicting the father – that was very much a part of my childhood.

PF: *But there's also a suggestion that the political malaise and uncertainty of the nation at large is echoed in the boy.*
LM: Dien Bien Phu was very important to me for personal reasons. One of my close friends was killed there. When it happened I was in the middle of the Indian Ocean with Cousteau on the *Calypso*. He was my first cousin. We were very close, we were the rebels in the family. He wanted to be an actor, then he was drafted, volunteered to become a paratrooper and ended up in Dien Bien Phu, where he died. The fact that I was away and only knew about it weeks after always stayed with me, like some strange guilt. I read a lot about Dien Bien Phu, and at one point even considered dealing with it in film.

PF: *The next film was in its way equally controversial, but on a political, national matter: the experience of the war and collaboration.* Lacombe, Lucien *was the first movie, I think, to look unflinchingly at collaboration. How much do you think that your film and subsequent films by other people on this subject were made possible by Marcel Ophuls's[3] 1971 documentary,* Le Chagrin et la pitié?
LM: I think my best work has always come through a long process of maturation. *Lacombe, Lucien* goes back a long way. It started when I went to Algeria in 1962 and spent twenty-four hours in a fortress in the middle of the mountains in east Algeria. This fort was held by a special unit, and we drove up there one afternoon and spent the night with them. It was just before the end of the war and everyone else in the French Army was thinking of packing up and going home. But these were

different; these were a bunch of die-hard professional soldiers, with a few fascists among them. I was with Volker Schlöndorff, who was my assistant then, and a friend of ours, a journalist for *Paris Match*. It was scary. We had dinner in the officers' mess; they were drinking a lot, and they started telling us – representatives of the media that they, of course, blamed for everything – what they really thought about the political situation and how much they hated de Gaulle.

They were a series of clichés: you had the young officer, an aristocrat just out of military school, who was from a family of professional soldiers; you had the sergeant who'd been fighting colonial wars all his life and hated the Arabs. The tension started to rise when we couldn't help expressing our own points of view. Around eleven o'clock, they decided to organize a night raid. So they woke up everybody – I think they wanted to show off for us. It was so absurd, so stupid. Suddenly, there were a hundred men starting out in a column under a full moon. It turned ugly when we entered a small hamlet; they woke up the peasants and scared them or beat them to find out about the Algerian guerrillas – it was just a horror scene. From a military point of view it made no sense at all. They eventually picked up a couple of so-called suspects, returned to the fort and everybody went to bed.

I was sharing a room with a young officer who had been fairly quiet up to then. He was an accountant in civilian life, doing his military service in Algeria; he started telling me that he was what they call the OR – *officier de renseignement*. He was in charge of gathering information. In other words, he was the one who was torturing. He was perfectly normal, perfectly well behaved, middle class – he was writing to his fiancée every day – and his justification for torture was that somebody had to do it, so he was doing it. There was something about him that I found enormously scary; it was the first time I was confronted with the banality of evil. I'm sure this man is now – well he's thirty years older – married, a good French citizen, probably very respected, maybe on the side of Le Pen, but I'm not even sure. But the circumstances that made him into a torturer, this very ordinary man, I found worth exploring. So I started making notes, but the Algerian war was too close; I found it difficult to deal with it. So I dropped the project. I thought about doing it after *Le Souffle au coeur*, when I spent time in Mexico. I love Mexico – I've been there a lot, my son was born there. There was a big scandal in Mexico at the time; the press had discovered that the police had been using kids from the slums that they had caught for larceny or petty crimes. Instead of putting them in gaol, they had trained these kids – they were eighteen or nineteen – brainwashed them, and made them work as para-police in civilian clothes. They would infiltrate students' demonstrations and suddenly break them up from the inside – sometimes with guns, sometimes with sticks. They had killed many students. I thought, this is a good variation on my original project. I want to work on it. I had lunch with Buñuel a little while after and he laughed at me: 'Even if you were a Mexican, they wouldn't let you do it. But for a foreigner to handle this story, forget it!' Of course, he was right.

Then for a while I thought of dealing with the Vietnam War, the American Vietnam War. These were the days of the trials of Lieutenant Calley[4] and Captain Medina and other Americans who had committed atrocities on the civilian population in My-lai and other places. But this was not my territory; it was not for me to do it. It would have to be an American director.

This was about the time when my own personal memory of what later became *Au revoir les enfants* came back to haunt me. I was not ready to deal with it then, but I thought I'd use this background of 1944 for my 'banal evil' project, and I started researching collaboration – not collaboration at the top level, but ordinary collaboration in the provinces, in the small towns. I was a little reluctant to deal with that period because it had been done quite a lot in the French cinema. But the moment I started researching it, I realized that this aspect of the period had never been really exposed except in Marcel Ophuls's *Le Chagrin et la pitié*, which had recently been released. Actually, I had something to do with that release because at the time my brother Vincent and I had started a small distribution company.

Ophuls's film had been produced by a Swiss company as a co-production with French television. Then French television decided not to show it, so we released it in cinemas. Of course, it triggered a controversy; there were lots of threats from right-wing movements when it was shown in two cinemas in Paris. The film did quite well, but we had to have volunteers guarding the venues. After Ophuls's film, I thought, I'm safe, this is it. He has dealt with collaboration head on, I can now deal with it in fiction terms. Little did I know. Because *Le Chagrin et la pitié* was made up of documents and interviews, it had the enormous strength of being about real people and real facts. The moment I invented characters and situations – even if they came directly from my research – I was exposing myself to controversy. I knew this was a minefield, so I was very cautious; for months I conducted research, interviewing ex-collaborators and members of the Resistance, seeing historians who were specialists of the period. Some of them gave me access to their archives.

I met a historian in Toulouse who had this huge iron cabinet full of documents about what had happened in different little towns and villages around here. He said, 'I'm not supposed to show them to you because there is a proscription.' In France it is forbidden to name individuals involved in possibly illegal activities without their permission. Of course, eventually he let me look at them. And I managed to find a number of collaborators who had survived; those who had not been killed by the Resistance, or put on trial and condemned to death after the war. Some ran away to Germany, and were found later, when justice had become milder. They were put in gaol for seven or ten years. These people changed their identity, changed their lives, but we managed to find a few of them and got them to talk.

I started writing a screenplay and came up with the character of Lucien, who is from a peasant family, and by a series of accidents gets to work for the French Gestapo in a little town. And then I got stuck. I had this idea from the beginning that he would deal with a Jewish family who had taken refuge in the attic of a house in the town. One day I was walking in the streets of Figeac, a small town where I actually shot the exteriors – about forty minutes from here – and I heard piano music coming from the top of a house – a very melancholy Beethoven sonata, played slowly. Clearly someone was studying – passages would be repeated. I listened to it, and I had this vision of a Jewish family with the daughter who is very much a Parisienne and is bored to death having to hide in an attic. That's when I decided to work with Patrick Modiano. Although he was born in 1947, his first two novels took place at the end of the Occupation, both dealing somehow with collaboration, and I liked them very much. I thought I should work with him because he had this enormous curiosity about the period. He helped me tremendously, especially with the part of the film that has to do with the Jewish family.

From the beginning I wanted to shoot right around here. We were just finishing the screenplay when I found out by accident that the central character actually had existed – or somebody very close to our character. I was in Limogne, the village right next to here, and was talking to the man who owns the garage. He said, 'What are you doing?' I wanted to ask him a few questions, because he was in the Resistance. I described what the story was about. He said, 'Oh, you're talking about Hercule.' Hercule was a tiny young man with a physical defect; he had one shoulder higher than the other, and he had worked for the Gestapo in

36 *Lacombe, Lucien:* Lucien (Pierre Blaise) gets a chilly welcome from
the Jewish tailor (Holger Löwenadler) and his daughter France
(Aurore Clément)

Cahors. He was eighteen at the time, and they had sent him to infiltrate
one of the Maquis here, and believe it or not my house was abandoned
during the war and the Maquis took refuge here for a few weeks in
January 1944. When I bought the house in 1965 there was the Croix de
Lorraine, the Gaullist logo, everywhere – you could still see the presence
of the Maquis.

The garage owner in Limogne confirmed that this young man Hercule
had stayed with the Maquis in my own house, which was really bizarre!
He was very active, denounced a lot of people. Thanks to him there was a
raid by the Gestapo and the German army in Figeac and they deported a
hundred people from the town. Eventually, Hercule was arrested and
executed immediately after the war. So the garage owner said, 'You're
telling the story of Hercule.' I said I'd never heard of Hercule before.
After all this research, and zeroing in on this region, I find that somebody
very close to Lucien Lacombe had actually existed and lived in my house!
I thought it was a sign of fate. It happened just a couple of months before
I started shooting.

PF: *From the start, had you intended that Lucien should be played by a non-professional?*

LM: From the very start. Not only did he have to be played by a non-professional, but it had to be somebody from here with the local accent – that was crucial to the story. And somebody with the same background. It took us months that winter of 1973. At the same time as I was working on the screenplay with Modiano, I had two assistants working full-time searching all around for the young man to play the part. We put ads in the papers describing the character. We saw literally hundreds of teenagers. My assistants went to schools, sports clubs, looking for a miracle to happen, because this part was so difficult to cast. I described the character for the local radio, and insisted that he be from a farmer's family with a rural background, not a student at Toulouse University.

And the miracle happened. After a long time. We were in the office of the *Dépêche de Toulouse*, we had seen something like fifty boys, some of them interesting enough that we got them to read a couple of scenes and took photos. Then we were finished and as we were leaving the building a boy came to me and said, 'Are you Louis Malle?' He had this tough, rocky, peasant accent. I said, 'Yes.' He said, 'Well, I was to come and see you, but I'm late.' Immediately, I saw something about him that was unique. I said, 'Let's go to a café and talk.' I discovered he'd been more or less forced by his mother to come; he had absolutely no interest in playing the part. His name was Pierre Blaise, he lived about an hour from Toulouse. The more we talked, the more I looked at him, the more I felt, 'He is the one.' I drove him back to his home in Moissac and met his parents. Then the next week he came here and spent a couple of days.

He was very wild, he was seventeen, had left school at fourteen and had gone to work with his elder brother, who was cutting trees in the woods. I gave him the script to read, and he said, 'Oh, I would never have done that', but I could see right away that he could completely identify with the character. I gave him the part and started working with him. First, I did something that I had already done with *Le Souffle au coeur*. We were going through the script and he was reading the scenes, and Modiano and I would listen to him. We adjusted the script because when he had a problem with a line he was usually right and we were wrong. I could see right away that he knew much more about the character than I did; he was not only playing the part, he was also my technical consultant on everything that had to do with the character's background, his emotions, his behaviour. He agreed to do the film somewhat reluctantly.

I think he was interested in the money and I liked the fact that he was not really interested in becoming an actor.

We started shooting, and for some reason we began in the middle of the week. When we got to the weekend, he came to me and said, 'I'm going home, I don't like it.' I said, 'But you can't do that, Pierrot, you've signed a contract. You're playing the lead.' My assistants and I had to talk to him for hours before he finally came round. I tried to understand what had happened. Actually, he was so wild and proud he resented the way, because he was just seventeen, the film crew bossed him around. The cameraman would say, 'Pierrot, don't move', and people would treat him like a child. So I had a meeting with the key technicians, and I said, 'Starting Monday, you're going to treat him as if he were Alain Delon. Don't think of him as Pierrot Blaise, this little peasant of seventeen, think of him as Belmondo. You have to be really cautious. He's got the whole film on his shoulders; he's so much more important than any one of us.' And from then on things went better. He started enjoying being the main man on the set.

PF: *What you describe relates to the dramatic and moral crux of the film to a certain extent. The knife-edge between becoming a member of the Resistance and becoming a collaborator, that results from his being rejected and affronted. It's very similar to the way you describe Pierrot's own reactions to you and the crew.*

LM: And the fact that he was very much of a rebel, and somewhat of a social outcast, although he came from a great family. I still see his parents. He died in a car accident two years after the film. I loved him dearly. He had no conventional culture whatever: he had never seen a film in his life, had never been to a cinema. Not only had he never seen a camera, but he'd never been to a movie! And never read a book.

PF: *So he was completely ignorant about the circumstances of the Occupation?*

LM: Yes. We had to give him a serious briefing. He knew the character was bad, and distanced himself, but he understood everything about Lucien. Something that fascinated me from the beginning – he had a natural culture. He was a passionate hunter; he would talk about birds, about birds in certain seasons, how to find them, how to hide yourself to shoot them. He had this intimate relationship with nature – not only being a peasant, but also he'd spent the last two years of his life in the woods. He was drinking a lot; he had a lot of violence in him. One of the difficulties for me with *Lacombe, Lucien* was that I knew very little about the character since he was someone whose social background was the opposite of mine. I'd been spending a lot of time here, I knew how people behaved, I'd heard stories from my neighbours. Still, I was in unknown territory. Pierre Blaise was helpful. And I always followed his instinct. I would watch him very carefully and I could see when he was uncomfortable with a line or a situation.

He was also extraordinarily gifted in another way. What is difficult about film-acting, and some actors never learn, is that if you're sitting in front of the camera for a close-up, and you lean on this elbow instead of that elbow, the cameraman will look at me and I have to say 'cut', because you're not in your light. You sometimes have to take seven or eight precise positions in the same shot; it's a technique you have to acquire. So I'd prepared myself, and arranged with Tonino Delli Colli that, while the shots were precise, his lighting didn't have to be a question of millimetres; we'd organize the camera movements so that we left the cast a great deal of freedom. This was necessary because most of them were non-actors or were stage-actors with no experience of film. But in a matter of days Pierrot knew exactly what his position was. It was a sort of natural rhythm that he had.

I could see from the first rushes that on the screen there was something so powerful, so ambiguous about him. In a way, you could look at him as the ultimate villain, but at the same time he was incredibly moving, as he was discovering power and money and how you can humiliate people who have been humiliating you for years. Pierre Blaise was so good, he got me into trouble. A lot of people saw the film almost as an apology for a collaborator because Blaise was so moving and disturbing that you could not completely hate him.

PF: *He does go through a process by which he becomes a monster, and then gradually something sad and pitiful. At the end did you see him as a tragic figure reaching a form of atonement he didn't fully understand, which precedes what we are then told is his death?*

LM: As in many of my films, I didn't want to be judgemental. I didn't want to simplify, I didn't just want to make a portrait of a villain. Rather, I wanted to explore a complex character in all his contradictions. At the same time, in no way did I try to excuse or justify him. His behaviour in many situations is objectively quite ugly, and described as such. At the same time I wanted to make clear that he was accidentally transported into a situation he was not prepared for. He didn't even have the cultural instruments to understand what was going on. He was carried away by the incredible gratification of doing what he was doing. I don't think he was morally aware of what he was doing. I think it's maybe *the* one of my films where I've something of a Marxist approach. You know, the famous definition by Marx of members of the lumpenproletariat collaborating with the repressive forces because they are not politically informed – which has happened frequently throughout the twentieth century. Algerians collaborated with the French because they were literally starving. Lucien Lacombe is a member of the under-class who eventually finds social revenge and all sorts of gratification by collaborating with the Germans and Gestapo. It would have been completely untrue to pretend that this boy had the kind of political and moral values that intellectuals have. He had no sense of ideology – that's what I'm trying to say.

PF: *But the countervailing force in the film is not the Resistance; the counter-force is the Jewish tailor who becomes the victim, who has this massive dignity and integrity.*
LM: Well, if there is a positive character in the film it would be him, in spite of all his contradictions, and the fact that he surrenders himself to the Gestapo at the end of the film, which for me is understandable simply because he cannot stand it any longer.

PF: *How did you come to cast Holger Löwenadler in this part?*
LM: It was another one of those lucky events. I was looking for a German or Austrian actor, because the character had come to Paris as a refugee in the 1930s and was a prosperous tailor until the Occupation. So he had to have an accent. I was having dinner with Bibi Andersson, who asked what I was doing, and as I was describing this character she said, 'Louis, there's a man in Sweden who has worked with Bergman. He is now in a play at the Royal Dramatic Theatre in Stockholm, he's one of our best stage-actors, and is absolutely perfect for your part.' I was not sure. Well, why a Swede? And then she sent me a photograph from Stockholm and I thought, 'He looks damn right for the part. I must see him.' Then I found out that Löwenadler was originally Austrian.

He came to Paris and I cast him at once. I thought he was perfect. He was the only actor with any experience in this cast. Except, of course, for Thérèse Giehse, who plays the grandmother of the family – she also played the lead in *Black Moon*. She was one of Bertolt Brecht's great actresses and created *Mother Courage* in Zurich. She was extraordinarily famous and respected in Germany at the time. Volker Schlöndorff said, 'You must meet her, she's such a great actress.' But I said, 'Volker, how can I offer her this part? She doesn't have a line to say.' But she accepted the part, and she did something wonderful with it. She was always in the background and she had almost nothing to do. But she became a very important character. It was so interesting to depict a Jewish family with three levels of assimilation. The grandmother, who has spent most of her life in a ghetto in Eastern Europe, is completely out of place in the French rural environment. Her son has become a prosperous Parisian tailor, but his accent and attitudes are still those of Mittel-Europa. His daughter, whom he has called France, is completely Parisienne. At some point she says: 'I'm fed up with being Jewish.' The line came from Patrick Modiano. I loved it, but it got me in a lot of trouble. She is the one who rebels constantly against her fate. Why should she hide when she is so French and feels so integrated?

PF: *Seeing again, only the other day,* Un Condamné à mort, *when the Frenchman who's deserted from the army is put into Lieutenant Fontaine's cell, I thought, where have I seen this man before? There seemed to be a strong resemblance between Bresson's actor and Pierre Blaise.*

LM: It's one of those subconscious things. When I was looking for Lucien, what I liked about Pierrot Blaise must have been that he reminded me of the boy in *Un Condamné à mort*. But I certainly was not aware of it. When we were editing *Lacombe* in this very house, one evening they were showing *Un Condamné à mort* on French television, and the editing crew and I were pleased to see it again. When we got to the last part of the film and the boy showed up, all of us had the same reaction: it was amazing how close he was to Pierrot. In the first scene Lucien works in a retirement home for old people. Originally, what I had in mind was to evoke my boarding school and to make him this very character who is so important in *Au revoir les enfants*: Joseph, the kitchen help who eventually goes to the Gestapo. In my first screenplay, he was this boy working in the kitchen of a school; he's kicked out because he's accused of stealing, and out of revenge he goes to the Gestapo – that was how he started to work for them. Almost immediately, I decided I'd better start with something else because it was another story. One day I was going to deal with it, and it didn't make any sense to use it as an introduction to this film.

37 Charles Le Clainche as Jost, the ex-collaborator sharing the hero's
cell in Bresson's *Un Condamné à mort s'est échappé* (1956)
38 Pierre Blaise as Lucien, the new collaborator, pondering the wages of
sin in *Lacombe, Lucien*

PF: *You said you thought that after* Le Chagrin et la pitié *this was an acceptable topic to be dealt with exactly as you wished. In fact, there was an extraordinary reaction against it, involving leading politicians, was there not?*

LM: Yes. I was not really worried about that when I was making the film, except that I knew certain things would irritate me. For instance, I read during my research that one of the torturers in the Gestapo in Bordeaux was black, from Martinique. Actually there were two. Again, it was a typical story; they had been recruited by the French army, had been stuck in Bordeaux, and had not been able to go back to Martinique. One of them had his family in France, and they were literally starving; eventually they joined the Gestapo, and were in charge of torturing. This is documented, this actually happened. Now before you put a black man in the Gestapo, you think twice about it. I had discussed it with Modiano. We thought: 'It is not because it actually happened that we should have it. It's because it's going to be so disturbing.' You remember in the odd motley group that constituted the French Gestapo in the film, he was the nicest of them all.

He was Lacombe's best friend, because both of them were outcasts, socially. He was obviously in a very strange spot. To have him among these fascists certainly was ironic and provocative, but his situation was somewhat similar to Lacombe's and I thought it would force the spectators to ask themselves a lot of questions. Of course, I knew it was not 'politically correct', as we would say today. I was in for trouble, and I was prepared. The picture was at first exceptionally well received by most of the critics. But suddenly something happened. I remember in *Le Monde* the critic called it a masterpiece. Then, four days after, there was an editorial in *Le Monde* saying, wait a minute, this film is dangerous. It really attacked the film. Then, in the following weeks, you had a series of editorials, opinions, for the film, against the film. People talked about nothing else for weeks. I was very happy about that. *L'Humanité*, the Communist paper, asked me to a debate with one of their editors who was from a village near here and had been in the local Resistance. For me, what was going on was fascinating.

Obviously, in the collective unconscious of the French this period is very murky. There was, for years, the official history, which had been created largely by those most involved in the Resistance – the Gaullists and the Communists. The official story was that the French people as a whole were against the occupiers. There were a few traitors, and from the Communist point of view they had to be from the ruling class, because it was inconceivable that someone from the working class could have been a collaborator. For the Gaullists, collaborators were few and they were vicious human beings, the scum of the French population. Of course, reality is altogether very different, and I'm not even going to get into that because it's too complex. But basically you can say that 95 per cent of the French population were just waiting. There were a certain number of people who went into the Resistance, and also a number of people who collaborated, for various reasons.

I remember one story that encouraged me to do *Lacombe, Lucien*, which was told to me by Jean-Pierre Melville. Melville was a great *résistant*, and once he was in the train from Bordeaux to Paris – it must have been 1943 – with a friend of his, also in the Resistance, and in those days the trains took for ever, they stopped all the time. And in their compartment there was a young man. They started talking and he told them he was very anxious to do something patriotic and he was going to join the French Waffen-SS. He was going to fight the Communists on the Russian Front. He was all enthusiastic: 'I want to do it for my country.' And in the course of the train journey they managed to turn him round: he joined the Resistance and became a hero. They made him understand that first, it was very bad judgement to collaborate. They said, 'If you're a patriot you shouldn't be with the Germans.' Simple as that.

It's almost too good a story, if you want. But it was typical of the period. In my research I found a family where there were two brothers: one was in the Resistance and the other was in the Milice, a fascist creation of Vichy that was arresting the Jews and fighting the Resistance. Strangely enough Cousteau was in the Resistance, and his brother, who was a very well-known journalist, was arrested and condemned to death after the war; he was writing in a weekly called *Je suis partout*; he was the editor, Pierre Antoine Cousteau.

PF: *Drieu La Rochelle wrote for it, didn't he, and Robert Brasillach, the film historian?*
LM: Brasillach was executed, Cousteau's brother narrowly escaped. His sentence was commuted.[5] When I was working for Cousteau, in the mid-1950s, his brother came out of gaol. He was a dour, right-wing ideologue, the first one of his kind I had ever met. Jacques Cousteau had saved his brother's neck in 1944 – he was a naval officer then, and decorated with the Medal of the Resistance – and he came to testify that his brother knew about his activities and never denounced anybody.

So from early on I was made aware of the dividing lines between people with the same background. And it's totally absurd to say that collaboration had anything to do with a particular social milieu. I belong to the high bourgeoisie, my mother's family is from the north of France and they had been occupied twice in some twenty years. There was a strong sense of the Germans as the hereditary enemy and there was no doubt in my family that they were to fight the Germans. God knows, they were against Communism, and God knows for a while they respected Pétain and believed that he would handle the Germans. But several of my cousins, older than me, joined de Gaulle, went to Spain and from Spain to Africa or to London and went into the Free French Army. My family was rigidly patriotic. But some of their friends were Pétainists to the very end and believed that the priority to save Christian civilization meant fighting Communism, rather than the Germans.

There's a scene in *Lacombe, Lucien* about all these letters of denunciation that the Gestapo was receiving. One of the historians I consulted told me that in a little provincial town in France the Gestapo ran away and left behind their archives, containing thousands of letters of denunciation from local citizens. They would denounce their neighbour just because his dog bit their daughter. Clouzot's film *Le Corbeau*[6] was very much about that.

PF: Le Corbeau *is a great film. At the end of the Occupation Clouzot was attacked, on the grounds that he'd dwelt on the corruption of French provincial life, and it was alleged, wrongfully, that his film had been shown for propaganda purposes in Germany. Were people conscious at that time of* Le Corbeau *being an allegorical depiction of life during the Occupation?*
LM: What do you mean?

PF: Le Corbeau *is not set in any particular time. There were no films made during the Occupation where the actual Occupation is represented, yet you have this phenomenon of the letters of denunciation, the poison-pen letters, signed 'Le Corbeau'. When people saw it during the war or afterwards, were they immediately aware that it was a film about the Occupation?*
LM: Oh, definitely. It was forbidden by the German occupying powers to deal with reality, except for propaganda. It was a very brilliant period of French cinema; film-makers were often dealing indirectly with what was going on in France at the time but they couldn't do it openly. It was impossible.

39 *Lacombe, Lucien:* the anti-hero finds a new aim in life at Gestapo headquarters under the gaze of Pétain

What makes *Lacombe, Lucien* strong and what made the controversy somewhat a series of misunderstandings is that in its description of characters and events the film exposes all the ambiguities and contradictions in behaviour that belonged to that period. For instance, in this part of France where Resistance and collaboration had been facts of life, the film was completely accepted. People who had lived through that period knew that this film was completely true and honest about what actually happened. And people who were not French took it for what it was: a reflection on the nature of evil. The controversy was between French intellectuals and politicians. Those who attacked the film did it on the grounds that it was fiction; we had invented and put on the screen a character who was complex and ambiguous to the point where his behaviour was acceptable. For them, it justified collaboration – which certainly is not what I was trying to do.

PF: *Marcel Ophuls told me that he was shocked by its ambiguity. Do you recall him writing to you or approaching you at the time?*
LM: He said that to my brother. I'm not surprised. *Le Chagrin et la pitié* is a very ideological film. Ophuls wanted to make a point, which was new

at the time, of examining what happened in a provincial town, Clermont-Ferrand. He really wanted to expose things that had been hidden. He was trying to prove something, and to expose French collaboration. He was very much into making a moral judgement. For me, the point was made. I wanted to go beyond that. Rather than passing judgement, I wanted to scrutinize a kind of behaviour that is very hard to understand and was certainly contemptible. After all, if people are shocked by ambiguity, they should not see my films. I think Ophuls's film and *Lacombe, Lucien* work from very different premises.

PF: *One final point on* Lacombe, Lucien, *which is the music. You used jazz before, and 'found' scores. There was a certain risk, I assume, in choosing something as jaunty as Django Reinhardt and the Quintet of the Hot Club of France.*

LM: Well, again, it's one of these examples in my work where the music came naturally. Of course, I don't remember listening to that music during the war when I was ten or eleven, but later when I got interested in jazz I started listening to Django Reinhardt, especially what he recorded in the 1940s. Before the war the Quintet was Django Reinhardt and Stéphane Grappelli, with whom I worked on *Milou*. They were very joyful, very 'up'. Grappelli was in England during the war, and Django replaced him with a clarinet player. It certainly was the influence of the time; those recordings of 1942–3, with the clarinet instead of Grappelli's violin, were very moody, very gloomy. And I thought it was a perfect background for the period. I used an early recording of Grappelli and Django for the credits, when Lucien's on his bicycle. It's a very 'up' piece, which I thought would fit perfectly the beginning, the exposition: he's going home, and he's happy. The rest of the music I used were the war recordings without Grappelli. It's slightly improbable that those Gestapo guys would listen to Django! I also had some recordings of singers of the period, an absurd song which was then very popular called 'Mademoiselle Swing', with a jazz background.

So I used music of the period, and I used it as source music. I never used it, except on the credits, as a score. And at the end of the film I used completely different music which came from recordings Jean-Claude Laureux, my sound man, had made in India. When *L'Inde fantôme* was released, a French recording company brought out three records of the music he'd recorded. The one I used was flute music from Bengal. I was looking desperately for a musical counterpoint to the elusive atmosphere of time being suspended when the grandmother and France and Lucien are hiding in the woods. Nothing happens, just a routine life, except that for these urban Jewish women to be there is astonishing, whereas Lucien is completely in his element. One of the things I really like about *Lacombe, Lucien* is this open ending, completely suspended. I remembered the music of this flute-player in Calcutta: I tried it on the images and it worked perfectly.

Lacombe, Lucien was the first time I put together a whole cast where practically nobody had any kind of film experience. Even Holger Löwenadler, an established stage-actor, had little experience of the camera. I felt very good about that.

This new relationship with my interpreters worked really well, trying to define precisely what I was expecting from them, and then giving them a chance, especially in the case of Pierrot Blaise, to really take his character and make it work. I remember I had to shoot a scene where Lucien was with his mother on the farm and he had to kill a chicken. I was a little uncomfortable setting up the scene, and he came in and said, 'This is not the way I kill chickens. Do you want me to show you how I kill chickens?' So I said, 'Well, show me, but don't kill the chicken.' He showed me that he would take the chicken by the legs and with a karate chop, a very fast movement of the hand, chop off its head. So we started shooting the scene. I said, 'Pierrot, this is the tracking shot. You're going to catch the chicken, then come back to your mother and on the way you'll kill the chicken. Let's see what happens.' We did one take. I was prepared to cover myself in case the take was a disaster, but I didn't have to. If you watch the film very carefully, at the moment when he chops off the head of the chicken, the head comes very close to the camera, and you can see the camera operator does a little jump! I don't think a professional actor could have done anything like that.

Aurore Clément was very frightened of the camera and I had to work hard to give her confidence. I realized that, in order to be good in my work with actors, I would have to treat each one differently. I would have to understand them, to know them and love them. They have different personalities, different problems. This is something that happened to me after India. I lost any kind of rigidity and stopped trying to apply, as many directors do, a systematic approach to directing actors. When people ask me, 'How do you do it?' I say, the only thing I can tell you is that I have absolutely no principles, no preconceived ideas. I just observe them.

It's a constant series of approximations, including, sometimes, dirty tricks until that moment when you say 'Action' – hoping, ideally, that they will find a state of innocence as if they were doing it for the first time and were improvising their lines. Some actors need to be bossed, to be told, to be pushed. Most of them must be treated like a piece of Sèvres because they are scared to death. Some actors are too technical; they prepare their work so much that you feel the need to disturb their routine. That's what's so interesting about directing; it forces you to become an acute observer of human behaviour. You have few chances to do that in real life – with that kind of intensity, anyway.

There was something else singular about *Lacombe, Lucien*. Not only all the images but also all the sounds were made here. Nothing was added which did not come from the shooting. The whole soundtrack – except for the music, of course – is from the original recording: either sync sound or wild tracks. There's absolutely no looping or post-synchronization. The editing room was in the little house over there. During shooting, we were never more than one hour away. We would see the rushes on the editing machine, then I put it together with Suzanne Baron. We went to Paris at the end, looked at the film and only added the music. Everything was the original sound. It never happened to me before or since. It certainly adds to the authenticity of the film.

PF: *The film we're coming up to now was also shot in this area, specifically in and around your own house –* Black Moon. *It has a distorted soundtrack, hasn't it, and at times is deliberately out of sync?*

LM: Completely out of sync! *Black Moon*, although it was shot in the same environment, was a very different proposition. I had no direct sound, I didn't have a sound man on the set. I decided that the soundtrack would be reinvented after. If you ask me where *Black Moon* comes from, it's rather complicated and a little obscure. I think it started from my adoration for Thérèse Giehse. I had such pleasure working with her when we did her last scenes in *Lacombe, Lucien*. I told her I would love to work with her again, to give her a more important part. She said, 'I've been watching you. I think you should make a film where people don't talk.' I thought, that's a weird observation. She said, 'Think about it.'

And she left. I edited *Lacombe, Lucien*, the picture was released, and we had the controversy. It got boring. I decided to move on and keep myself busy. I was actually living here in this house. I would go to Paris, but I had written, shot and edited *Lacombe, Lucien* here and I decided to stay on. I had a dream of Thérèse Giehse in my bed – not an erotic dream, just a dream where she was occupying my bed and refusing to move. I had a couple of other dreams and I started writing them down. Then I thought, maybe this is a chance to do something that I've always thought of – the equivalent of Surrealism's automatic writing, but in film. Of course, it's a contradiction in terms, and literally impossible, because whereas you can take a piece of paper and start writing whatever comes into your mind, film-making means putting twelve people somewhere and telling them what to do. You have to organize, prepare, you have to feed them – it's impossible to improvise 100 per cent, except of course I've done it in my documentaries. So I said, 'Well, I'll start with the screenplay.' The screenplay was very short. It was always understood that it would just be a starting point.

Black Moon is a combination of many things. It certainly conveys my admiration for and curiosity about *Alice in Wonderland*. And in the part I deliberately cast this English girl, Cathryn Harrison – Alice's slightly older sister.

PF: *And the title is English, not French.*
LM: Yes, don't ask me why. It came that way. *Black Moon* sounded much better than *Lune noire*. So, I had an English girl in the lead, and Thérèse Giehse, who was meant to speak in this invented language (which gave me a lot of trouble, by the way, but I didn't have to bother about it during shooting). There was also the incestuous brother and sister. I had cast Alexandra Stewart, and for months I tried to find her a male look-alike. At the last minute, I chose Joe Dallessandro, which is one of the most surprising casting decisions I've made in my life. I had very much hoped to cast Terence Stamp but, I don't know, he was afraid, or worried about the project.

PF: *Was it his appearance in* Theorem *that had given you that idea?*
LM: Yes, as well as the fact that he could have been great as Alexandra's twin. But it didn't work and then I found out that Joe Dallessandro was in Italy. I still think of the English version as the original version. It's actually better than the French. Doing the sound in post-production, we made two versions immediately. But I always felt the original version was the English one, maybe because of the reference to Lewis Carroll.

PF: *One part of the film contains emblematic and, in some cases, mytho-logical birds and beasts. One is an eagle and suddenly, looking at a picture in your room here, I realized the image of Joe Dallessandro pursuing the eagle with the sword comes from Indian mythology. The badger has various resonances, the talking rat has his parallels in*

Lewis Carroll's mouse, and there's also the talking unicorn. Was it just your subconscious dredging up memories and associations?

LM: For instance, take the image of the eagle – that comes directly from Indian mythology, the warrior with the sword killing the eagle, cutting the eagle into two. I was simply looking at this image on my desk when I was writing and it entered the screenplay, almost against my will. I was trying to work from dreams and free association. It ended up that one aspect of the film is somehow a home movie, in the sense that it is a series of visual moments, all taking place around or inside my house. I was using the house as a central character. It's as if it was a microcosm of the universe – the different rooms, the stairs.

This is a curious house, where every room is on a slightly different level; you go up and down steps to get to rooms, there are half-floors. It's a house with many, many doors, opening to the outside. But because it has so many doors, when there are a lot of us inside, it's impossible to find where people are. You call them and shout, and they answer, and you think they're on this side of the house, but they're on the other side. So that entered the screenplay and it was a very good equivalent of Alice's Wonderland, because it is quite realistic, a fairly straightforward description of the topography of my house. At the same time, it became an imaginary place, a place where the imagination could wander. Then I realized I had no choice but to shoot it in my own house. It was a terrible idea, of course, but I had to do it, because I was never going to find or build a house like mine.

I don't know how to describe *Black Moon* because it's a strange *mélange* – if you want, it's a mythological fairy-tale taking place in the near future. There are several themes; one is the ultimate civil war, I would call it, the war between men and women. I say the 'ultimate civil war', because through the 1970s we'd been watching all this fighting between people of different religions and races and political beliefs. And this was, of course, the climax and great moment of women's liberation. So, we follow a young girl, in this civil war; she's trying to escape, and in the middle of the wood she finds a house which seems to be abandoned. When she enters the house, she obviously enters another world: she's in the presence of an old lady in bed, who speaks a strange language and converses with a huge rat on her bedside table. She goes from discovery to discovery – it's a sort of initiation.

PF: *To do with her adolescent change, puberty and her rising woman-hood. Even the title,* Black Moon, *could refer to menstrual cycles.*

40 *Black Moon:* the incestuous siblings (Alexandra Stewart and Joe Dallessandro) in the garden of Louis Malle's house near Limogne-en-Quercy on the Causse de Limogne

LM: It's about the emotions and fears of puberty, no question about that. Although I was trying to film without analysing what I was filming, that aspect was obviously quite clear. What is strange about the film is that, though I was trying to convey something completely imaginary and unreal, I ended up shooting it very realistically. I don't think it was a conscious decision. I suppose it happened because I was shooting the house in winter, and the landscape around was disturbing and strange enough for me not to need to reinforce that visual impression.

PF: *Was the decision to invite Sven Nykvist[7] to collaborate as the cinematographer connected with this? Were there any particular Bergman films that had a quality you wanted to catch – manifestly allegorical or mythical Bergman films like* Shame, *for instance, which has a similar apocalyptic framework?*

LM: I knew Sven, and we had talked about working together before. And I felt this would be the perfect occasion for our collaboration. What I always find so interesting and disturbing in Bergman's films is the combination of character and mood and moments that are obviously of the mind and imagination, without the mannerism usually connected with the cinema of the fantastic – on the contrary, it is done in a very realistic manner with this cold light of the North. When I prepared the film with Sven, we agreed that there should be no sun, it should be all cloud and flat light with no source and no shadows. The first three weeks here, we had blue skies every day. But we stood our ground, and we shot interiors, or at the very start of the day before the sun was up, or at sunset. There's not one scene in the film with sun. When I explained to Sven what I was trying to do, I think he understood, he felt ready for it. There was something about the project that immediately interested him.

PF: *In discussing the screenplay with the cast, did you tell them from the outset that you didn't want to advise them on motivation, that you merely wanted them to seize their characters and do various things as if in a dream?*

LM: I prepared them for that. I was certainly not going for psychological motivation of any kind. I tried to convince them that they should go into themselves and I think Cathryn Harrison was quite comfortable with that. She's the one character who refers to a tradition in a certain way, the adolescent who discovers all these fears expressed by the sounds in the opening scenes. When she's in that tiny car and runs over the badger – we were so worried about not killing that badger – she's entering a

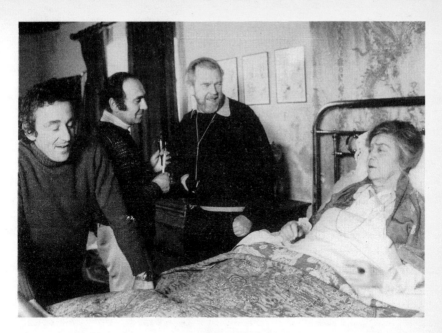

41 *Black Moon:* Sven Nykvist (centre) prepares a shot at the bedside of
the Old Woman (Thérèse Giehse)

42 *Black Moon:* Lily (Cathryn Harrison) and the Brother (Joe
Dallessandro) bury an enemy

world, the world of her mind. She was fifteen at the time – pretty much the age of the heroine – and so she understood the character. It was more difficult for the others. I don't think Joe Dallessandro ever really understood what it was all about. But he didn't mind.

PF: *He's no stranger to the bizarre, one might think.*
LM: He was perfectly prepared for something that was eccentric, and I suppose for him it was no more difficult than a lot of things he'd done with Warhol and Paul Morrissey.[8]

PF: *The girl is subjected to severe accusations of the kind that one gets in* Alice. *The unicorn accuses her of being a disturber, a troublemaker. Is this a projection of her own guilt?*
LM: I think so. That part is pretty close to Lewis Carroll in the sense that it's about this fear children have of being accused, their own inner turmoil. She was about to become a woman, and there are all these fears. The other side of guilt is discovering a sense of responsibility – which brings with it the fear of not being able to become a responsible adult. This is something which is a recurrent aspect of my dreams – being accused of all kinds of things. It certainly goes deep into our unconscious. I believe it's almost genetic, something that you have to live with to reinforce a certain sense of obligation. I think it comes with adolescence – or earlier, of course. But it gets to a crisis point when you're just about to become an adult.

PF: *Did you have any feedback on the film from child psychologists and psychoanalysts?*
LM: Oh yes. I had a lot of that. The film was very difficult, somewhat opaque. It was one of my great flops at the box office, but I was prepared. You can always expect a miracle, but I knew it was a difficult film. Again, it's one of those films I felt I had to do. I did it mostly for myself, for my own sake. I was certainly not thinking of the audience when I made it. Generally, I never think about the audience, but in this case I'd just made two commercially successful films in a row and I felt this was my chance to do something that was obviously not going to be a box-office hit. However, as with *Zazie*, I think I was unnecessarily obscure. I think I could have achieved the same unconscious goals that I was after without making it so difficult – which ultimately led to its rejection by the audience. Although the film had some kind of a cult following, it was not even released in many countries.

PF: *It was never released in Britain.*

LM: Twentieth-Century Fox had acquired the rights for America and a few other countries, and I was happy about that because they helped me finance the film. They agreed to open it in America, but they never bothered to open it in England and many other countries.

Somehow I would like to revisit it one day, because it was certainly very intimate, very important for me. I think I could have given myself more time, and been clearer about what I was after. At some point, I decided to go into shooting but it was too rushed. It was part of the experience that I had this short screenplay which defined what the scenes were about; in the process of shooting it I changed the scenes considerably, and kept improvising, hoping that I could apply the technique of automatic writing to the shooting itself. It was difficult to work that way. I was living in a little house next door, and I'd come to the main house with Sven a half-hour before everybody else and would try to explain to him how I was going to shoot that day. Then people would start to arrive. But sometimes I'd not made up my mind. I realized when I was shooting that I had to be clear enough to explain to other people what it was about, otherwise I should have worked all by myself with a small video camera. But within the routine of normal film-making, it didn't always work. When I was clear about what I was trying to do it was a lot easier!

I had the same problem when I was editing the film. I put together a first cut, as always with Suzanne Baron. I remember we went to a cinema in Cahors to look at it and realized it didn't make sense at all – which was perfectly fine, except that not only did it not make sense but some moments were much stronger than others; some were disturbing and achieved what I was after, and some didn't. So I remade the film in the cutting room. I changed the order of scenes and made cuts. I even reshot, because we always agreed with Sven that we would come back and do some additional shooting. I brought back everybody except Thérèse Giehse, and we shot some more scenes. So I was going as far as you can, within the normal way of making a film, ignoring all the rules and routine and habits, asking the actors not to take the screenplay seriously. However, I realized that maybe this situation of constant improvisation was not really suited to my temperament. Well, let me put it differently: it's not difficult to improvise in the context of something which is fairly realistic or understandable for everybody. You can improvise a dialogue – for instance, a love scene between two people in a café. You can invent the situation and lines, the intervention of the waiter, anybody can do that. But because it was so odd and mysterious, there were days when I couldn't even come up with ideas how to start a scene.

Yet it was a very interesting venture. I've always had a certain nostalgia for this experience. The part that had to do with Alice and the homage to Lewis Carroll was fairly easy, because it was on terrain where I had reference points. But some of the other moments – especially the parts which were mythological, half-way between fairy-tale and science fiction – were more difficult. I don't think cinema is the perfect medium for that – or maybe I failed, I don't know.

PF: *When you talk about making sense, the film isn't actually supposed to make sense in the conventional way. Obviously, the kind of thinking behind the film reminds one of the avant-garde films of the late 1920s – say, like Dali and Buñuel's* Chien andalou, *of which they said that in writing the film, whenever they discovered that an idea came from their rational conscious mind, they would then reject it. They wanted only that which did not make any rational sense.*

LM: It's obvious to me that I had the same sort of approach. I remember, when I was writing the script, each time something appeared which looked like a plot-line, I would cross it out. The fact that *Black Moon* was a full-length film made it difficult. This is something I considered seriously in the editing – cutting it down. I even had a cut which was just one hour; I had taken out a lot of scenes that didn't quite work. *Black Moon* is one of the least known of my films. I always insist on having it included in retrospectives of my work. Opaque, sometimes clumsy, it is the most intimate of my films. I see it as a strange voyage to the limits of the medium, or maybe my own limits.

Notes

1 Dien Bien Phu: the now legendary fifty-six-day siege of this sprawling garrison town near the Laotian border in northern Vietnam ended in a humiliating defeat for the French in May 1954 at the hands of Ho Chi-minh. Six months later the French were engaged in another colonial war in Algeria. Dien Bien Phu is Vietnamese for 'seat of the border prefecture'.

2 Pierre Kast (1920–84): Second World War Resistance activist, co-founder of the University of Paris Cinéclub, film critic (for *Cahiers du Cinéma*) and director of documentaries and features.

3 Marcel Ophuls (b.1927): son of Max Ophuls, he was born in Germany, grew up in France and the United States, and returned to Europe in the 1950s. Associated with the New Wave through his friendship with Truffaut, he directed a couple of fiction films but

didn't come into his own until he embarked on a succession of lengthy political documentaries, beginning with *Le Chagrin et la pitié* (1971). His most important recent film is *Hôtel Terminus* (1988), a four-hour documentary about Klaus Barbie.

4 Lieutenant William L. Calley Jr was convicted by a US Army court martial for his role in the murder of 500 Vietnamese citizens at the village of Son My on 16 March 1968, the notorious My Lai Massacre. Captain Ernest Medina was his senior officer.

5 For a clear account of the pre-war and wartime activities of Robert Brasillach, Drieu La Rochelle and Pierre-Antoine Cousteau see *Les Collaborateurs 1940–1945* by Pierre Ory (Éditions du Seuil, 1980).

6 *Le Corbeau* (1943, dir. Henri-Georges Clouzot): a doom-laden *film noir* examining the tragic effect of a poison-pen letter writer on the citizens of a provincial French town. Because of its alleged anti-French propaganda (though the film was never shown in Germany, as his critics claimed), Clouzot was prevented from working in post-war France until 1947. In 1951 Otto Preminger transposed *Le Corbeau* to a French–Canadian town as *The Thirteenth Letter*, with Charles Boyer in the role created by Pierre Fresnay.

7 Sven Nykvist (b.1922): great Swedish lighting cameraman who has photographed virtually all of Ingmar Bergman's films since 1960, as well as working with Polanski, Malle and others. His many awards include an Oscar for *Cries and Whispers* (1972) and the Special Artistic Achievement Prize at Cannes for Tarkovsky's *The Sacrifice* (1986).

8 Paul Morrissey (b.1939) American director from the New York Underground school and important figure at Andy Warhol's 'Factory'. He directed the Factory's leading male star, Joe Dallessandro, in such films as *Heat* (1972) and *Andy Warhol's Frankenstein* (1974).

CHAPTER 4

America and the Pursuit of Happiness

PF: *Was there a feeling after* Black Moon *that you had completed a phase in your career and that you needed to move on or move elsewhere, and actually to America?*

LM: My decision to go to America was a combination of various events in my life. After *Lacombe, Lucien* and *Black Moon* I felt that I was becoming a local, regional film-maker. Of course, I was happy to just live and work here, to continue in that direction. But I got scared that I was going to get stuck. As often happens in my life and work, I felt the need for a change of environment; I needed to re-examine everything from scratch. And I had always intended to go to America at some point. Actually, through the 1960s there were several American projects that collapsed. Of course, I was well aware that this was alien territory, that I was on dangerous ground. I knew enough about the American film industry, I knew that their way of making films is different from my way of working – I like to be totally independent and control my work from beginning to end. But I felt I had to move on, I had to leave France for a while. My curiosity was getting a little exhausted. The end of the 1970s was – at least, that was the way I felt at the time – extremely dull in France.

PF: *You'd made your first visit there in 1956. We're talking now about twenty years later. Clearly you knew American music, literature and films. How well did you know the country physically? Had you travelled widely in America at that time?*

LM: Yes. I had always been interested in America and went there under various pretexts – the most obvious one being to present my films at their American openings. After 1958, when I went for *Les Amants*, I spent time in America practically every year, especially in New York, which has always been my favourite city, and still is. I also managed to spend time in many other parts of America: California, of course, Los Angeles; but I also knew the South-west, the South. So I knew the country. And I was aware of the fact that America is a very difficult country to comprehend. Behind the façade, which makes all of America seem pretty much the same, you have an incredible variety of mini-cultures. This is because of the composition of the American population, the fact that it's a country of immigrants. This is something that I have been trying to explore in my American films – both documentaries and fiction films. So I knew it would be very challenging. I certainly was not naïve about that.

The reason that I decided to go is that one of my long-term projects had concerned a book I'd read on early jazz in New Orleans. It was a history of the red-light district, Storyville, and contained a lot of documents, a lot of photographs, and interviews with witnesses from the period. In the late 1960s, when I was finishing *Le Voleur*, I was tempted to make a film about the beginnings of jazz. I've always been fascinated by the jazz pianist Jelly Roll Morton. By the late 1930s Morton had become completely unknown and was playing in a bar in Washington; he was discovered by a young folklorist called Alan Lomax, who worked for the Library of Congress.

He recorded Morton talking and playing the piano – a sort of interview with music. Jelly Roll tells his version of the beginning of jazz, claiming he had invented it single-handed. As a result he had a revival; he made some great recordings in the early 1940s, and eventually died. And Lomax wrote a book, from which I worked on a screenplay with an American playwright called Jack Gelber.[1] But I was not happy with the screenplay – that was in the late 1960s – and I didn't proceed with the project.

Then I came across the book on Storyville, and when I was preparing *Black Moon*, in the summer of 1974, a friend sent me a recently published book of photographs by Bellocq[2] that had been rediscovered and printed very carefully by a great American photographer called Friedlander and published by the Museum of Modern Art in New York. Not only were they remarkable photographs, but they were very close to my story because Bellocq's photographs were of Storyville prostitutes. So after I finished *Black Moon* I put the two things together. In the book on Storyville was the story told by this old woman, who had been born and raised in a whorehouse as a child prostitute called Violet. I wrote a twenty-page synopsis putting those two characters together: Bellocq meets Violet and falls in love with both her and her mother.

So I had the premise of what became *Pretty Baby*. Originally, I saw it as a continuation of *Lacombe, Lucien*, except that it would be about the politics of sex, another kind of corruption. She was raised in a whorehouse and, since child prostitution was a big thing at that time, she was naturally prepared to sell her virginity at some point, an event for which her mother and the madame prepared her. For her it was like First Communion, the moment when she would enter life. To isolate this little girl in this very specific environment and to reveal a world whose moral values are completely different from those that are generally accepted – it gave me a chance to examine the incredible hypocrisy of the world around her.

PF: *It was set in the years leading up to 1917, and ends just as the brothels were being closed down, America was entering the First World War, New Orleans was being cleaned up, and jazz moved north.*
LM: Yes, it was certainly a pivotal moment in the history of jazz, but also a big turning point in American history. The film takes place a few months before the end of that era. I felt very strongly about this project, and it seemed absolutely natural for me to go to America. When people ask me today, 'What made you leave France and go to work in America?' I honestly have to say, 'I was not actually going to settle in America. I wanted to make that particular film, and it just happened to take place in America.' When I went to present *Black Moon* at film festivals in New York and San Francisco, I also visited Los Angeles and fairly quickly made a deal with Paramount for two pictures. I had no idea what the other one would be about, but that seemed to be normal.

So I started work on *Pretty Baby* early in 1976. I knew it would take time because things move very slowly in the American film industry. But I wanted it to be that way. I didn't want to rush, because I was working in an unfamiliar environment. So in my mind I was going to stay there for two years. Since I'd signed for two films I thought I'll see what happens with the first one, and maybe I'd continue, or perhaps do the second one somewhere else. I had no plans for the future, except that I knew I would be busy for two years, which is what happened.

PF: *You chose for only the second time to work with a woman writer. Did that seem essential to this subject?*
LM: I had a good friend who was head of production at Paramount, David Picker, whom I'd known when he was at United Artists in the days of *Viva Maria* and *Le Voleur*, and I liked him. I told him from the beginning, 'I want to be my own producer', and he accepted that, which was unusual. I said, 'I certainly want to work with a writer, I'm not going

to write this screenplay in English by myself, but I have very precise ideas about the film.' Because of the nature of the story it seemed obvious I should work with a woman and at David Picker's suggestion I met with Polly Platt, who had never had a screenplay credit before. She was a production designer, and had been married to Peter Bogdanovich, not only designing his films but also collaborating on the scripts. She is a remarkable woman. I was interested in the fact that she was not really one of those professional Hollywood screenwriters, the kind of people I was afraid of because I thought they would betray what I was trying to do. I had several discussions with her, and I could see that we were really on the same wavelength. We did a lot of research, we spent time in New Orleans. Then, when we had the structure of the film, she started writing it.

That's when I started having problems, the kind I've always had with American writers. They don't work the same way we do in France, where – at least from the time of the New Wave – it's taken for granted that cinema is a director's medium. So when you work with somebody like Jean-Claude Carrière, or any French screenwriter, you work in close collaboration. That's not the way writers work in America. Very often it's completely the other way round. Usually a producer asks a writer to write a screenplay, or a writer himself does a screenplay – either an original or from a book, or whatever. Most of the time, the director comes later – which, of course, is not the way I'm used to working. And even with this project, though *Pretty Baby* was something that came from me entirely, at a certain point she took everything we had discussed together, and went away and came back with a screenplay. Although I liked the screenplay, I felt somewhat betrayed. We worked together on the second draft, but it was still different from what I had in mind. I wouldn't be able to explain precisely what it was. It's just that I felt estranged. Maybe it was simply because I was working in English for the first time. And the truth is, it's happened to me many times since. I am much more comfortable with the scripts that I have written or co-written myself!

Then we went into casting and pre-production. At the last minute the studio got very nervous because they suddenly realized that the subject matter was controversial. Here was a film where the central character was a child prostitute. So a few more months were wasted before they finally decided to go on with the project. It was a battle of nerves. Then we had to rush into filming so as not to lose the winter season. I had the problems most European directors experience when they make their first

film in America. I had enormous difficulties because it was crucial for me
to bring in Sven Nykvist and he had trouble with the cameramen's union.
One of the things I found irritating is that in America it's absolutely
forbidden for cameramen to operate. Sven is an extraordinary camera-
operator: for him, as for many European cameramen, he is more than the
director of photography; operating is a continuation of his work. We
ended up giving in, and had a succession of camera-operators because we
were not happy with them.

I had a fairly mediocre crew; they didn't quite understand what I was
doing. Sven and I both felt isolated; we were fighting constantly with
everybody. It was not easy. A friend of mine who came to the set at the
end of the shooting was talking to a grip, and asked, 'How is it going?'
And the grip said, 'Well, I'll tell you, I'm fed up with working with an
artist!' They thought I was fussy, because I was searching, which has
always been my way of working. I would do five takes and realize
something was wrong. When I saw that the actors were uncomfortable, I
would move the camera, find another way of doing it that was simpler,
clearer, more elegant. There are great crews in America, but this one was
not; they thought I didn't know what I wanted, that I was not really a
professional director, that I was just fooling around! They resented it.
And so did I. It was really a war. On the other hand, I had a wonderful
cast. I was especially happy with the casting of Brooke Shields.

PF: *Had she acted before? She was a much sought-after model, was she
not?*

LM: She was twelve when we made *Pretty Baby*. Her mother had put her
to work as a model when she was one. It was a very difficult part to cast. I
had a lot of mixed thoughts about asking a child to go through these very
disturbing scenes. I felt I had a moral responsibility. The studio was
afraid of the controversial subject matter, but when the film was finished,
there was nothing graphic or exploitative about it. In the end, they were
not so happy about that, because if it had been scandalous at least people
would have gone to be titillated. Actually, it was very austere and
nothing was really shown. It was even more disturbing for that reason. In
that sense, I was never too worried about the child, but still it was a very
difficult part for a twelve-year-old to play.

I tested a number of girls, but I had met Brooke Shields early on and
always kept coming back to her. She had been exposed at an early age as
a model – I'm not saying it's the same thing, but she had been
selling her body all those years. I think she was mentally strong enough to

43 *Pretty Baby:* child whore Violet (Brooke Shields) with her own
baby doll

be able to handle the part. Also, there was something about her astonishing beauty that in the context of the story was both very disturbing and
incredibly moving. Because of the complex nature of her family life in
those days she was as tough as nails. And because of that there was a
certain vulnerability I could see right away that she was not going to be
able to express, that I was not going to get from her. So I had to adjust
the screenplay, give up certain things, especially the love affair with
Bellocq, which I had to shorten considerably. I regretted that of course,
but I had no choice. But, apart from that, I was quite pleased with her,
and, especially as photographed by Sven, she was astonishing.

PF: *The visual style of the film is quite different from* Black Moon, *and
also different from the diffused lighting that Sven Nykvist had used in
most of Bergman's colour films.*
LM: I showed Sven the paintings of Vuillard, especially those that date
from the late 1890s and the beginning of this century. These paintings
have always fascinated me. We discussed the light and Sven agreed with
me that there shouldn't be any backlight. As in these Vuillard paintings,
it would be very flat light. In some of those paintings, it seems as if the

characters are part of the wall. The light doesn't cast shadows. So we worked that way, constantly fighting with the gaffer, the man who set the lights under Sven's direction. He was always adding backlights. It became a joke; Sven would always ask him, 'Could you turn off this one, this one . . .?' And he would say, 'Are you sure?' They couldn't understand why there was no backlight. If it resembled anything, the lighting was pretty close to *Lacombe, Lucien*, which Sven very much admired. It was certainly different from *Black Moon*, because it was a totally different visual context. That's one aspect of the film that I completely controlled. We took over a huge house in New Orleans and transformed it into the whorehouse. We chose the colours of the walls and wallpapers, the different combination of colours. We spent a lot of time on that in pre-production.

PF: *What about Keith Carradine and the concept of the character of Bellocq? You were having to invent, from a small amount of biographical information, a character who was some kind of voyeur, an emotional cripple, but who was not essentially perverse in wanting to marry Violet. Did you have someone in mind like Toulouse-Lautrec and his fascination with the lives of brothels and sketching whores?*

LM: When Bellocq was rediscovered, when those glass plates were found, it was a matter of controversy. It was very difficult to attribute those plates; some people claim they're fakes, but I don't think so. There *was* a Bellocq who actually existed. And because of the Toulouse-Lautrec syndrome, he was described as a monstrous man, as a cripple. I did research on Bellocq and found out that he was not the only photographer doing that in New Orleans; the prostitutes loved to have their portraits taken. So at some point I deliberately decided that he would be strange, and probably very shy, obsessed with his work and fascinated by the world of prostitution. But not a libertine – somebody rather austere in his private life, and simply obsessed with photographing these girls, especially the young ones. Very quickly we understood that we had to create our own Bellocq. Basically the context is historical, but the character was our invention.

PF: *Since* Pretty Baby *comes after* Black Moon, *were you aware of the relationship between Alice Liddell and the photographer Dodgson – Lewis Carroll – and that between the little girl in the brothel and the photographer Bellocq?*

LM: Absolutely. Also it was very obvious to me at the time that somehow

44 *Pretty Baby:* Louis Malle tells Keith Carradine (as New Orleans photographer E. J. Bellocq) where to point his camera

Pretty Baby was a continuation, and a variation, of many of the themes of *Lacombe, Lucien*. My ambition was to make a sort of American *Lacombe, Lucien*. Since I was just coming out of *Black Moon*, I was still obsessed, I suppose, with the central character being a young girl. I had this vision of a little girl playing in this brothel, which was a little bit like the house in *Black Moon* – a sort of imaginary world. Since she was not allowed to go out, she would be in this very claustrophobic environment, but she would have the whole world of her imagination. There were other children, all girls of course, in the house, and I found it fascinating, these children playing their games in the middle of the activities of the whorehouse. There's some of that at the beginning of *Pretty Baby*, but it's a dimension that was not explored as much as I wanted.

One of the things I'd read that struck me about those houses was that the hygiene was terrible – there were all those rats everywhere. I don't know why I have this fascination with rats; I had in mind that Violet would have a rat for a pet. Polly thought it was absurd and didn't make any sense. She convinced me to give that up. She might have been right. After all, I'd done that in *Black Moon*. In general, though, I wanted the whole story to have much tougher edges.

For instance, the part that was enormously important to me was the moment when the whorehouse is closed down and she's thrown out on the street; her mother is getting married, she is going to live with Bellocq, and they have this life for a while where they are like husband and wife. It was very disturbing, this twelve-year-old prostitute becoming a housewife. For various reasons I didn't really have a chance to develop that part of the story. It is in the film, and there are some strong moments, but it doesn't go as far as I wanted.

Pretty Baby was well received critically in America, in spite of the controversy, but not so well here in France. It was a little bit like the reception of *Le Voleur*. Maybe because it was a period film and either I didn't quite make my point or people didn't get it. This is a film I cared a lot about, and looking back it had the potential to be one of my best achievements. It may have been a mistake to make it as my first film in America. When I did *Atlantic City* the screenplay was brilliant, and the pretext was a sort of thriller. Because I was much more in control of what I was doing, I managed to make a film that was altogether better – but my ambitions for *Pretty Baby* were much greater.

PF: *One final point before coming on to* Atlantic City *– about the end of* Pretty Baby, *which I think is particularly fine, where Bellocq is being*

deserted. He is the art photographer, the girl is being borne off into a future of mass society and conformity, and the final scene has the girl being photographed by this boor, her stepfather, with a box Brownie that anyone could use. Was this your final comment on the relationship?
LM: I loved the ending. The idea of the Brownie came from Polly Platt. I thought it was the perfect ending; we had that in mind from the very beginning. What I especially like about it is the ironic twist, the fact that the mother who had made her child become a prostitute eventually succeeds in marrying a shopkeeper and becomes the perfect suburban bourgeoise. So to have the mother come back, insult Bellocq for corrupting her daughter and then take the daughter away was very strong and very simple. I was really happy with the scene at the railway station.

PF: *Your next film, the one that many of your admirers most like, was* Atlantic City. *It's also about a city at a point of crucial change, and indeed it proved quite prophetic, because it seems now to stand for the state of America during the 1980s.*
LM: Yes.

PF: *I take it that the idea of the city at that time preceded the screenplay? One has the sense that this was the setting for this film, it couldn't have been made anywhere else.*
LM: Absolutely. But I have to give you the genesis of the film. After *Pretty Baby* I spent time on a project that didn't work out. I was a little disconcerted; I was not sure I was going to stay in America. Fortunately, I went to shoot a documentary called *God's Country* in Minnesota, which was a very happy experience, very interesting, great fun, and it brought me back to basics.

Now, by accident, when I was coming back from Minnesota, I was approached by some Canadian producers I knew. These were the glorious days of the Canadian tax shelter: the joke was that they were raising money from dentists in Winnipeg who, instead of paying taxes, would rather give their money to the film industry. They were desperate: they had organized the tax shelter, they had the money and they had a book. I said, 'What do you want me to do with this?' It was a terrible book – though they eventually made it into a film. They said, 'Well, do you have an idea, do you have a project?' This was July – and they had to spend the money by the end of the year. So I said, 'There's an excellent playwright, John Guare³ – I'm interested in working with him. Let me talk to him.'

So I went to see John Guare. Fortunately, he had just finished a play and had time. We started talking. In the preceding winter, literally every day, the *New York Times* had something about what was going on in Atlantic City. They had just legalized gambling there. It was very controversial, and there were all these stories about 'Will the mob move in?' Two casinos had just opened and they were building several more. So the conversation turned to Atlantic City, and I said, 'Maybe this is something we should look into.' And John said, 'I couldn't agree more and it so happens that one of my parents' old friends is the manager of the first casino to open, Resorts International.' We called him, we rented a car, drove down to Atlantic City and spent something like twenty-four hours there. I don't think we slept at all. His friend took us around, explained what was going on, and we saw for ourselves all the contrasts, all the gloss. The rest of the town was literally a slum. Before they legalized gambling, Atlantic City, which had had a glorious past in the 1920s and 1930s and 1940s, had almost become a ghost town.

PF: *It also had these emblematic associations with the Miss America contest, and the setting for the original Monopoly board game.*
LM: Yes, it was one of those mythical places. Over the years I've met a number of people who had spent their holidays there. It had been very popular as a resort, and had fallen into complete decay. The contrasts were astonishing. They had refurbished the Boardwalk, but you could walk three blocks and you'd be in the middle of the worst slum, mostly a black population. And there was this craziness: they were building new casinos and they were pulling down all the great old buildings of the 1920s. So, driving back to New York, we started putting together a fairly simple plot, some kind of a thriller.

We thought of this two-bit gangster who by accident suddenly achieves his dreams, and this old lady in bed – some memories, obviously! – and this young girl who came to Atlantic City and wanted to become a croupier, and all their dreams and expectations. We were trying to combine the old and the new. The character of Lou, the Burt Lancaster character, represents the old, glamorous Atlantic City. When he talks to the hippy who has stolen the cocaine in Philadelphia, Lancaster tells him, 'I wish you'd seen the Atlantic Ocean in those days.' He says, 'Ah, the Atlantic Ocean was something then.' People were always quoting that line, it's one of Guare's great lines. So he represented the past, and Susan Sarandon's character, who lived in the same building, represented the people coming from all over America with their dreams.

For both of us, it was very obviously a metaphor for America itself.

I hate to generalize about America, but things move quickly, the past is abolished, so these images of buildings coming down and buildings going up worked well for the story. The last image over the end titles – the enormous wrecker's ball knocking down one of the great buildings – we were lucky they were doing it when we were shooting those scenes. So I got terribly excited. And I remember telling John, 'If this doesn't work, I'm going to come back anyway with a 16mm camera and do a documentary on what's going on in Atlantic City.' I ended up making it as a fiction film, but there was no doubt in my mind from beginning to end that Atlantic City would be the central character. It was really about the city and what was going on – it was also a documentary about America.

So I came back to my Canadian friends with a synopsis. In the meantime they had inquired about John Guare and, since he was described to them as an avant-garde playwright, they were a little scared. I said, 'He's your only chance. If not, I won't do it. Let me do it my way.' And I must say they were gracious enough to accept that. I had to come back here because I had to spend the month of August with my children. John came with me and we worked on the script. I knew immediately John would be a great person to work with. What I like about *Atlantic City* is that it's about things happening in contemporary America, whereas *Pretty Baby* was somehow a continuation of my French work in the sense that it was about the past. It was a period film, a reflection about something that didn't exist any more.

PF: *Atlantic City is not a film of hindsight, but a film of foresight; this is the city that Donald Trump helped to create, and now is as tarnished as the dreams that he embraced.*

LM: Yes, absolutely. It was shot at the end of 1979 and was a vision of the following decade. Of course, we didn't know it at the time, except that after those two years in America I felt I was a fairly acute observer of the American scene, and I found in John Guare somebody who had a very original (slightly distorted by his imagination) vision of his own country, which of course he knew better than I did – especially his singular knowledge of American mass culture and icons. So it was a great collaboration. We complemented each other; basically the same vision, though at a slightly odd angle. I had a chance to combine my experience of both documentary and fiction.

My only obligation was to cast a certain number of Canadian actors

because it was meant to be a Canadian film, and to obey the rules of the
Canadian industry. They let me cast Burt Lancaster and Susan Sarandon,
but the supporting cast were Canadians. Of course, there were wonderful
Canadian actors working in America, like Robert Joy, who played Susan
Sarandon's husband, and Kate Reid, who played Lancaster's tyrannical
companion.

We were really short of time, and I was quite scared. But in the same
way that everything didn't seem to work quite my way in *Pretty Baby*,
everything did seem to work my way in *Atlantic City*. John Guare stayed
with us for most of the shooting and sometimes, when scenes didn't
work, I had the chance to reshoot them. We had a tight budget, but we
could do it, because I had a smaller, faster crew. We shot in Atlantic City
for about five weeks and the studio shooting took place in Montreal. The
crew was part Canadian, part American, part French – all enthusiastic
and very good. I felt really comfortable, pretty much in control. I
improvised more than I usually do, but it had to do with the material and
the fact that we were constantly adjusting to what was going on in
Atlantic City. For instance, we found out that they were going to pull
down a particular building and we decided to move a scene so that we
could have the building being demolished in the background. And there
is the scene where the husband of the Susan Sarandon character is
murdered on the top of this bizarre parking place with elevators – an
absurd structure I have never seen anywhere else. It was so inconvenient,
but it was typical of the place.

PF: *It was a lift to his scaffold, wasn't it?*
LM: Yes, of course! I brought John to this place and said, 'He has to be
murdered here, at the top, with the whole city and the Ocean in the
background.' I think we had intended that he would be murdered in the
corridor of the hotel. But I said, 'We can organize it so it's here.' My
obsession was to have Atlantic City ever present and to shoot as much as
possible outside. The Canadians weren't too happy about it; they
thought that we would shoot two weeks in Atlantic City and then do the
interiors in Montreal. But I convinced them. So it went well, except that
we didn't quite finish by the end of the year.

PF: *Burt Lancaster's role was perfectly suited to him – there's one strand
of Lancaster's work going right back to his first movie in 1946, the minor
criminal, the doomed boxer in* The Killers. *Did he immediately see it as a
part that suited him when he read the script?*

LM: I have to be honest with you – my first choice was Robert Mitchum. The Canadian producers thought Burt Lancaster was a bigger star, although neither of them was a box-office name any more. You know how it goes in America, it takes five years and it's almost Burt who? Because audiences are so young, things move very quickly.

PF: *I think Mitchum would have been wrong for the part, because I don't believe he could have produced that particular change from being the loser to the winner. He's too laid back, he couldn't be as pathetic as Lancaster at the beginning or as ebullient at the end.*

LM: The reason I wanted to work with Mitchum is because I have always been a tremendous admirer of his. I think he is one of the great American actors. It had always been my dream to work with Mitchum. I went to Los Angeles and met both of them on the same day, and just by meeting the two of them I realized immediately that Lancaster was the right choice. Mitchum was interested, but I was not sure that he was very interested. On the other hand, Burt had read the screenplay and the first thing he said was, 'A part like that, especially at my age, happens every ten years, if you're lucky.' He knew it was a great part and I really appreciated that he understood that right away.

PF: *Also, he had the experience, unlike Mitchum, of working with a number of European directors, including Visconti and Bertolucci.*

LM: Yes. We started getting along well, although Burt had always had the reputation of being difficult and a lot of people had warned me about him. I remember I was in France when they were shooting *The Train*, which Burt produced, and after a couple of weeks he fired Arthur Penn, who is a good friend of mine. But as soon as the conversation turned to Visconti – whom I admire enormously and Burt idolized – we were on very familiar ground and we got along right away. It was a little difficult for Burt's ego when we started rehearsing and trying on the costumes, but he understood very well that the character was essentially a nobody, a two-bit failure, and would have to look really run-down. He would certainly have won the Oscar that year but for the fact that Henry Fonda was known to be dying when the voting took place. Every critic in America, though, voted his the best performance of the year.

I admired Susan Sarandon even more for handling her character, which was much harder to tackle. The Lou character was perfectly defined and his arc was quite clear up to the end. The woman, with all

45 *Atlantic City:* Burt Lancaster on the Boardwalk with Louis Malle
46 *Atlantic City:* hippie Dave (Robert Joy) on the Boardwalk with
gangster Lou (Burt Lancaster)

her contradictions and dreams, not knowing what she wants – it was a difficult part to play, and she really did it well.

PF: *At the beginning of the film she has our sympathy completely, and then she loses it. Whereas he is pathetic, but as he gradually realizes his tawdry dreams, even of being a killer, he takes on this heroic stature at the end. This is presumably something that was always in the script?*
LM: Yes, it was always in the script. The only real argument I had with Burt was over the scene at the very end, in the motel room, when he's calling the Kate Reid character to explain to her: 'The killer, it's me, I did it.' And she says, 'Ah come on, come back home.' Sarandon is never going to make a life with him after the exhilarating night before. So they have this awkward scene, which is wonderfully written, where she says, 'Maybe I should go and get a pizza,' and we know she is going to leave, but Burt wanted his character to be in control – *he* was sending her away. I didn't think it was right; I thought he really was dreaming of showing her off to his friends now that he has all this money. 'We'll go to Miami,' he says. But she just wants to sneak out. What Burt had in mind was that it was his decision to let her go.

PF: *But at that point he has come full circle, because he has seen her steal the money from him, just as at the beginning her hippy husband has stolen her wallet from her.*
LM: Yes, it's a perfect circle. I think the way the scene ended up was quite right. Both of them knew intimately that what he was talking about all evening was not going to work. And after she leaves, he comes back to Kate Reid and gets her to exchange the rest of the cocaine for the rest of the money. He's very happy with his old mate. When they're walking on the Boardwalk, he's in charge, he's very grand, and Sarandon's character is going away to Europe with the money she's stolen. So it was a bittersweet ending and very right. I realize now when I look back that it was a difficult film to pull off because every moment and every character was always on the edge of becoming a cliché or predictable. But I think it's a rare quality of John's script, especially in his dialogue, that he always surprises you – that's what I really like about his writing.

When the film was finished, for some reason I thought it might not even be released. I was very worried about it. I'd finished the final sound work and final mix in Paris and we had a screening there for a French distributor. The reaction was mixed, which was a foretaste of

what was going to happen, because in France, in spite of the fact that I
shared the Golden Lion in Venice the following autumn, the picture was
strangely ignored. I had mixed reviews, and even the good reviews were
rather condescending. Then I brought back a print to America and had
a screening in New York for about fifty people. The reaction was
incredibly enthusiastic. And I realized that this film was going to be
better understood by people who knew the context. Then we went to
Venice and I remember there was a screening for the press, and the
foreign press – the non-French press, the British and Italians and Germans – were very enthusiastic, and eventually we won, sharing the
Golden Lion with John Cassavetes.

PF: *Yes, for* Gloria, *another of these off-beat gangster films. You talk
about mixing the film's soundtrack. Although Michel Legrand is
credited with the music, nevertheless everything in it is all source music,
a very elaborate mix of popular songs and jazz, including 78 rpm
gramophone records of Tommy Dorsey.*

LM: Yes, it was required by the screenplay. I got great help from John's
intimate knowledge of American popular music. We injected a number
of the songs that he had found. So we had that to start with. I went to
Michel Legrand because he's very flexible and can write all kinds of
music. Some of the music already existed, we had recorded it during
shooting, but there was some other music I wanted. For instance, the
Susan Sarandon character is coming back from the hospital after the
weird scene where Robert Goulet's dedicating the Frank Sinatra Wing –
there is one, by the way – and Lancaster offers to walk her home. When
they stop in the coffee shop, I wanted some cheap country music – but
without words, because of the conversation between the two of them.
And Michel did that extremely well.

Also we ended up having to do an original recording of the Bellini
aria – the Casta diva from *Norma* – which is so important at the
beginning. During shooting the reference was the famous Callas
recording, but we couldn't use it because the rights were incredibly
expensive. So we had to do a recording with Elizabeth Harwood, a very
distinguished English opera singer. The first day, or half-day, in the
sound studio in London, we had the whole London Philharmonic, and
Michel wanted to add several pieces of score, since here was an opportunity for him to work with a huge orchestra. So, for the scene in the
elevator parking lot, he had one of those big instrumental symphonic
pieces. And there were several others. To my great shame, I cut every-

thing out in the final mix because I realized I didn't need it; we had a number of sound effects that I felt were more interesting, and much stronger, than the score. I think Michel was disappointed, but he understood.

PF: *Everybody in this film is on the make one way or another: stealing, exploiting financially or emotionally, without exception. And one of the people is a Frenchman, a croupier. Now I'm sure there are croupiers instructing people at schools for dealers in Atlantic City or were at that time. But was this put in as a personal signature to show that you yourself or your fellow-countrymen were not excluded from the processes of corruption and exploitation?*

LM: I don't think I thought of that. We needed a sort of sleazy character who would be teaching the young dealers, and because the Susan Sarandon character is constantly dreaming about Monte Carlo, we thought it would be interesting – and I think it was John's idea – for the croupier teacher to be French, so that she could ask him, 'How is it in Monte Carlo, the elegance?' Eventually, he ends up suggesting that she prostitute herself. He says, 'Just go with him and bring him luck, he'll give you a lot of money' – a pretty horrible character. And then I was stuck when I was casting the part, because this is a very small role but it has to be extremely well handled. I tried to find a French actor in America, but couldn't find anybody. I had in mind, all the time, that it would be wonderful to have Michel Piccoli playing that part. So I ended up calling Michel in Paris – I'd never worked with him, but we were friends – and that's the greatness of Michel: he said, 'Sure, I'll come, I'd love to work with you, and even if it's only three days, I don't care.' So he came and he was just wonderful, except that I had some problems with his accent in English – he was so difficult to understand! But he made the part work. And I promised myself that one day I would give him a great part, which eventually I did, in *Milou in May*.

PF: *I mentioned earlier that some of the people you met in India seemed to me to presage these two left-over figures of the counter-culture and hippy flower-child world, the Sarandon character's husband and sister, one of them absolutely corrupted, the other perhaps too foolish to be corrupted. Were you aware of dealing with a decade which you hadn't touched on dramatically?*

LM: Yes, it was taking place at the end of the 1970s and in those days hippies were already somewhat of the past. But the Susan Sarandon

character was meant to come from a remote part of Canada, Saskat-
chewan. Moose Jaw! I don't even remember if John made it up and
then actually found out it existed, or just knew that it existed! Anyway,
we thought it would be interesting to give her a hippy past. She'd
become this woman who wants to make it and have money. She wants
to conform to the rules of capitalist society, but she has a past. So it
seemed natural to make the ex-husband and her sister hippies – rem-
nants of the past. Especially her.

Of course, the character of the younger sister was very much a caricature. The girl who played it was a young Canadian actress who had
been quite successful in a couple of Canadian films. She had played
Ophelia the preceding summer and was the great hope of Canadian film
and theatre. She played the part of the hippy sister seriously, and as
soon as the shooting was finished she went to India to an ashram. I
don't even know what's happened to her, I think she's still there. It was
very ironic and very disturbing, in a way. I realized early on that she
was going to play the character really sincerely, which made it even
more bizarre.

When we made the film we didn't have an American distributor, and
it took months to convince Paramount to release it. They did because I
had a good relationship with them, and the man who ran Paramount at
the time, Barry Diller, saw the film and loved it. Everybody around him
warned him that it was not going to make any money. Eventually they
released it, and to their great surprise – I'm not saying it was a huge
box-office hit, it was not – it was incredibly well received, and ended up
with five Oscar nominations for best screenplay, best actor, best actress,
best film and best director. And for many American critics it was the
best American film of the year. This was the moment where I felt
working in the States was going to be easy for me. I had just met
Candice and we got married in September 1980. I went on to make *My
Dinner with André* that winter. Both films were released in 1981, and
both of them were well received. *My Dinner with André* became a cult
film, as you know. I thought I was hot. It was a paradox, because both
films were, in every way, marginal to the industry.

PF: *Two things unite* Atlantic City *and* My Dinner with André. *The first
is that they are connected with American cities; one of them is a very
New York film. The second is that they bring together your interest, in
different ways, in documentary and drama. You spoke about the documentary background of* Atlantic City. *The way in which* My Dinner

47 *Atlantic City:* waitress Sally (Susan Sarandon) lunches with her
elderly neighbour
48 *My Dinner with André:* Wally (Wallace Shawn) dines with
an old friend (André Gregory)

with André *is presented, a lot of people believed you were acting as a documentary director, filming a conversation between two old friends in a New York restaurant – Wally Shawn as a sort of Sancho Panza figure, and André Gregory as the Quixote of the mystical side of the theatre. Yet this, to put it mildly, was deceptive.*

LM: Wally Shawn has a very small part in *Atlantic City*. He was a friend of John Guare's and I got to know him while I was working with John. We cast him in that funny part of the waiter in the restaurant in that big scene between Lancaster and Sarandon. He only had a couple of lines, but there is something about Wally, he looks so odd and interesting. I'd known André Gregory for a while and admired him as a stage director. While I was working with Wally in Atlantic City, he told me, 'I'm finishing writing this screenplay, it's called *My Dinner with André*. It's about a dinner between the two of us, and it's based on the fact that we'd worked together and life had separated us and André went on all these travels, and we met again and we thought it would be interesting to confront our experiences of the 1970s.' Although Wally is occasionally an actor, he is essentially a playwright. He always saw it as a screenplay. It was very nearly finished and he was going to send it to me. Of course, my first reaction was, 'Well, good luck.' The description of what it was about, I felt – film these two guys talking in a restaurant? This is all I need! I was very sceptical.

When I finished editing *Atlantic City* I came back to New York. I was having this great love affair with Candice, in the spring of 1980, and one day I received the script. It has never happened to me before or after – I wish it had – but when I finished reading it I felt I was so interested, so impressed, so curious about it, and immediately identified with both characters. I picked up the phone and called Wally, and then André, and said, 'Well, listen, let's do it. I don't know how, we'll need to talk about it a lot, but I'm definitely interested.' So we started meeting.

I thought the script was too long, I thought it was incredibly difficult to pull off, and I was not quite sure that both of them would be up to the difficulties of the parts. For a while I played devil's advocate, and said, 'Maybe the parts should be played by Dustin Hoffman and Robert Redford.' They were horrified. I was mostly unsure about André, because Wally is a wonderful supporting actor. Although Wally has an enormous role in this conversation, the more difficult part was André's. The first problem was that although they were meant to be themselves, they had to approach it as characters. For instance, André had to learn his lines. It seems to be improvised, but it was written to the dot; even his hesitations were written in the script. Although it was about André and his own experiences as he told them to Wally, the way it was written he had to reinvent his own character. I thought that was terribly interesting.

I've never rehearsed as much before shooting with actors as I did with these two. We spent months working. We'd meet in my apartment in New York in the afternoon, and we'd go through a segment of the screenplay. At some point I would tape them and show them what I felt was wrong or right. I would insist that they think of it not as themselves but that they become actors playing characters. I even went as far as asking Wally to play André's role and vice versa. It was a very systematic and long and fastidious preparation.

In the meantime, we had tremendous difficulties raising the money – even though it was a small sum, and in the end we did it very comfortably for $400,000. We always received the same reaction – 'It's terribly interesting, but it's not a movie.' The only thing I could say was, 'We're going to make it, and it's going to be a movie.' I said, 'Leave it to me, you have to trust me.' A movie can be anything. But, of course, people were scared it would be extraordinarily boring.

PF: *Did you cite the examples to anyone of Rohmer's* Ma Nuit chez Maude *or Jean Eustache's* La Maman et la putain?
LM: Oh, absolutely. And, of course, it worked for people who knew a little more about cinema, but the reaction of would-be financiers was negative. So the project was postponed a couple of times. In the meantime they went to London to do it in the little upstairs theatre at the Royal Court. And my name was in huge letters on the poster as the director of the play – actually I had very little to do with it, they were just sitting at a table on stage. I told them, 'You have to do it differently from what we rehearsed, you have to raise your voices, and frankly I think it's going to be a little bizarre, but it's good practice.' In the process of rehearsing we had tightened the screenplay. Wally was so precise and fierce about everything he had written, but little by little he agreed to make some changes and adjustments. At some point I felt we were ready.

The ultimate irony is that although this is a piece which is about New York and New York intellectuals, we shot it in Richmond, Virginia, because we had to do it non-union for budget reasons. We shot it in a huge hotel that had been closed down. We made the ballroom of the hotel into a sound stage. We re-created a New York restaurant. One of my problems, visually, was where to put these two people. Because I had to have a sense that it was really just between the two of them, I had to put them in a corner. But I realized that if they were going to be in front of two walls, it was going to be difficult to watch for over two hours. Our very good designer, David Mitchell, came up with the idea of having mirrors. And, although I didn't do anything complicated, I had to change the position of the camera slightly for every take. And, of course, if you shoot in front of a mirror, and you move the camera six inches, you have to reset all the lamps. So the solution we came up with was not mirrors, but a series of little mirror-squares that we could move slightly. It was a nightmare; every time I moved the camera we had to reset every square little mirror. But I think it worked in the sense that it gave a little bit of the background of the rest of the restaurant. We had these extras and we'd move them around so they would be in the reflection. It saved the film from becoming too abstract and gave a life to the background without interfering with the conversation.

I was hoping very much to do it with Sven Nykvist, but at the last minute he couldn't, because the film he was finishing was behind schedule. So I had to quickly choose a cameraman I had never worked with before, Jeri Sopanen. We had enough money to shoot for almost three weeks with a very small crew. We had shot the beginning in New York: in the subway when Wally's going to the restaurant, and there's a very nice coda where he's going back home in a taxi and he's reflecting about the evening and his memories of childhood. The rest, the restaurant, was shot in Richmond.

I had told everybody that I was going to approach the shoot very slowly and rather than more rehearsals I'd prefer to start shooting and find my angles. I wanted to experiment. Would I use tracking shots? I wanted to play around a bit. First, I realized that if it was going to work it was going to work in the cutting room. I took that for granted. Second, I needed reaction shots of both of them all the time so that I could cover myself and be able to cut back and forth constantly. The shots on Wally and those on André – the transitions had to be so smooth that the spectator would not really notice the cutting. I think we got that. I think it's perceived by people as a sort of flow. I don't think they're aware of the cutting. Spectators get the impression that they are both constantly on the screen. But that was difficult to do. At the end of the first week we'd shot an enormous amount of footage.

PF: *And shooting in sequence?*

LM: Yes. Pretty much in sequence. Long takes of the conversation. Of course there were breaks, when the waiter was bringing a new dish, so I had to deal with that. The 16mm magazines we were shooting with were ten minutes, so each take would be ten minutes long. There was a film lab in Richmond, to my surprise; they developed the negative and printed the rushes. The next Sunday I went to see the first five days of shooting with France La Chapelle, the continuity girl, just the two of us. We watched rushes from eight in the morning until ten at night, and I was completely confused. But watching these takes, I somehow figured out how to deal with both of them. It became clearer to me that in shooting André, when I wanted him to be funny or slightly pompous, a certain angle was the best, and when I wanted him to be moving, it worked better for him if the camera was a little higher. And the following week, plus a couple of days in the third week, I reshot everything, with very subtle changes in the positions of the camera. I had abandoned very quickly any kind of tracking because I thought it would interfere with the cutting. Also, tracking in and out would just show the camera, and it was essential that people forget about the camera immediately.

After a week, the two of them started to relax, which was great. At the beginning André talks non-stop for something like twenty-five minutes, and it was really hard to pull off. I thought, if the audience doesn't leave the theatre in the first twenty-five minutes, I'm fine. What André was saying was quite interesting, but it was odd, slightly pompous. I suppose my contribution to the screenplay and making it work as a film was that I don't think it was originally meant to be as funny as it eventually was. I was really happy to hear how much people laughed the first time I saw it with an audience. That was exactly what I had hoped for, but you never know. If you read the screenplay it was not obvious. I pushed André to give certain details in his performance that would provide this – the humour, the foolishness at times. But I also used Wally's reaction shots. They were essential. And we injected them very carefully. At the beginning I wanted the audience to be terribly curious about Wally, who didn't say anything, but by the way he was reacting you knew he didn't quite understand what the other one was saying and he was somewhat disapproving of it. So it prepared what was to follow.

PF: *You say that in this debate between the mystic, intellectual seeker André Gregory and the sort of* homme moyen sensuel *of Wallace Shawn, in this debate about life, aesthetics and experience, you saw yourself in*

both of them. Yet the laughter that you're describing came from leading
the viewer – inevitably you were interpreting the debate by the reaction
shots of Wallace Shawn.

LM: Well, I said that I could identify with both of them. Obviously, I felt
closer to the Wally character, although I understood what André had
been going through. I'd had my own crisis; I'd been to India and dropped
out for a while. I could understand this quest. The André character was
not necessarily André, by the way – it was much more subtle than that.
Because it was written by Wally, the André character, even in the screenplay, was slightly irritating. You could immediately see it was written by
the other one. I just put the accent on that; I exaggerated it. At the same
time, I knew André could be funny, even ridiculous. In a way, what is
great in the evolution of his character is that at the end he becomes
extraordinarily moving. He is redeemed; for instance, when he talks
about the child and how the child becomes a man – a wonderful moment.
It was essential at the beginning to look ironically at this intellectual
adventurer who's always coming back and just by accident spending days
in Richard Avedon's house, between trips to Poland and Tibet. It all
came from the text – I didn't betray the text. I loved the André character,
I identified with him, but there was something about him that disturbed
me. In my own quest I'd never gone as far as he did, but I could have.

PF: *You had two very striking physical types to work with; they remind*
me of those two characters out of John Ford's Stagecoach, *the gambler*
Hatfield, played by John Carradine, and the little whisky salesman,
played by Donald Meek – they represent, physically, different levels of
society, different kinds of social expectation.

LM: When the Wally character starts talking, somehow in his writing he
ridicules himself. And, of course, Wally is a wonderful character because
he's totally in control, but at the same time he's authentically bizarre,
consciously or not.

By the end of the shooting I had this enormous amount of material. I
was basically happy with it. It was just before Christmas. At the beginning of the following year I brought in my editor, Suzanne Baron again. I
warned her, 'Suzanne, this is going to be a very tough one to pull off. It
will happen or not happen in the cutting room.' We proceeded by
successive approximations. We very quickly found out which were the
best moments. What she did wonderfully was to choose – sometimes it
was a question of two frames – the moment to cut so it would not be
noticeable. Also, it had to follow the conversation and respect the

emotion of the moment. Outside documentaries, I think it's the most elaborate job of editing I've ever done.

It was first shown at the Telluride Film Festival,[4] which takes place around Labor Day in America at the beginning of September, and I couldn't go because I had to do something in France, but André and Wally went, and it was incredibly well received. It became the one film of all the festival that everybody talked about. When I came back to New York I met a woman I knew slightly, the wife of a producer, and she said she'd seen *My Dinner with André* and she went on and on about how great it was, and then at some point she said, 'I saw your name and I knew you were involved, that you directed it, but what exactly did you do?' I thought, 'This is the ultimate compliment.' For most spectators, except those who know a little about film-making, it seemed like I'd put one camera on one side and one on the other side, and shot it in an afternoon with the two of them improvising. To end up giving that feeling to a normal spectator was, for me, quite an achievement, and I was very happy with that.

PF: *And also it was a film that people emerged from carrying on the debate – it had an open-ended feeling to it: it put questions, it didn't provide easy answers, even though people may have felt greater sympathy for one side or the other.*

LM: The film did quite well in every English-speaking country, extremely well on its own terms. It was an independent film, it didn't do as well as a Spielberg film, but it was very successful. Of course, in France nothing happened. It seemed absurd to dub it, although we did it eventually and ended up presenting it with subtitles – there were, like, three lines on every image. I told my friends, 'You have to see it twice. You have to see it first to read the titles, and then see it again and look at the images.'

I suppose my contribution was to emphasize that it was not so much what they were saying, but the way they were saying it; to bring out that sometimes they were not quite sincere or they were not quite telling the truth, or they were reinventing their memories. Through the reaction shots I could emphasize that. Something was happening on their faces, beyond the words. So the film was working on two levels: the discourses, the conversation, and getting to know those two characters extremely well. You never have a chance in a normal film to get so much time with close-ups of two characters. It ended up as being about this intimate relationship and people came out of the movie and wanted to continue the conversation.

This film stayed in cities like New York and Boston for something like nine months; I think it was in the same cinema in Boston for a year. People were telling me in Los Angeles, and in Texas, 'We had *My Dinner with André* dinner parties, where we'd have dinner, play the tape, and then continue the conversation.' It came out just as this ugly decade of the 1980s was starting, and the film is somehow a melancholic coda to what had happened in the 1960s and 1970s. It was very much about a certain category of people, very much at a certain moment when sensibilities started shifting. It was perceived as such, and was, in a way, strangely topical, which nobody knew in advance or could anticipate. That probably explains why people were so interested.

PF: *After* My Dinner with André, *one of your most fastidious films, came the coarsest thing which you've been engaged in,* Crackers. *The only thing they have in common is Wallace Shawn. How did you get involved in it, how happily did you go into the project?*

LM: Both *Atlantic City* and *My Dinner with André* were released in 1981 in America – *Atlantic City* in the spring and *My Dinner with André* in the autumn. Both were very well received. I got interested in a scandal that had been very much in the papers, and eventually somebody wrote a book about it. It was about an extraordinary character, a swindler who was offering people an offshore tax-evasion scheme. He took money from a number of suckers and eventually was caught. The FBI was about to start an investigation on corruption among politicians and they forced this character – I don't remember what he was called in reality, but in John Guare's screenplay he was called Shelley Slutski – to work for them. They used a fake Arab sheikh who was offering money to politicians and this fake sheikh was an FBI agent. The swindler was to approach the politicians, because the sheikh would either be trying to acquire American nationality or be terribly interested in investing money in their constituencies.

PF: *Is this what became known as the Ab Scam?*

LM: Yes, Ab Scam. Again, I wanted to do something different. I thought this would be wonderful material for a political satire and comedy. I discussed it with John Guare, and he was quite enthusiastic. Early on we thought it would be a great part for John Belushi – in fact I wanted to pair Belushi and Dan Aykroyd. It was at a time when Belushi was an immense star in the States. I was crazy about Belushi when I met him. I thought he was incredibly inventive, rather confused as a person, but with enormous potential as a comic actor. So from the beginning

Belushi and Aykroyd were involved.

Everybody in Hollywood wanted to finance the project. John Guare came up with the title: *Moon over Miami*. We set it up in Florida and started working on the screenplay. And then my mother died and I had to go back to France, just when we'd delivered the first draft to Columbia. One morning John Guare called me and told me that Belushi had died of an overdose at the Château Marmont in Los Angeles. I thought immediately, 'This project is gone.' What I anticipated happened: the studio people were not terribly enthusiastic about the project. The screenplay was very funny, very provocative and they would have agreed to shoot the phone book with Belushi, but the moment he was dead I knew they were going to turn it down. Then I spent a number of excruciating months trying to replace Belushi; I talked to Dustin Hoffman and a few others. Eventually I thought the best choice was Bob Hoskins. I'd seen *Guys and Dolls* on stage, where he was very convincing as an American. Except in those days in Hollywood it was, Bob who? Nobody knew who he was. As you know, he is now very popular over there.

PF: *And playing Americans.*

LM: Yes. Aykroyd was very loyal, but we realized quickly that we weren't getting anywhere. Guare wrote a second draft and we lost patience. I got very restless because we'd spent almost a year on this project. I didn't know what to do and I had this producer who had been calling me for a couple of years trying to convince me to remake the Mario Monicelli film *I soliti ignoti*. I forget the English title.

PF: *It was known in Britain as* Persons Unknown *and in America as* Big Deal on Madonna Street.

LM: I turned it down several times. And then somehow I was sucked in. They said, 'You can always pull out when you want', and I refused to commit myself. The screenwriter was an extremely nice man – Jeffrey Fiskin, who'd worked previously with Ivan Passer on *Cutter's Way*, which I liked. We got along very well, and neither of us was too sure there was a way to make the story work in America today, but he was signed to write the screenplay and made some money, so I thought, well, I'm going to see what happens. I was not even under contract yet, but for some reason, I never understood why, they really wanted me to do it. It happened little by little – I put the tip of my finger in and I ended up completely in the machine.

I became intrigued when Fiskin said, 'We should look at San Francisco.

There are interesting mixed neighbourhoods there.' So we went to San Francisco and looked round. We ended up in the area called the Mission District, which was very mixed, with ex-hippies, artists and drop-outs living in what, essentially, was a Latino neighbourhood. It had a *quartier* life – cafés with tables outside – that you rarely find in American cities and we thought, maybe we could set the story today in this particular part of San Francisco. It was the early 1980s when a lot of people were out of work.

Jeff came up with a screenplay, and my first reaction was, 'I don't want to shoot that.' It wasn't a bad script, the characters were interesting (they were characters from the *commedia dell'arte* transposed to America), but it had nothing to do with me and I didn't want to do it. I don't know what happened – they managed to convince me. I blame myself entirely. I'm not going to use the excuse that Hollywood screwed me, because I didn't have to make it. I was just very anxious to get back to work. What I should have done was take a 16mm camera and go somewhere to shoot a documentary. I would have saved my soul. But instead of that I said, 'Well, if I start another project from scratch it's going to take another six months. I've always been ready for a new kind of experience, and this'll be my one and only experience within the American studio system. It's not even a project of mine, so why not?'

I began pre-production and immediately started getting into trouble. The picture had a budget of something like $12 million, but I realized very quickly that out of the 12 million I would only have 4 or 5 to make the film. The rest would go in overheads and absurd salaries – including mine, as a matter of fact. I kept coming back in the evening and telling Candice, 'I don't think I should do it', and she kept saying, 'Then why do it?' and I would say 'Well, I'm going to pull it off.' I was lucky enough to put together an exciting cast. It's the only positive thing that can be said about the film. It had a really funny, interesting cast – Donald Sutherland, a wonderful actress called Christine Baranski, and Wally Shawn, and Sean Penn, and Jack Warden, plus a number of unknown very good black and Latino actors.

PF: *You say it is a good cast – they are good actors – but one of the principal reasons why the original film was successful was because the gang of hopeless low-life crooks were played by immensely glamorous performers: Vittorio Gassman, Mastroianni, Claudia Cardinale. You had a cast, in fact, of beaten-up realists.*

LM: Yes, I was excited by the cast, though certainly by Hollywood

49 *Crackers:* the gang's all here – Larry Riley, Donald Sutherland,
Wallace Shawn, Sean Penn and Trinidad Silva

standards it was an odd one. Trinidad Silva, the Mexican-American
whose character in the Italian film was Cardinale's brother – he was not
really an actor. He'd been in a couple of films, but they didn't even know
who he was. The girl who played the Cardinale part had never acted in
front of a camera before. Wally was an odd quantity by Hollywood
standards, but at least they knew who he was because of *My Dinner with
André*. I even had to fight for Donald Sutherland, because they didn't
think he was a box-office attraction. Of course, I was digging my own
grave. My number-one supporter in this venture was the man who was
the head of Production; the second week of shooting he left Universal
and was replaced. I knew then I was in deadly trouble. What they call
'musical chairs' in Hollywood – where the key executives move constantly from one studio to the other – is terribly dangerous for us
film-makers. You start a project with somebody who is very enthusiastic
and then you're left with somebody who knows nothing about it.

But I want to go back to what you were saying, which was absolutely
right, about the Italian cast, though they were not all as famous then as
they eventually became: Claudia Cardinale, Renato Salvatore, Marcello
Mastroianni, Vittorio Gassman and Toto. It was a fabulous cast. My

casting was odd, bizarre and interesting, but it certainly had none of that appeal. Of course, I watched the Italian film several times, and I realized the film only worked because of the extraordinary performances – the fact that these people were so entertaining and worked so well together. I should have done my film with a kind of equivalent of that cast. But I went the other way – a great mistake. Although I enjoyed working with the cast I'd chosen, I hated being on the set. I kept asking myself, what am I doing here? It was shot in the Hollywood manner, with an enormous crew; it was such an enormous crew that it took me practically the whole film to get to know everybody.

We shot exteriors in San Francisco for several weeks, then we came back to the sound stage at Universal. Not only was it a huge crew, but also it was constantly changing – not the key members, but the grips, electricians and special-effects people would rotate; they'd move to another film. I was introduced to an industrial way of making films, which I could not even begin to handle. Frankly, my judgement about the film today is that I did a terrible job. To be honest, a mercenary director, somebody who is talented and used to working from a screenplay that was not his, used to being hired at the last minute – and there are some good directors working that way in America (actually it's the majority of them) – would have done a much better job than I did. My sense of comedy is completely different from the material I was working with. It would be too easy for me to blame the project itself or the screenplay – actually, Fiskin's screenplay was workable. I was just not used to working that way. I was like a cog in a big machine, and I didn't feel I was really in charge. Although it was probably the biggest budget I ever dealt with, I constantly felt the pressure that we had to finish that day because we had to move the next day. So I had less freedom than with *My Dinner with André*, or any of my French films, or *Atlantic City*. Then I started editing with Suzanne Baron, and because it was a studio film I ended up with a crew of something like fifteen assistant editors, when I'm used to working with a maximum of two. It was a complete mess. We realized early on, piecing together the scenes, that it didn't work. We came up with a first cut; we had a disastrous preview. It became a total nightmare, and it kept me in the cutting room for much longer than I cared to be. Eventually, the picture was a flop. Some people like it – not too many.

PF: *Yet having done that you then made a film which is very much in the American, indeed the Hollywood, grain.* Alamo Bay *is directly in the tradition of the Warner Brothers social-conscience picture. Darryl*

Zanuck, who created the genre at Warner Brothers, said he would snatch
stories from the headlines and make hard-hitting melodramas. You did
snatch this story from the headlines about the Ku Klux Klan recrud-
escence, the redneck reaction of the local fishermen in the Texas Gulf to
Vietnamese refugees coming into the area to work as fishermen.

LM: It started in the late 1970s and early 1980s. I think the film was shot
in 1984. While I was working on Moon over Miami, I became interested
in the stories I was reading about in the papers – there was a piece in the
New York Times Sunday Magazine written by a Texan journalist called
Ross Milloy. I thought it exposed fascinating contradictions in America:
this notion that the Vietnam war was continuing on American soil in
Texas. Here were these fishermen who were Catholic and had left Vietnam with their priest and resettled in the Gulf in Florida and Texas.
Almost immediately they started competing with the American shrimpers, and because they were terribly good at what they were doing and
very organized and hard workers, they started to threaten the American
fishermen's economic survival. That set off a series of ugly incidents. The
KKK moved in immediately and tried to organize the fishermen and
encourage violence. I'm always interested when, due to historical events,
people are forced into behaviour that would not normally happen, that's
created by circumstance. Suddenly people change. They find out who
they are – sometimes revealing the ugly side of themselves.

This was obviously the case in those fishing towns in south Texas.
They were rednecks, which is a bizarre culture in itself: very macho.
People drink a lot, they drive around with their pick-up trucks, and
behind their heads they always have these hunting rifles hanging in the
cabin of the truck, which is very impressive for a stranger. There was also
the irony of these Vietnamese who had left their country because they
had been trying to help the Americans win the war, only to find themselves being denounced as Communist spies, the Yellow Peril, invading
Texas. It was ugly and violent, but it was also strangely ambiguous.
These rednecks were perfectly normal people, going to church every
Sunday. They were not a bunch of Fascists or criminals, just fishermen.

PF: *They were finding in the Vietnamese scapegoats for their situation, in*
the way that the Jews in Germany were used in the 1920s and 1930s by
people embittered by their economic conditions.

LM: Exactly. It gave me a chance to expose the roots of racism. The
Vietnamese became scapegoats because these Americans felt threatened.
The economy of these little towns was in bad shape anyway; they were

over-fishing and the shrimps were disappearing. When the Vietnamese came and started to shrimp – sometimes working on shifts at night – it got everybody crazy. I read about how the Americans were horrified by cultural differences. All the clichés of racism: Vietnamese children peed in the streets; they were dirty; ten people shared a room; the food they ate was disgusting. If you compare it to what happened in Europe with the Jews, the similarities are striking. I thought it was an opportunity to examine what seems to be a pattern.

When I first went to Texas to meet Ross Milloy and he took me around, it had finally quietened down. It was extremely tense, but it was quiet. My first instinct was, maybe I should go with a 16mm camera. But it was too late. Ross encouraged me to make a fiction film out of it, but I kept telling him, 'Maybe it would be better if it was made by an American director.' I knew that I was bound for trouble and decided not to do it. Then I went into Crackers – that very unfortunate experience. When I came out of Crackers I needed revenge. I really thought I should make a film on my own terms. So I came back to what became Alamo Bay. I researched with Ross, and decided to work with a writer called Alice Arlen.

PF: *Presumably you'd liked* Silkwood,[5] *but did that come about because you decided that the conscience of the film should be the woman returning to the town from outside, with a perspective on the local situation?*
LM: Well, I knew Alice, and I liked her writing. For the script of Silkwood, she shared the credit with Nora Ephron. The director Mike Nichols had told me that she'd been very helpful. Because she spent her childhood in Wyoming, she knew about rednecks. I took her to Texas, where the situation was calm but still extremely tense. We talked to people, including some of the Americans who had sided with the Vietnamese and had been threatened. And she wrote a first draft of the screenplay. I wanted to do it very quickly. We very consciously had as a reference point those Warner Brothers films of the late 1930s and early 1940s.

PF: *They started fairly early on.* I Am a Fugitive from a Chain Gang *and films like that were early 1930s. There was another film I am reminded of, a John Sturges film from the mid-1950s,* Bad Day at Black Rock. *There are even certain physical resemblances between Ed Harris and Robert Ryan. They both strut around in this aggressive way, wearing baseball caps, and have a relationship with a younger woman who stands for different values. They are also about the relationship between south-western American xenophobes and, in this case, the Vietnamese and, in the Sturges film, the Japanese-Americans.*

LM: Actually, Alice offered to take *High Noon* as a model, but twisting it around. The idea was to use a genre that Hollywood had employed quite often of a stranger coming into town and little by little being caught between two communities. The young Vietnamese would come to town with great expectations and be adopted by his compatriots, but he would ignore the unwritten rules and behave like, and try to become, an American. At the end of the film he's standing by himself against the whole town.

Again, I was in the situation of having a teenager at the centre of the film. First I looked at some Vietnamese, or even Chinese-American, actors and couldn't find anybody young enough or convincing enough. So I had to go into the Vietnamese community for someone authentic who could play that part. As usual I went into this long search and one week before we started I was still interviewing. I had chosen this young Vietnamese boy, but although there was something interesting about him, and something moving, I knew it was going to be difficult. I could see that he was uncomfortable. So at the last minute I went into a frantic search to find somebody else, but I couldn't find anyone, so I had to start with him. I'd been extremely lucky from *Zazie* to *Le Souffle au coeur*, *Lacombe, Lucien* and *Pretty Baby*, but with this one I felt I was in trouble.

Alice Arlen was with us on location and I had two wonderful actors, Ed Harris and Amy Madigan, and during the shooting, and even more so during the editing, they became the central characters. This is not what I expected to do. It was a betrayal of the original idea, which was to take this young man and, through his eyes and experience discover what is going on.

PF: *But making the Ed Harris and Amy Madigan characters the centre emphasizes the connections with and criticism of the myth of the West as it carries on in Texas – and the Western itself: the name* Alamo Bay, *the whole ironic reworking of the Texans defending themselves, the racist character nicknamed after 'Shanghai' Pearce, one of the great cattle-drovers. You have also the emphasis on the fact that in Westerns the voice of reason is usually that of the woman, often the schoolteacher. Though the violence in this film, given the genre, is inevitable at the end, I don't think you could have avoided that, given the form you had chosen.*

50 *Alamo Bay:* Dinh (Ho Nguyen) takes a back seat as liberal Glory
(Amy Madigan) confronts xenophobic Pierce (Ed Harris)

*You build up expectations that, whatever the values of the film, the
villains are going to get their come-uppance, not by being won over to
reason but by acts of violence, by the shoot-out.*

LM: From the beginning, I was interested in telling the story within this
particular genre. It's so stylized, it almost becomes operatic. I was quite
aware of that, and was definitely trying to work in that direction. And in
that sense I think there would have been a better balance if the Vietnamese boy had been more convincing than he was. I have to blame
myself because I have usually been successful in creating odd characters
and finding the right people to play them. In this case, I even had to do
something that I did reluctantly – his English was so difficult and broken,
although one of my assistants, a very smart man from the Texas film-
school, worked with him every day on his lines, that I had to reloop him
entirely with a Chinese-American actor in New York. Actually, it worked
quite well. But that tells you how desperate I was. We had this strange
triangle with the woman at the centre, a very powerful villain and this
weak hero.

I must say, apart from that, I was happy with the film when it was all
finished. I thought I had made my point, I thought it was accurate, I
thought the depiction of the rednecks was not at all a caricature –

although that's what the American critics complained about. The New York and Los Angeles critics know nothing about the redneck culture. I knew a lot more about it after making the movie than they did. I was not expecting that it would necessarily be well received but I thought the film had real integrity.

Crackers was immediately dismissed – for good reasons, I must say. It was a tremendous flop, and disappeared as soon as it came out. I notice that American critics, when they talk about my work, never talk about *Crackers*. They're being polite. *Alamo Bay* came out in 1985, the tenth anniversary of the fall of Saigon, and Americans were trying to revisit the Vietnam war and make peace with it. It was in the middle of the Reagan years. I couldn't have found a worse moment to release the film. But what I didn't quite expect, although I should have anticipated it, was the feeling that here was this French director who had been working in America and had been well treated, and suddenly he was dealing with something that was very disturbing, an ugly series of events in recent American history. Critics in New York and LA dismissed the film without actually saying that, but the less sophisticated ones in the smaller cities didn't hesitate to say, 'Mind your own business.'

PF: *Wasn't there that feeling when you were making it in Texas? What was the reaction of the local people when they knew what the subject matter of the film was?*
LM: It was like we had come to reopen hostilities! The shooting was very tense. We found ourselves re-enacting something that had happened four years before, although I purposely chose a town where it had been a little quieter. When I picked that little town I started recruiting a lot of locals. Outside Ed, Amy, the young Vietnamese and a couple of actors, all the others were real fishermen. And, of course, the Vietnamese were all local Vietnamese. Both communities were very much against the project. Eventually, the Americans, or some of them, were interested in appearing in the film and making money. They played some of the scenes with a kind of intensity that was a little strange. Many of the people playing the extremists among the fishermen, the ones who wanted to get rid of the Vietnamese, were convinced that their characters were right.

On the other hand, I had enormous trouble convincing the Vietnamese community to take part. They turned me down; when I was looking for extras nobody showed up. I had to convince the priests that it was important to make this film. I had to go to the Bishop of Corpus Christi so that the Catholic hierarchy would take a positive attitude. Actually, he happened to be a remarkable man and was very helpful; he came and talked to the Vietnamese and told them they should work with us. Shooting the scene with the KKK burning the cross and trying to scare the Vietnamese was very tense, let me tell you. We received a lot of anonymous threats.

Ed Harris and Amy Madigan came into this little town two weeks before we started, and I was impressed by the way Ed, in a matter of days, started to mix with the fishermen and become one of them. He was so much part of the community, so much of a redneck, that sometimes I was not sure if I was dealing with an actor. This was the kind of work that American actors do so well, but push it to such an extreme. He went into drinking and some very erratic behaviour, which I definitely think was part of his preparation in becoming his character. And that helped us, because the locals in the cast were crazy for Ed, they loved him, they were all buddies. Amy and Ed have always been liberal in the American sense, they've always been involved in leftist causes. Yet Ed was practically taking sides with the rednecks. Which is something I wanted – I wanted to do justice to them, in the sense that the presence of the Vietnamese was definitely an enormous threat.

I went back there not so long ago to visit Ross Milloy, who still lives in Austin. We revisited the coast, and there are practically no more American fishermen there – they've been wiped out. And almost no more shrimps. The shrimpers that are left are Vietnamese. The Vietnamese were much more organized, worked harder, were dedicated to success, which is what has made them so successful in America.

PF: *I don't think you minimize in the film the challenge they represent, also the way they don't understand the rules or the laws. A final point on the visual and aural texture of the film. Amy Madigan was brought into movies by Walter Hill in* Streets of Fire, *and another person introduced to the cinema by Walter Hill was Ry Cooder. You used him on this film, and you had as the cameraman Curtis Clark, much of whose work had been in documentary.*

LM: I've always liked Ry Cooder as a musician, a film-musician. He had just got a lot of attention for the score of *Paris, Texas*. Originally, I had intended to use existing country music. I even made a deal with a country-music publisher from Nashville, who ended up playing the Baptist preacher. He was very enthusiastic about the project and we even started putting pieces of existing country music that he had prepared for us on the images. Then I realized, because the film was in this operatic

51 *Alamo Bay:* Louis Malle organizes a Ku Klux Klan rally
52 *Alamo Bay:* Ed Harris leads white-sheeted rednecks against the
Vietnamese fishermen

vein, that I needed a score – which doesn't often happen to me. So I went
to Ry, because I felt I needed a consistent score, and he did a beautiful
job. He understood the film quite well.

The choice of Curtis Clark came about partly because we had a very
small budget. There are two unions in America, IATSE, the official
union, and an independent, basically New York union called NABID,
and from the beginning we decided to do business with the second union,
because they were younger and it would be easier for me to work with a
smaller crew. Because we had a limited number of shooting days, we
knew that we would end up with a lot of overtime, so we went to
NABID and I brought to Texas an excellent New York crew that I was
really happy with. Curtis had started his career as a cameraman in
England and I found out that he was back in America and was actually a
Texan. I had admired his work for Peter Greenaway, especially *The
Draughtsman's Contract*. So I decided to work with him. It was his first
American film, and he's been working in America ever since. I don't
know what to say. We didn't get along very well. But he's a very good
cameraman.

I always have problems with slow cameramen. I've worked with very
few of them. One of the things I've always admired in the great
cameramen I've worked with – people like Henri Decaë, Sven Nykvist,
Tonino Delli Colli, or recently Renato Berta – is that they work fast.
We spend a lot of time discussing the lighting before we start, and then
things go. I always like to keep the momentum going. For me that has a
lot to do with the actors, keeping the rhythm with them. I especially
hate to work with a cameraman who changes his light between takes. A
lot of American cameramen do that – and some French cameramen too,
I should say. You're just getting to that moment you want to get your
shot, everybody is there with you, and the cameraman asks for twenty
minutes to modify his lighting. So that made my relationship with Curtis a little difficult, and probably unfair, because by American standards
he's not slow.

PF: *Before you made* Alamo Bay, *in fact back in 1979 before* Atlantic
City, *you shot documentary material in a small town in Minnesota called
Glencoe. You didn't assemble it for the public until 1986, as* God's
Country, *when you revisited the town to add a little coda. Then you
subsequently made another American film* And the Pursuit of Happiness.
*How did these two films relate at the time to your American fictional
works?*

LM: Through the end of the 1960s and the 1970s I made several documentaries, my Indian documentaries, and *Humain, trop humain* and
Place de la République in 1972. It's a little difficult to explain why, but I
always intended that after the Indian films I would try to alternate my
fiction and my documentary work. Most of my French films after *Feu
follet* are set in the past. It seemed that in terms of fiction I needed
distance. It was not a conscious decision, but it always seemed easier to
deal with a theme or subject or story that was in the past because it
would, maybe, give me a better view of it and a more lucid approach to
what I was trying to do. It just happened that way. Dealing with something in the present in fiction was dangerous; it would be influenced by
what seemed topical. I seemed to need the distance of time. As an
antidote to that, and because I was curious about things happening at the
moment, I thought I could confront the present better with *cinéma direct*,
in 16mm, in a documentary form.

PF: *What is the difference between* cinéma direct *and* cinéma vérité?
LM: Well, *cinéma vérité* is not a term that I like to use; *cinéma vérité* is
cinéma mensonge. *Cinéma vérité* has a moral implication: it's meant to
define the truth, which is very pretentious and not necessarily true. I like
cinéma direct because it's more a technique than anything else. What I
call *cinéma direct* is a kind of documentary where you completely
improvise, you work with a minimal crew, you don't try to organize
reality, you just try to find where your interest or curiosity takes you, you
try to film what you find interesting or surprising, and later try to make
sense of it in the cutting room. It's a cinema of instinct, of improvisation,
a cinema very much of the present. As something happens, you try to
catch it. Then you examine what you have and why you shot it that way.
That's my personal definition. It seems to me that *cinéma direct* is the
best way to describe what I was trying to do in India or the documentaries I did in France in 1972, or those American documentaries I did
later on.

I made *God's Country* in the spring of 1979, at the end of which I did
Atlantic City. I had worked on a fiction project with which I was not
satisfied, and I had not been encouraged by the first reaction of studios or
financiers. In the meantime, I had been approached by Susan Weil, who
was the head of programming at PBS at the time, and she had said,
'Louis, we admire your documentaries and we would like you to make
one in this country if you are interested.' So I went back to her. I had
chosen a subject: I wanted to study the phenomenon of the American

shopping mall. They were not completely new at the time, in 1979, but for Europeans they were quite new. The mall had been invented in Minnesota, for the simple reason that Minnesota is so cold in winter, and had become almost like a mini-culture. I'd read a couple of interesting articles about the birth of the idea of shopping malls – the architecture, economics and sociology of the mall. I said, 'I don't need much money to make the film' – we were talking about something like $50,000.

So I went out with a small crew, five of us altogether, and we went to Minneapolis and started looking at shopping malls. I also decided that I would handle the camera myself. In my previous documentaries I'd been lucky enough to work with Étienne Becker, who'd become a director of photography, but I don't think he was anxious to come and work in the States. Since all the crucial decisions in this kind of filming are made by the cameraman, I thought it was maybe just as well. By taking the camera myself, I discovered it added a dimension to my work which made my relationship with the people I was dealing with more personal and intimate than just standing beside the camera or handling a second camera as I'd done before.

I went to Minnesota and realized this idea of the shopping mall was never going to work, for one stupid reason – muzak is part of the environment, it never stops. This absurd and terrible music was on low, but not low enough for us. It would always be in the background, and any kind of editing would be impossible because the music would be constantly cut. I tried to convince the manager of one of the malls to cut the muzak, and of course he refused, because for him a shopping mall without muzak was not a shopping mall, it wouldn't work. He said it would be detrimental to business. So here I was with my crew in Minnesota. We had a van. I said, 'Why don't we look around? Maybe we'll find something interesting.' It was not an accident that I'd chosen Minnesota. I knew I would find shopping malls, but I was also interested in dealing with the Midwest, which is basically still very rural, with a population composed of European immigrants, Scandinavians and Germans and Poles and Lithuanians. Also, the Middle West is somewhat mythological; in America it's seen as the real country, the real people, the real values – except that nobody ever goes there, specially people making films. They fly above it, from New York to Los Angeles; they never stop.

I decided to look for a rural community, and spend time there getting acquainted with people, talking to them and eventually filming them. We started driving at random; we shot several things; we went into a mining town for a bit. It went on for three weeks and I was getting worried, until we entered this little town of Glencoe. It was a Sunday, and the annual festival. The town had about 5,000 inhabitants – everybody was out, there was an orchestra playing the polka, the traditional German/Polish accordion music. Everybody was dancing and drinking a lot of beer. Most of the inhabitants of Glencoe were of German origin.

We stopped and started filming that afternoon: the people, the games. We had a very good feeling, we were very well received, people were sunny and warm. We stayed about three or four weeks. In that first day, because everybody was around the band and in the street, we got to know people. We took their telephone numbers and said, 'Can we come and visit you?' The next day we went out of town to see a farmer, and asked him if we could film his work and family, the interior of his house. So that's how we did it.

I was terribly curious about these people. They were more interesting than I expected, because the cliché, I suppose, about Middle Westerners is that they are conventional – which they *are* in a way – and live in very tight communities, they're churchgoers. All these clichés are true if you want. My filming and the narration were slightly ironical, but I fell in love with these people. They were actually quite smart, sometimes surprisingly aware of what was going on, and it was a period when things were good for the farmers. This little community was economically in very good shape. I had wonderful surprises. For instance, this tiny little community lost in the fields of Minnesota had a theatre and they were putting on plays that this wonderful woman, the wife of the lawyer, was writing. And we had the chance to film a wedding, which was great fun. I had a wonderful time.

Also, I found echoes of the Vietnam war. I couldn't help remarking that this was a community where there were literally no blacks at all; a few Mexicans, agricultural workers, more or less transient families. And we ended up talking politics. I could see some traces of racism, but sort of gentle, if you can define racism as gentle. I remember one of the young farmers, one I really liked, said at one point, when I asked, 'How come there are no blacks in this community?' 'Well, it seems that blacks don't like it here, they don't stay, they don't seem to fit.' People just took for granted that blacks wouldn't show up.

PF: *You were trying to be both non-judgemental and also aware of certain precedents that you wished to avoid, the kind of patronizing and exploitative documentary often made by Europeans, the kind that François Reichenbach[6] used to make about America. Not as bad for instance as* Mondo Cane, *but looking for the colourful and bizarre and often finding evidence to support his own views about Americans.*

LM: Certainly François Reichenbach and myself are completely different in sensibility; I don't think we're attracted to the same things. What was so interesting about Glencoe was that it was really a little town where nothing happened. It was a hopeless topic for a documentary in a way, like when I went to Thailand. They were so remote from the centre of decision-making, so remote in every possible way, yet that's precisely what I found interesting.

The part I personally like best in the whole documentary concerned a young girl who was working in an office. I had met her at the theatre, she was one of the amateur actors in the company, and I said, 'I would like to talk to you.' So we went to see her at home at the weekend, and we started a conversation about what it is to be a woman in Glencoe, the fact that it was still a very macho culture, the fact that it was difficult for a woman to have a free sexual life, that it was impossible to be homosexual – you would have to leave Glencoe, it would not be accepted. She started talking about her own experience; she started expressing a certain amount of bitterness, and when we were cutting the film we used to call her the Madame Bovary of Glencoe. She had dreams, she wanted a more interesting life, she hated the place for its bigotry. She was a rebel. She left and ended up in Florida. We kept writing letters to each other for a while after, so I knew what happened to her.

Anyway, I sat in front of her with the camera and we started talking, and it became a sort of confession. I was shooting roll after roll. I realized there was something about being behind the camera myself. It was as if she was having this conversation with the camera. It was as if the camera was asking the questions. And she was talking, sharing her confidences with the camera. It would not have worked that way if she'd been talking to me. There was something about her, the way she said certain things, because she was looking at the camera, which made it a lot more intimate and disturbing. When she finished she suddenly got a little frightened, and said, 'I never thought I would tell you all that.' I said, 'I think it's fine. Take my word, I'll make the best out of it.' And she was great in the film, very moving and interesting.

Then I came back to New York, got involved in *Atlantic City* and put everything on the shelf. I told PBS, 'There's no hurry. I'm going to make *Atlantic City*, and when I'm finished I'll come back and cut *God's Country*.' Then it took them something like five years, which is typical of PBS, to raise the additional $50,000 that I needed for editing. After

Alamo Bay I started thinking about *Au revoir les enfants*. But in the meantime, in 1985, I decided to edit *God's Country*. Suzanne Baron had already made a first long cut in Paris, actually. We had something like two or three hours. I decided to re-cut it and it immediately crossed my mind that since six years had passed I should go back.

So I returned for something like one week. Because I'd started editing, I'd seen which were the most interesting segments that we had shot, and knew which people would be in the film, so I wanted to see what had become of them. When we went back, the farmers of America were in the middle of a huge economic crisis; it was that time in the middle of the Reagan years when it seemed that the bottom had fallen out. All these farmers were going bankrupt and having to sell their farms. The mood was very different, very gloomy, and I would talk to the same people, who told me, 'We're in big trouble, I don't know if we're going to make it.' One of the farmers I had dealt with had sold his farm and left. My friend, Madame Bovary, had gone to Florida. I go back to Glencoe from time to time. I'm still friendly with everybody there.

PF: *Also, when you went back there, there was a sudden reaction of paranoia, even involving anti-Semitism, on the part of one of the people you met, which contains echoes of* Alamo Bay. *And there were the seeds there of the Costa-Gavras film,* Betrayed, *and right-wing farmers organizing in the Middle West.*

LM: It's the same old story. When you're in big trouble, you need a scapegoat. I remember this very surprising declaration by one of the big farmers, who had been extremely well off in 1979. He had obviously overspent and was in financial trouble, and he started blaming it on the intermediaries, the dealers, the Jews. If necessary they would fight the government. They were very anti-Washington. In spite of the fact that it was Republican territory, they were very bitter and angry at the Reagan administration for letting them down. So you could see this right-wing ideology coming back. I didn't expect that, because they were fairly quiet and rational people.

PF: *Having looked at the native Americans in* God's Country *and their problems, you then went on in* And the Pursuit of Happiness *to deal with the new wave of immigrants. Was this connected at all with trying to explore in documentary fashion the two aspects of* Alamo Bay *with which you'd been engaged between the two films?*

LM: When I went back to Glencoe in 1985, I found people were so bitter that they would blame everybody else – the government, the Jews, the foreigners – I thought it was surprising, coming from these people, and it certainly was a prolongation of this very dramatic experience of *Alamo Bay*. The reason I got into making a documentary about recent immigrants, which I did at the beginning of the following year, was because I was some kind of immigrant myself. I was a de-luxe immigrant, but I had a sense of what it was to be a stranger in America. I was naturally interested in people starting at the bottom of American society and how they dealt with it. And it's certainly part of my curiosity about the Vietnamese in *Alamo Bay*.

PF: God's Country *came from setting out on a voyage of discovery, not knowing what you were going to find, and coming across a place that became the centre of the film. In the case of* Happiness *you had not a thesis but a question to put.*

LM: I had a theme, a plan. *And the Pursuit of Happiness* was quite different in origin. All of my documentaries have been somewhat random; I just took a camera and went somewhere that I was curious to look at. In the case of *And the Pursuit of Happiness* – it was the beginning of 1986 – I already intended to go back home. I'd started taking notes for *Au revoir les enfants*, which I wrote the following summer here in France. But I wanted to stay in America because my daughter Chloë had just been born, in November 1985, so I wanted to stick around with Candice and the baby. At the same time I was impatient to do something. They were about to celebrate the centenary of the Statue of Liberty, and HBO, the pay-cable television, asked me if I would be interested in doing something around the theme of the Statue of Liberty. There were a lot of celebrations about the immigrants and Ellis Island. So I met with them, and told them, 'If I was to do something about immigrants, I'm not interested in Ellis Island, or the past, or evoking the boats with the Poles and the Jews and the Russians and the Germans and the Italians. I want to do something about immigration today, recent immigrants.'

For instance, I had to do some casting for *Alamo Bay* in Dallas, and when I arrived at the airport with my assistant the taxi-driver was Ethiopian. So we started talking, and I thought it was very interesting that a Dallas cab-driver should be Ethiopian. He said, 'There's a lot of us here.' So I did a bit of investigating and found out that there was an important Ethiopian community; there were even Ethiopian restaurants in downtown Dallas. So I decided that that was what I wanted to film – recent immigrants from Latin America, Africa, Asia. I said, 'European immigration has been dealt with, it's pretty much the past.' HBO agreed.

It was January 1986 and I promised to deliver the film so that they could run it on the Fourth of July. I didn't have much time. We had a bigger budget, so I could afford a larger crew. Shooting was basically the same: I was handling the camera with an assistant; there was a sound man and a production person, and that was it. But I had several people to help me with research and scouting. We started shooting almost right away. We shot the arrival of the Cambodian refugees at Kennedy Airport in January. I would go to Florida to deal with the Cubans, and the Asians, and there was this funny encounter with the Somosa family – then I would come back and work with the editors, while the researchers would be looking around. We went to California, and to this very remote part of the country, western Nebraska, just to meet a Vietnamese doctor in the middle of nowhere.

PF: *Was it by chance you found him examining a Greek immigrant who had arrived in Nebraska in 1907?*
LM: Oh, it was absolutely by chance, except that the doctor was the only Vietnamese for 100 miles around. But there were a lot of old European immigrants in that part of the country, including a Greek community.

PF: *There is the contrast between* God's Country, *with its 1986 coda, and* And the Pursuit of Happiness *– the enormous optimism that is generated by the recent immigrants and the grave doubts and fears of so many of the Americans themselves.*
LM: Yes. *And the Pursuit of Happiness* is interesting and I like a lot of it, but I prefer *God's Country* because it is closer to what I really like, the sort of chance filming that I really enjoy and that has always worked well for me.

PF: *There are parallels between the two. If you go back to the early 1970s to the appearance in the same year, 1972, of* Humain, trop humain *and* Place de la République, Place de la République *is* cinéma direct *as you precisely described it – being there, making random discoveries. At one point you even hand over the microphone to one of the people you meet to let her conduct interviews and take part in the film. On the other hand,* Humain, trop humain *seems, in the form in which it reached the screen, a very formal picture in its structure and its observation and in its editing. It seems to be in three parts. It begins as almost a parody of a traditional film about the industrial process – it's rhythmically cut, it*

makes the people on the production line look as if they are a team
working towards a final product. You follow the whole process through
from the first strip of steel to the completed car then to the motor fair,
people examining the product. The second part – separated by the
consumers seeing the car – is almost a deconstruction of the first part. It's
edited in quite a different way. You see people at random in the factory,
you see their feet, you feel the weight upon them. The questions that are
raised in the first part – why are we not hearing what the people think
about their work? – are answered visually in the editing and photography
in the second part. Is this a proper interpretation of the film as it turns
out?

LM: These were the days of the aftermath of May 1968, when a lot of
radical students managed to infiltrate plants like Renault near Paris,
trying to politicize the workers. But I was not tempted to make an
ideological film. No propaganda whatsoever. *Humain, trop humain* is
the only one of my documentaries in which there is no narration. I didn't
want the spectators to hear my voice. The point of the film was just to
spend, literally, one week in that Citroën plant, which was very difficult
because the management were so suspicious. I chose this particular plant
because it was the most modern, the most recent assembly-line plant in
the country.

Interestingly, at the plants around Paris, like Renault or the other
Citroën plants, a majority of the workers were immigrants. Citroën had
settled at Rennes in the heart of Britanny because they knew they could
find workers there; 95 per cent were peasants, farmers from the neighbourhood, who were going through hard times. Most of them would
work on the line and their wives would keep the farm running. Essentially they were French. I did interviews with some of them and basically
they were happy. For farmers these were well-paid jobs. The unions were
very quiet. It was like the triumph of capitalism, in a way. Unlike certain
other plants, especially around Paris, there was no tension between
workers and management. It was modern and clean.

For one day we didn't shoot, we just watched, and I told the cameraman and the sound man, 'We're just going to make long takes, it will be
very repetitious but that's what it's all about. Stay on the same man or
woman, repeating the same five gestures maybe twenty times. We're not
going to cut, because it must become obsessive.' I wanted the spectator to
come out of seeing this film exhausted, as if they had worked an eight-
hour shift. The soundtrack was quite loud on purpose, capturing the way
it was in those big hangars – you could hardly hear yourself. I wanted to

give a physical sense of the fatigue and boredom – the completely inhuman aspect of assembly-line work – without having to say it, by just showing it, in a very sensual way, in images and sound.

Humain, trop humain and *Place de la République* were shown in a cinema in Paris right after *Lacombe, Lucien* was released. When I had finished editing them I had a screening in a university where the students were very radical, and I got into this enormous fight about, 'How come you don't denounce the system?' Immediately, other students dissented from that opinion, because they felt the film was making its point. But the militants reproached me for not *saying* it, which was what Godard was doing in those years.

PF: *Godard made a film in 1970 which was considered too tedious to be shown on English television,* British Sounds, *about the Ford plant in Dagenham.*

LM: I remember that very well. He was quoting Marx a lot, and there were some very pretty tracking shots. I tried to make the students accept that my film, by not being judgemental, by apparently not taking sides, by just showing how it was and making the spectator understand what it's like to stay on your feet for eight hours repeating the same movements, how you feel it in your body and your mind, that this was much stronger than talking about it. And, of course, it also had a strange beauty. It would evoke those industrial films of the 1930s, or even *Modern Times* if you like; it was the beauty of the industrial world, but turned around completely. When it was edited, and we started with this huge shot with the steel rolling, I said, 'It's almost religious, it's like a cathedral.' So that's why I put the Gregorian chant at the beginning. That was my only subjective intrusion, trying to give the spectator a sense that there was a bizarre religious aspect to what we were filming.

I had no preconceived idea. I was not even sure what I was going to find, or if the workers would let me film them. I thought it was interesting to show assembly-line work at its most efficient, as it was in those days. Of course now, twenty years later, it's all robots, so the assembly line is almost gone, which is very good. In those days it was not computerized, and it was still basically the same as when Ford invented the assembly line. I am conscious of the fact that it is hard to watch. But it's not a distortion, or a caricature.

PF: *Talking about* And the Pursuit of Happiness, *you described yourself as a de-luxe immigrant. Although French directors have worked in*

America – Duvivier, Clair and Renoir in wartime exile, for example – the
only significant one before the war was Maurice Tourneur. So you are
unique among your generation in having established yourself there, yet
you still thought of yourself as an immigrant. Do you think in English
when you speak in English? And do you constantly feel yourself an
outsider in American society?

LM: It's hard to stay an outsider – after all the time I'd spent there,
especially from 1978 to 1986. I never wanted to become an American
citizen, which I suppose would have been easy for me. I felt that there
was no point in it. If you take the example of Maurice Tourneur, he
became an American director, the same way Billy Wilder is an American
director, the same way William Wyler from Alsace became an American
director. These people came fairly young. When I came to America I was
in my forties and I had a lot of work behind me and was established
already as a French director. Although I decided to stay in America all
those years, I felt that it was very important for me to keep a slightly
different angle, to try to stay an observer of the American scene.

I think it's very interesting to be an expatriate. There are a number of
notable cases – for instance, in literature – of writers who took advantage
of being expatriates. You could mention Henry James or Joseph Conrad.
I was trying in my work to look at what was going on in America, in
fiction or documentary: I thought I had to keep my difference, my not
being born and raised in America. I remember many times asking John
Guare or Candice questions about things that I'd seen or read in the
paper; I wanted to understand better what was going on, and sometimes
they would tell me, 'It's interesting what you ask; I've never thought of
it.' When you're part of a culture from birth, you tend to take it for
granted. In the same way, sometimes in France foreign friends tell me
things about what they perceive, and I have to say I didn't think of it.
You don't notice certain oddities in the culture that you've lived in your
whole life.

But I felt strongly all the way through my stay in America that I should
not become an American director; I should be a European director
working in America. At some point it became difficult. I remember when
I was coming back to France I sometimes felt estranged from recent
events or changes in French culture. I knew less about it than I knew
about the latest things going on in the States.

Of course, the question of language is crucial to all this. I don't believe
in bilingualism. I think you never become completely bilingual, and if
you do you're in danger. There is a mother tongue that relates to

your early years, to your formative years; a language that is essential to what you are. Obviously, for me it is French. Of course, because I did not speak French sometimes for months, I started thinking in English. When I came back to France and started writing the first draft of *Au revoir les enfants*, I would catch myself starting a sentence in French and finishing it in English. You're always searching for the *mot juste*, and sometimes it comes faster in the other language. That was disturbing, and I took care of it very quickly.

When I am taking notes about something – an idea, a dream or a film I've seen – I don't keep a diary, but I've piles of little notes that I keep in files. When I look at these notes they are written in both languages. I don't really work on my writing; I just put down quickly what comes to mind, and it comes in both languages. Sometimes completely in English, sometimes completely in French, sometimes in both. It is dangerous: it could make you a bit schizophrenic. I'll never really be able, or even want, to write completely in English. I might work on a screenplay and write a treatment in English on my own, which I did recently, but I would never consider writing dialogue in English, the way I do in French. Dialogue must have something of its own, and I'm not really capable of writing interesting English.

PF: *But you can judge good dialogue when you read it.*
LM: Oh, I can judge good dialogue. It took me a while to be able to direct actors in English with the same sort of intensity and detail that I could in French. I think by *Atlantic City* I had overcome that handicap. But when I was in New Orleans preparing *Pretty Baby* I had to learn, for instance, that there's not one Southern accent. Of course, when actors put on a Southern accent in Hollywood films it's a conventional Southern accent, like the Marseilles accent in French – it's just this drawl, it's a caricature. But I found out while scouting locations and spending time in the South that there are twenty different Southern accents. One of my surprises was that in urban New Orleans people actually had a sort of Brooklyn accent – for reasons I've never quite understood – which had nothing to do with a Southern accent.

PF: *Making documentaries must keep you in touch very sharply with different kinds of accents and rhythms of speech.*
LM: Yes. And if I come back to *And the Pursuit of Happiness*, one of my great problems with making the film was the people I was dealing with – their English was usually frightful. Sometimes I could hardly understand

them, and I knew it would be worse on the soundtrack. When somebody was saying something interesting but it was not easy to catch, I more or less had to repeat it in my narration. Of course, it's a wonderful way to get to know a country and a language. The way people talk, the language they use, it gives you a great sense of their background, their culture; and, of course, their rhythms, their hesitations, their difficulties are very revealing. It's part of finding out about other human beings, and doing it with a camera and tape-recorder is a wonderful way to understand other people.

Notes

1 Jack Gelber (b.1932): Chicago-born dramatist best known for his long-running off-Broadway play *The Connection* (1959) about jazz-loving drug addicts. It was filmed in 1961 by Shirley Clarke with most of the original cast and musicians.

2 E. J. Bellocq: little is known of this dwarf-like, possibly French-born photographer who was active in New Orleans between the late nineteenth century and the 1930s. Following his death, eighty-nine glass plates were found in his desk, all but a couple being photographs of prostitutes taken in the Storyville red-light district around 1912. Their purpose remains unclear. The photographer Lee Friedlander acquired them in 1966 and the Museum of Modern Art, New York, published a selection of thirty-four of them in 1970: *E. J. Bellocq: Storyville Portraits*, edited by John Szarkowski.

3 John Guare (b.1938): New York-born dramatist and graduate of Yale Drama School, who had his first major success off-Broadway with the black comedy *The House of Blue Leaves* (1971). In 1991 his *Six Degrees of Separation* (a social comedy inspired by the true story of a confidence trickster fooling rich white New Yorkers by posing as Sidney Poitier's son) began a long Broadway run. In addition to scripting *Atlantic City* he collaborated with Jean-Claude Carrière on the screenplay of Milos Forman's *Taking Off* (1971).

4 Telluride Film Festival: held every September since 1975 in the small mountain town of Telluride, Colorado. It rapidly became America's most fashionable festival and the restored version of *Napoléon* was presented there in 1979 with Abel Gance in attendance.

5 *Silkwood* (1983): political thriller, directed by Mike Nichols and co-scripted by Alice Arlen and Nora Ephron, telling the true story of Karen Silkwood (Meryl Streep), the politicized plutonium factory worker, who died in mysterious circumstances while blowing the whistle on her negligent Oklahoma employers. At one stage Streep expressed interest in appearing in *Alamo Bay*.

6 François Reichenbach (b.1922): first a song-writer (for Edith Piaf and others), then a prolific French documentary film-maker and leader of the *cinéma vérité* movement. A number of his films, such as *Les Marines* (1959) and *L'Amérique l'insolite* (1960), relish absurd and outlandish aspects of American life.

CHAPTER 5

Coming Home

PF: *In 1986 you came back to France. Was this because you wanted to make a French film or was it that the time for* Au revoir les enfants *had at last arrived?*

LM: *Au revoir les enfants* is based on something that actually happened to me. The film is very close to my own experience. There are some striking differences in the sense that when I wrote the first draft and checked it (I talked to other witnesses, my own brother and other students and a teacher who was at the school at the time) I realized there were certain distortions, almost as if my imagination during those forty-five years had taken over and fertilized my memory. Memory is not frozen, it's very much alive, it moves, it changes.

There's a good example that my family always makes fun of: I remember a demonstration outside my family's factory in 1936 (the time of the beginning of the Popular Front), and I remember vividly seeing the red flags above the wall of my parents' garden. My sister said to me, 'That's ridiculous, Louis, you were not even in Thumeries at the time.' I checked, and of course I was. And my mother told me, 'I would never have let you out, you've invented it.' But up to this day, I believe I was there, because the image is so vivid, the red flags, people singing 'l'Internationale'. I couldn't see the people, but I could see the flags above the wall, which was about 2 metres high. I was following them on the other side of the wall, where there was a row of raspberry bushes. It's one of the early images of my childhood; I was not even four. Now, whom do you believe? It's my memory; even if I made it up, it doesn't make any difference. Some of that happened with *Au revoir les enfants*.

For years I just didn't want to deal with it, but it had an enormous influence on the rest of my life. What happened in January 1944 was instrumental in my decision to become a film-maker. It's hard to explain, but it was such a shock that it took me several years to get over it, to try to understand it – and, of course, there was no way I could understand it. What happened was so appalling and so fundamentally opposed to all the values that we were being taught, that I concluded that there was something wrong with the world, and I started becoming very rebellious. I'm not saying that it would not have happened, but it would have happened differently. I think it sort of focused me or at least made me extremely curious about things happening outside the very privileged environment in which I was raised.

I wouldn't even talk about it. It's not that I wasn't thinking about it – it kept haunting me all these years. But I wouldn't tell that story to anybody. I would sometimes discuss it with my brother, but with the people I met or lived with I never did. Not until the 1970s, which is about twenty-five years after. It's possible that my decision to situate *Lacombe, Lucien* in 1944 may have had something to do with suddenly remembering and wanting to remember; many details came back about what had happened to us at that boarding school. I did a lot of research on the period and that may have brought back my own memory of the time.

It was then, in 1972–3, that I took for granted (a) that one day I should deal with this, but (b) that I was not going to deal with it right away; probably a lot more time would have to elapse. During the shooting of *Alamo Bay* I started writing notes one Sunday about *Au revoir les enfants*. I had told the story to Alice Arlen and she said, 'Louis, you have to deal with it.' I knew the time had come. It was scary, because it was so important to me, it was my main reference point, certainly the most significant event of my childhood, quite possibly of my life. And I felt it was going to be very difficult to re-create it on film. I would have hated myself if I had failed. All these years I was buying time, because I wanted to be absolutely confident that I could at least be in the best of shapes to make it right. I'd been through hard times in America with *Crackers* and *Alamo Bay* and I felt I needed to go back to my roots, which meant *Au revoir les enfants*.

In the summer of 1986 I came back to this house with Candice and my children, and I started making notes, lots of notes. I told them, 'I'm going to try to write this, and I'm going to see if it works.' There was nothing obvious about that story when you think of it. It could be seen as a sort of variation on the Holocaust and there'd been so many films already about this subject. I was convinced I should deal with it, but was not sure I would go all the way. Eventually, in August 1986 I went back to Paris, and spent two weeks in complete isolation writing the first draft. I am very grateful to Candice for almost forcing me to do it.

PF: *Was* Au revoir les enfants *the working title, or did it come later?*

LM: It was always the working title. When I finally got a distributor, the first thing he said was, 'It's a terrible title.' I even changed it for a while; up to a few days before we started shooting it was called 'Le Nouveau', meaning 'The New Student' – a really bad title. They told me *Au revoir les enfants* would never work, but then they had said the same thing about *Le Souffle au coeur*. It was always *Au revoir les enfants* because it was the last sentence said by the priest, Le Père Jacques, when he left the courtyard of the school – that was what I remembered of the crucial scene in the courtyard that morning.

So I finished the first draft. I came back here and read it to Candice and my daughter Justine, and when I finished they were in tears. Strangely enough, that got me worried. I suddenly perceived how incredibly emotional it could be for others. I had to make sure it would not become sentimental. When I was writing the screenplay I started with the last scenes; those were the scenes I didn't want to change. I wrote it directly from memory. I didn't try to fine-tune the dialogue, it just came. The scene in the classroom when the man in civilian clothes, the Gestapo man, comes in, and then the scene in the infirmary, and in the courtyard – I knew that sequence was not going to change. This was the whole point of the film. So I worked almost backwards. As I kept working on the screenplay, I decided to check with other witnesses, people who had been in the school at the time. I realized that there were some discrepancies.

Interestingly, the main one was that I had made up the character of Joseph. I'll never quite know if I made it up because of *Lacombe, Lucien*; I think it's rather the opposite. I was fascinated by this very young man who is badly treated as a servant in this school for rich kids, is somewhat unjustly kicked out because of a black-market scandal, and decides to get revenge by denouncing the presence of the Jewish children. What I found out was that this boy existed, but he didn't do it – although it remains a little controversial even today; there are different versions. Some people say the denunciation came from neighbours; some say it came from an ex-student who had joined the Resistance and had been arrested and tortured. Actually, the Jewish kids had been hiding in the school since the spring before, whereas in the film I have them enter the school a few weeks before they are arrested. Without a moment's hesitation, I decided to stick to my version, because I felt it was more interesting. Ever since *Lacombe, Lucien*, I was convinced that Joseph had done it; Joseph was one of my sources for that film.

PF: *Having Joseph betray the presence of the Jewish boys in the school means that their being taken away by the Gestapo is brought about ironically, tragically, by a moral decision taken by the priests themselves.*

LM: Yes. I must say, dramatically, it worked incredibly well. Also, Joseph was a friend of Julien. They were doing a little black marketeering together; Julien was genuinely interested in Joseph and liked him. So there's this terrible moment in the courtyard when Julien suddenly finds out that Joseph did it. Again, it's the discovery of evil. But Joseph doesn't seem to realize the importance of what he's done. He sort of shrugs it off. That was enormously disturbing for Julien, and also, I think, for the spectator: that it all started with the petty story of the black market and the priest being so rigid about it. Rather than making Joseph a straight villain, I was trying to give him a dimension, and in that sense he was certainly a cousin of Lucien Lacombe.

PF: *Part of the strategy of the film, although you have these horrendous events at the end after the betrayal, was that in the early part you have what is a mildly anti-clerical boarding-school story, set against the background of the Occupation, about the friendship of the two boys – rather like a naturalistic treatment of* Zéro de conduite, *for example. It belongs to that French tradition.*

LM: Although I cannot complain, because *Au revoir les enfants* was exceptionally well received, I've resented the fact that a number of people only saw the friendship between the two boys, the Gentile and the Jew, a variation from a non-Jew's point of view of the Holocaust. I think it has many more dimensions. For me it's also a portrait of a child, obviously close to the character of *Le Souffle au coeur*, and I most deliberately put the emphasis on his very emotional relationship with his mother. The mother appears twice in the film: she's at the beginning, saying goodbye at the railway station, and then she comes to visit – one of the key sequences in the film being the restaurant scene. And, for the first time, I tried to give an accurate portrait of my own mother.

I was also trying to render what was happening to us, me and my brother, in this privileged boarding school. Of course, it was very cold at night, the food was terrible, but we were privileged compared to most other people at this time. We were surrounded by walls, somewhat pretending the war was not taking place, feeling protected. When I examined what the structure should be, I thought it was important, little by little, to see the war breaking in. The central story is the arrival of this new boy and how he and Julien become friends; there's hostility at first

53 *Au revoir les enfants:* Julien (Gaspard Manesse) waves to his
beautiful mother
54 *Atlantic City:* gangster Lou (Burt Lancaster) peeps at his beautiful
neighbour

and then step by step we see the birth of a friendship between two children who are equally curious about certain things, probably a little smarter than the rest of the students, and how they find their affinities.

And there were other facts and details. For instance, the forest scene was also based on a personal memory. Strange as it seems, in this rather dangerous period, they would send us out – as a form of character-building – in winter when the days were very short, at the end of the afternoon before dinner, on a treasure-hunt in the Forest of Fontaine-bleau. I remember getting lost with a friend and being scared to death. I invented the ironic incident of the German soldiers being extremely nice and bringing them back.

PF: *In the restaurant scene the German officers are trying to impress Julien's mother by their gentlemanliness, contrasting themselves with the Militia, who come in and intimidate the diners.*

LM: Yes. It's a comment on what was going on then. The French collaborators were more aggressive and active than the German soldiers. There is this table of German officers from the Luftwaffe, the aristocrats of the war, and they're drinking champagne and having a good time and they don't want to be bothered, so one of them says, in German, 'Oh, the French with their politics!' They're showing off to Julien's mother. The restaurant scene is a key scene because while I was trying to make the mother into a lovable character, at the same time I wanted to show that she has all the prejudices of her background. When she talks about Léon Blum – the bourgeoisie hated Léon Blum – she says, 'I've nothing against the Jews.' But she's shocked when Julien asks, 'Aren't we Jewish?' The conversation is taken directly from my own childhood memories. My father's family was from Alsace and we had an aunt we always called La Tante Reinach; we always tried to convince my mother that my father's family was Jewish. I would be unfair if I said that my mother was anti-Semitic. It's much more complicated than that. But she had those reflexes. If we children said, 'Maybe we're Jewish after all' – she'd say, 'My God, stop this. The Reinachs are good Catholics.'

The film has many shifts and contrasts, and exposes many ambiguities and contradictions. And yet it was mostly perceived as a straightforward story about the horrible behaviour of the Nazis, a variation on the horror of the Holocaust, which was, of course, at the centre of the story. But it was also a fairly accurate look at French society, especially the haute bourgeoisie.

PF: *The priests have a greater complexity here than they do in* Souffle au coeur. *We see their rigidly harsh behaviour, and then gradually perceive that they have in fact an heroic role. They also have a socially critical role, as in the sermon that is delivered when the parents visit the school, which greatly disturbs the bourgeois parents. But there's also this point when, while they are protecting the Jewish boys, they cannot bring themselves, when Jean comes up to the altar, to give him the sacrament, even though this might help provide protective cover.*

LM: Well, that's something I added. I used a couple of things that didn't come from my own experience. For instance, the scene where Bonnet stands up in the middle of the night and says his prayers was something a Jewish friend told me. I happen to have many Jewish friends of my generation who survived because they were hidden in Christian schools. One of them is Gilles Jacob.[1] I had lunch with him and told him I was just about to start shooting this film and he said, 'But Louis, this is my story. I survived when the Militia came only because myself and my brother were hiding in the church behind the organ.' And I've heard many of these stories, especially after the film was released. I also added the sacrament thing. In my school, and it was something we found immediately suspicious, Bonnet was not going to mass, he was staying in the classroom. Frankly, I thought this was not very smart, but it was agreed. Somebody else told me that story of the Communion. It's not quite clear in the film if it's partly provocation or partly Bonnet trying to be as much of a conformist as possible, wanting to do what everyone does. So he goes to the communion rail. The truth of the matter is, it's a great sin to give the host, which is the body of Christ, to somebody who is not baptized. It's absolutely forbidden. So the priest was shaken and, for an instant, he didn't know what to do.

PF: *Except for* Zazie, *the few references to other movies in your films are very discreet. In* Au revoir les enfants *the whole school is drawn together by attending a performance of Chaplin's* The Immigrant. *Even Joseph is there and the priests. The musical accompaniment – is it Saint-Saëns the priest plays? Tell me about that. How did you choose that film and the music?*

LM: That was based on memories, plus poetic licence – it was in the following years that they showed films in the school on Sundays; that's when I saw the first Charlie Chaplin shorts. They were projected in this strange format that was rather popular in the late 1930s and 1940s, the 9.5mm, which had a perforation in the centre – a terrible invention.

Chaplin was forbidden during the war, of course, by the Germans, not only because he was Jewish but also because he'd made *The Great Dictator*. But his films, I was told, were still being shown, very discreetly, in schools and cine clubs. It was one of the great memories of my childhood, those Sunday evenings; we'd darken the room, there'd be a white sheet, and everyone would sit and watch those films. I chose *The Immigrant* because, first, it was one of the great ones, and second, it was an evocation of freedom for those Jewish children when they see the Statue of Liberty, America being the Promised Land.

I don't know why I wanted to have the violin accompaniment, or how I ended up with this virtuoso Saint-Saëns piece. I knew it would be something quite bizarre. From the very beginning I had this scene in mind, and it works well. It was difficult to shoot: when I was shooting towards the children, because of the lighting, I couldn't show them what was going on on the screen. So we had the master shot with the children in the foreground, including the screen. But when I did all the reverses and group shots of childen laughing or dreaming, I had to get them to laugh or react to something they were not actually seeing.

PF: *You were working for the first time with a youngish cameraman. How did you obtain the curious, sombre tone of the film in which one senses some shadow of disaster lurking over it which isn't just the January weather?*

LM: First, I could always picture the precise look that the film should have. It crossed my mind that I should shoot the film in black and white. Very quickly I decided this was too simple. What I remember visually of the Occupation period was that there were no colours. The school walls were white or grey, and we were all in navy blue: the beret, the sweater, the short pants – all blue. The priests were Carmelites, so they wore dark brown. It seemed obvious to me that I should make the film in colour, yet it was going to be a film without colour. The first time I discussed the look with the woman who made the costumes, I told her the only red I wanted to see in the film was the lips of the mother. Outside of that, I didn't want a trace of red. There was not really an art director, but this great veteran designer Willy Holt helped me transform the school we'd chosen outside Paris. We repainted certain rooms and made up the dorm – always with the sense that the colours would be cold and essentially blue. So when I discussed the lighting with Renato Berta we already had the environment.

We had the great luck, which also made shooting very difficult, of

55 *Au revoir les enfants:* Jean (Raphaël Fejtö) and Julien (Gaspard
Manesse) enjoy Chaplin's *The Immigrant*

having one of the coldest winters in January and February 1987. There
was a lot of snow, which I had been hoping for. The problem with
snow is that it never matches, and you have snow when you don't want
it. But I was so happy when it snowed, we rushed certain scenes. Basically, it was to be a very hostile environment, cold in every sense of the
word. Night would fall very quickly. And there was very little artificial
light, because electricity was restricted; and in those days you would
have one electric bulb hanging in the classroom and that was it. I don't
know how we didn't all go blind. So I asked Renato to work around
that. And, of course, he had to use lighting. So we discussed using fast
film and I told him, as I had told Sven for *Black Moon,* 'I don't want to
see the sun.'

  In terms of the shooting schedule, even though we shot everything in
the school and in the surrounding little town, we knew that after four
or four-thirty we couldn't shoot because we couldn't balance the night
outside. So I said, 'It's just as well. We're going to start early in the
morning, and we'll do as much as we can until one o'clock. After lunch
we'll come back and finish.' So we had short hours, which was much
better for the children; something I learned very quickly about kids in

films is that they can give you four, five hours and then they're gone, they can't concentrate. You have to accept that.

PF: *In casting the two central boys, were you concerned not only that you had to get performances from them but also that they themselves had to develop a friendship of the kind that was essential to make the film convincing? Did you bring them together when you did tests?*

LM: I knew even before I started writing the screenplay that the film would succeed or fail on the casting. I had to find two exceptional boys. Once I had decided I was going to do it, it was already September. I had to shoot in winter, I had to start in mid-January, so we were really rushed. I immediately sent several people out looking for the boys. We did what we always do: we described the character in TV programmes for kids of that age, in radio stations with young audiences, we put posters in the *lycées*. I wanted both of them to be Parisian, so the search was mostly in Paris. The girls in charge of the casting saw hundreds of them; we would ask them to send their photo, then we'd make a first selection and when the children were off school they would come to the office and we would make a video test. Then, when we found interesting ones, I would read the scenes with them and tape them again.

It was a very long process, and I was very anguished. Fairly early, I met Gaspard Manesse, who was to play Julien. I hesitated for a while between him and another boy, but there was something about Gaspard: he was like quicksilver, he was so alive, very sharp and insolent. Arrogant and shy at the same time. When we started reading with him I could see he was on pitch. I said, 'I'm not going to cast him until I have the other one, until I have Bonnet', because it was all about the chemistry between the two of them. And that's when we ran into trouble; we had a much more difficult time, I don't know why, finding the Bonnet character. It was literally three weeks before we started that I found Raphaël Fetjö and decided to go with him. I was very confident about the boy playing Julien, not quite sure about the other, because he was so introverted. I was not sure whether he was coming across.

Before we actually started, we spent three days with all the kids, not only the two principals but also the supporting cast of children, and we worked in the classroom where we were going to shoot, rehearsing with them and with the camera crew. We filmed the rehearsals, and when I saw Raphaël on the big screen I realized it was going to work. He needed a little more work. He was a little bit like Pierre Blaise from *Lacombe, Lucien* – he was not quite sure that he wanted to do it. I think he was scared.

56 *Au revoir les enfants:* Louis Malle rehearses his juvenile *alter ego*
(Gaspard Manesse)

PF: *Did you teach them to play boogie-woogie piano for the scene in which they realize their mutual appreciation of jazz and the wonderful camaraderie that it expresses?*

LM: Well, it's always like that in films – the one who played well was the one who was not supposed to. Raphaël was supposed to be a good pianist, and he'd never played the piano. The other one was very much a musician. So I had to force poor Raphaël to learn to play this Schubert piece. He learned the boogie-woogie better; he learned to do the pumping, though we had some problems in post-synchronization. But it was at the end of the shooting and the two of them were so comfortable. The two boys very quickly became so confident, they seemed to master the technical difficulties of film-acting so easily, that sometimes I had to be hard on them because it was almost too easy for them. Of course, I'd spent time explaining to them the historical background of the story. The irony is that they're both half-Jewish – but the one who played my part is actually more Jewish, because his mother is Jewish. Raphaël's mother was Egyptian, and his father was Jewish. They knew little about that period, but they could relate to the situation, to the emotions of the characters; they could understand.

And the miracle was that all these kids with their Reeboks and sweatshirts and jeans with holes in the knees – many from that very school where we were shooting – we put them in the uniforms and the shoes – those horrible shoes of the period, with wooden soles – we cut their hair (which they hated) and instantly they became children of 1944. We were struck by how natural the transition seemed. It made me think that the period was not the point; I am convinced that children today can completely understand what it was like being a child in 1944. And the boys really took over their parts and jumped back forty years. It gave me hope, because I could suddenly see that children of today watching this film would be seized by what was going on and completely identify with the boys on the screen. In France it was seen by a lot of children.

PF: *The film came out at a time when anti-Semitism was rearing its ugly head again.*
LM: Yes. When I was trying to raise money for the film, I got rather negative reactions from the industry. People would say, 'You're not going to tell that story again: the boarding school, the Occupation, the Holocaust. No.' They discouraged me. Although the budget of the film was very small, it was difficult to raise the money. But just as we had finished shooting and were editing, there was the Klaus Barbie trial. They had captured Barbie in South America and brought him back. He was one of the worst German war criminals in France during the Occupation. The effect of the trial in France was very emotional, and very good, because suddenly it brought back the period; it was on television and widely watched.

When I started the project, it seemed to the French that the Occupation was a thousand light years away; they had decided it was over and would not deal with it any more. There was no question that the Barbie trial brought it back, to a new generation particularly. The trial was very moving, with all these old people testifying how they'd been tortured and deported. They were not looking for vengeance; they were looking for justice. So, my film was suddenly topical. Also, two weeks before my film opened, Le Pen managed to make one of his stupid gaffes. He said something idiotic about the Holocaust and, of course, there was a torrent of protest.

PF: *The relationship between the two boys is partly to do with Julien being intrigued with the mystery of Bonnet; it's also the discovery of kindred affinities. They are natural soulmates and they share interests. Was your own relationship with the Jewish boy as strong in that way; did you share interests in music and literature?*

LM: No. We were rivals. I was a good student in those years, but he would always beat me, and I slightly resented that. We were in a position of emulation. The real Bonnet was very shy and probably was also instructed to keep some distance from the others. I was, of all the class, the closest to him. Like the film, we had a shared interest in books and reading, and we had conversations. When the Gestapo came we were in the process of really becoming friends. It never went as far as it's described in the film. Let me put it this way. The very intense relationship between the two boys in the film is more my imagination than my memory, in the sense that I wish it had been that way; I wanted it to be that way. I was terribly interested in him and wanted to know him better, but we didn't become real buddies like they had become at the end of the film.

What I invented for the film is the moment when Julien discovers, through the prize book, that Bonnet is not his real name and concludes that he is Jewish. That's not the way it happened. At my school, the older students were told that those three children were Jewish. It was a dangerous thing to do, but the priests wanted to trust their students. My brother was older and he knew about it and told me. He was not supposed to, but he couldn't help telling me that the boy in my class was Jewish. My first reaction was: I didn't believe my brother. I was so surprised. My brother was always pulling my leg too, always telling me lies. I never really talked about it, and of course I never mentioned it to Bonnet. I think I was still wondering if it was true when the Gestapo entered the room. In the film I made the relationship evolve into something which I suppose would have happened in the following months. It made for a much more interesting and intense relationship.

The same is true of the scene in the classroom at the end, when the Gestapo agent asks for Jean Kippelstein and Julien knows it's Bonnet. The Gestapo man turns his back and Julien can't help it, but for a fraction of a second he looks back towards Bonnet and the Gestapo man catches his eye and goes to Bonnet – people took it as an expression of my guilt, especially children. After the film was released, I went to talk in *lycées*, because teachers asked me to discuss the film with kids the same age as Julien and Bonnet, and it was always, 'Did you really do that?' – almost as if I'd denounced him. As if it was me, not Joseph, who had done it. I kept telling them that they would have found him anyway. I didn't even bother to tell them that it didn't actually happen that way. I wrote it that way in the very first draft and left it because I thought it would make it more emotional for Julien. I never intended that Julien –

57 *Au revoir les enfants:* Pope Pius XII looks the other way as the
Gestapo arrest Jean Bonnet (Raphaël Fejtö)
58 *Au revoir les enfants:* 'I will remember every second of that January
morning until the day I die'

or I – would seriously feel responsible for Bonnet being arrested. Although, maybe that's what I was trying to say, unconsciously.

PF: *At the age of twelve you must have known that to be arrested by the Gestapo would almost certainly result in something terrible happening. How aware were you of the extermination camps?*

LM: We knew. And people who pretend that they didn't know are just – well, we knew. I was not even twelve and I knew. I remember my parents talking about it, how horrible it was. There had been this enormous event in Paris in July 1942 when the French police rounded up the Jews. Essentially, the Jews they arrested were foreign Jews, and they were put in the Vélodrome d'Hiver. That's one of the most shocking episodes of the Holocaust in France. I'm not sure we knew that they were almost certainly going to die. It was only after the war that we found out exactly what had happened. The director of the school, not being Jewish, was given a different treatment. They hesitated before they deported him because he was a priest. But this Père Jacques, whom I made into Père Jean, when all the people with him in the camp were put in a train, he asked to go with them. He didn't want to be treated differently because he was a priest.

When I hear or read that most people in France didn't know anything about the fate of the Jews – that's an incredible lie. If they didn't know, it was because they didn't want to know. As I said, my parents knew and told us about it. I remember how shocking it was when the yellow stars first appeared.

PF: *In the very last minute of the film, your own voice comes up on the soundtrack, saying that this was the key memory of your life, you've thought about this every day since then, that you'll never forget it. At what point during the making of the film did you decide you would speak those lines and make a personal intervention in this dramatization of your own experience?*

LM: These lines were the first thing I wrote before I even started the screenplay. My voice was also at the beginning. I thought it might be helpful to establish from the beginning that the story was a flashback, to show that it was my memory. Over the railway-station scene, I had my voice saying I was going back to school and hated it – but it was redundant because the scene with the mother said it all, so I took it out. But the line at the end and the fact that I would inject my own voice – suddenly jumping forty years – that was always my intention. Some people advised me to put it in writing instead of using my voice, but I knew it *had* to be my voice. I thought it was important for people watching the film to understand at the end that this story was a true story and actually came directly from my memory. And I knew it would come on the close-up of Julien.

PF: *After* Au revoir les enfants, *you remained in France and went from a winter film to a film of spring/summer. This film also has an historical setting: 1968 and* les événements *of May. Do you remember that time? You weren't down here in the country then, were you?*

LM: Oh no. I was in India for months, and I came back to Paris in early May 1968. I remember it well. I hadn't the faintest idea what was going on in Paris, and after those enchanted months of drifting around India, I was very reluctant to come home. I was simply going to refuel, look at my footage and go back. I arrived at Orly Airport around noon and it was very difficult to find a taxi-driver to take me where I lived, near the Latin Quarter. There was a huge demonstration going on. It was not yet a revolution, but there were a lot of people in the streets, young people, mostly students. I was stunned and exhilarated. I started phoning people and that night went out to dinner. On the Place St Michel I said something to a policeman which he didn't like and suddenly there were ten of them jumping on me and my brother, clubbing us.

That was my introduction to May 1968. From then on I was definitely on the side of the students! I was not supposed to stay in Paris. I'd been asked to be a member of the jury at the Cannes Festival; I thought this was a good idea because I'd not seen films for a long time except Indian films. So the next day I left for Cannes. Quickly, the students' insurrection got bigger, the demonstrations more violent and the government lost control of the situation. They were completely taken by surprise. I was getting impatient in Cannes, where the Festival was proceeding as if nothing was going on elsewhere.

PF: *Who were your fellow jurors?*

LM: Roman Polanski, Terence Young, Monica Vitti – these are the ones I remember.[2] And the president of the jury was an old French writer called André Chamson.[3] In my hotel I was glued to the TV, and kept thinking, 'I don't know what I'm doing here, I must go back to Paris.' After a while, I don't remember the exact date, a group of French directors came down from Paris – Truffaut and Godard and a few others – and they gathered together with those of us in Cannes like Lelouch and Claude Berri.

We had a meeting and they said they had been sent by the film union in Paris and represented a newly formed Comité Révolutionnaire du Cinéma, or something like that. They said that the Cannes Festival had to stop. I thought it was an excellent idea, because I was anxious to get back to Paris – although it was already difficult to travel: no trains, no planes, no petrol. Of course, a lot of people were against the idea: the producers and people involved in the film industry thought the Festival should continue. Our argument was valid because we felt that if the whole country was going on strike it was absurd and obscene that the Cannes Festival should continue, that people should put on tuxedos and go to the screenings as if nothing was happening, as if we were in Lichtenstein or Monte Carlo.

My role was to encourage the jury to resign; the Comité thought that if the jury resigned, there was no more Festival. So I went to a meeting of the jury, and Terence Young said he had received a phone call from the French union, and as he was a member of that union he would follow its orders. And I convinced Monica Vitti. Truffaut talked to Roman Polanski who said he would resign, and then almost immediately regretted it; we had a big fight after that. So the majority of the jury agreed, or were persuaded, to resign. I went back to the Palais du Festival, where film-makers were occupying the stage. It was a ridiculous moment: they were trying to have a screening, Truffaut was holding the curtains so they couldn't start the show and people were literally fighting on stage. I came across, took the microphone and said, 'The jury of the Festival has resigned.' There were boos and applause. This really triggered the closing of the Festival.

Of course, I got the blame. I was *persona non grata* in Cannes. The shopkeepers were furious. Word had spread that I was responsible, that I had single-handedly stopped the Festival, so when I went into the coffee shop next to the old Palais, the Blue Café, they refused to serve me.

I remember going back to Paris with friends in a car and having a terrible time finding petrol in the Lyons region. In Paris at the time there was a permanent meeting in the School of Cinema, called pompously États Généraux du Cinéma. One of the great aspects of May 1968 was that everybody was meeting all the time: at the Sorbonne, at the Odéon. Everybody came up with projects to change radically the way of making films. Generally, most of the projects were about the State taking over production and distribution. Milos Forman was in Paris then and he said, 'But you're crazy. You want a *socialist* cinema? Do you know how it works in Czechoslovakia? It's a disaster.' But it was exciting and Utopian and great fun. We would go to those meetings and write projects to transform the legislation and make films outside the capitalist system. And some of us would go to the demonstrations, which were practically twenty-four hours a day. We made sure we were represented, the États Généraux du Cinéma, in all the parades.

I never really believed it was going to become a revolution. I remember a conversation with my friend Pierre Kast. We were in the middle of this tumultuous meeting, there must have been at least 1,000 people in an amphitheatre and somebody was on stage defending a project when he was violently attacked and denounced as a mandarin – it could have been Chabrol. Every one of us at some point was insulted, by very young film-makers or students, as bourgeois *cinéastes*. And I said, 'This is what the Convention must have been like during the great Revolution.' And Kast said, 'Yes, but the difference is during the Convention heads were rolling.' That was the big difference: we were not risking our lives.

PF: *So you constantly had a sense of the absurd?*

LM: Yes, of some kind of 'happening' – with all the good sides of it. People had stopped their routine completely and were talking to each other. People who didn't know each other would start arguing in the street. There were no cars, people were walking or on bicycles. It was a great moment; suddenly, the whole country stopped and people started thinking about their lives and about the society in which they lived, coming up with all kinds of solutions, most of them not very practical. When it was over, I thought: 'It should be institutionalized. There should be a May 1968 every four years. It would be a catharsis, much better than the Olympic Games.' We knew it was not going to become serious, although I suppose a lot of people in the bourgeoisie were afraid that the Communists might try to take over, that there was the possibility of a civil war.

The government had literally collapsed, and didn't seem to know what to do. Like at the end of *Milou en mai*, de Gaulle suddenly disappeared for two days at the end of May and nobody – not even the journalists – knew where he was. It was discovered later that he went to Germany to talk to the five most important generals of the French army. There was bad blood between de Gaulle and the army because of the Algerian war, so he wanted to make sure that he could count on them. Eventually, he came back and was his old self again – strong and threatening – and announced that he was dissolving the Assembly and that there would be elections within three weeks. At the same time, the Gaullists organized a huge demonstration on the Champs Élysées, 1 million people. There came a point where Parisians were fed up with the constant chaos. And that was it. Suddenly, order was restored. The whole happening of May 1968 instantly died. I suppose the 'heroes were tired'. It seemed as if it had been, well, a great moment.

PF: *At the time did you think of making a documentary of* les événe-ments, *or using them as the basis for a feature film?*

LM: Well, I decided not to touch a camera – I'd been shooting for all those months in India, and there were a lot of cameras out on the streets already; a lot of people I knew were filming what was going on. So I didn't feel it was necessary. After it was over, there were a vast number of militant films, using the footage of *les événements*. When I was editing my Indian films we let our young friends who were radical militant film-makers use the editing room at night to finish their films. At the time, it never crossed my mind to use that period for a fiction film. Actually, it was not even the origin of *Milou*. I intended to come back to this part of France to make a third film here, to make one about a country house and the end of a family – a sort of Chekhovian theme if you want. I wanted to use my memory. I was still dealing with the past, less obviously than *Au revoir les enfants*. And because *Au revoir* had such a tragic theme and was such a sombre film, I felt the need to do something lighter.

I was very happy about *Au revoir les enfants*, and especially happy that it was so well received. But when a film of yours is very successful, it usually tends to destabilize you. When you have made a film which is a flop, the next month you're back to work, because it's hard to take and you want revenge. It inspires you – at least in my case it does. But when something like *Au revoir les enfants* happens, it is quite overwhelming, and, frankly, I didn't expect it. Because I cared so much about the film, I started following it when it was presented in many different countries; even in France I went to schools and universities and introduced it. I was curious to talk to the public about their reactions. So I stayed with the film for many months after it was released.

Then as a reaction I thought I should use my memory again, but definitely for a comedy. Also, I had been intrigued by the idea of making an ensemble film. Instead of putting a character or two at the centre I was curious about a portrait of a social group, in this case a family. Of course

I thought of *The Cherry Orchard*. I decided that it would be set in the 1960s. Early on I came up with the death of the matriarch as marking the end of the family. Because in a situation like that, considering the laws of inheritance in France, this huge house, this beautiful estate, could not be divided, so these people, who were actually broke, were going to sell it. This was the premise of the story. Then it occurred to me that it would be interesting to put it right in the middle of May 1968.

It didn't come completely by accident. I started to think about *Milou* in the spring of 1988, when the French media were celebrating, with a certain fanfare, the twentieth anniversary of the events and re-examining what had happened. There were a lot of pieces in the newspapers and on TV. And what I remembered was quite different. There was something very pompous about the way the veterans of May 1968 were evoking it. Of course, they were twenty then and it was the great event of their lives; now they are bureaucrats or socialist politicians or in advertising. There was a lot of nostalgia.

May 1968 was very good as a background for my script. It gave me the chance – an old device of mine – to examine how people react when taken out of their routine by a series of events: the private one, which is the death of the grandmother, and the historical one, May 1968 – even if the story is taking place in a remote and very peaceful part of the country. News of the revolution comes to them secondhand and distorted. Suddenly, my characters are facing a situation where they have to improvise and re-examine who they are. They haven't seen each other for many years and they don't especially like each other. What they intended was to come back quickly, bury the old lady, sell the house and go back to where they belong: London, Paris, Nice, Bordeaux. But they are stuck. And, of course, things happen. First, because all of them were raised in that house, they rediscover their past, their roots, their childhoods. Then there's the formidable presence of Milou, the one who stayed in the house and represents continuity, tradition. He is completely destroyed by the death of his mother. But he's not against the revolution because, after all, he is free, he has nothing to lose; he is generous and open to new ideas.

The film is a satire on a certain bourgeoisie, but though I wanted to make fun of my characters, I also wanted them to be moving. They go through different shifts, critical and selfish at first, then when they find out that they cannot bury the grandmother, they loosen up, and start dreaming the dream of a utopian society: a commune on the estate, sexual liberation, all the ideas *à la mode*. It is spring, the weather is wonderful, nature takes over. And then there's the final twist when they find out de Gaulle has disappeared – 'He might be dead', somebody says – and they panic.

PF: *There is that scene where they misinterpret the news on the radio – I thought that it resembled in some ways the panic in America as a result of Orson Welles's* War of the Worlds *in 1938, when people took to the hills. At what point did you bring in Jean-Claude Carrière? You hadn't collaborated with him for twenty years, but you had met him in Paris at the time of* les événements, *shortly after your return from India.*
LM: Jean-Claude and I are very, very close friends. For various reasons I had not worked with him since *Le Voleur*. Actually on *Au revoir les enfants* he helped me quite a bit. I consulted him. He's an expert on script structure. Also he'd had that experience of being a boarder in a school during the war – so he gave me some ideas. I worked for several months on *Milou en mai* on my own, and in November 1988 I realized I needed help, I was stuck. I had all the characters, and I had the plot, more or less. But I had problems, especially with the second half. I remembered how easy and helpful it had been to work with Jean-Claude, and I asked him, although he's a very busy man, if he could give me one month. I brought him what I had, seventy or eighty pages, and we started from that. This story is close to home for him, even more so than it is for me in a way.

He comes from that part of France, from a farming area in the wine country. So he knew well that mini-culture of people with a few acres of vineyards who for several generations, from the end of the nineteenth century until the 1950s, were pretty well off. They had very little to do because wine-making doesn't take that much work, and also they were selling their wine quite well, even if it was mediocre. Typically, where we shot we had a problem because there were no more vineyards left. The vines had been pulled out in the 1960s because the government had convinced most of the wine-producers to cut their production, and go for quality; a lot of these people replaced their vineyards with fruit trees or just went out of business – which is the story of this family.

Jean-Claude knew everything about that, he had lots of stories. I always wanted to have Milou going for crawfish; my own memories as a child were of fishing at night with lights, which was strictly forbidden. But he said, 'I know another way. You put your hands down under the bank of the river, that's where the crawfish are, and they bite your finger.' He provided a lot of other details that enriched the story.

We worked quickly, since I was anxious to shoot in the spring or early summer of the following year, 1989. It was very much a seasonal film. I originally wanted to shoot near here, but I realized that the landscape should be a little less austere, more smiling and lush. So we looked around in the *département* called Le Gers. I kept telling the people scouting with me, 'We're never going to find what we need – a house with a big cherry tree in front of it.' And one day we drove up a long avenue to a house, I stopped the car, got out and saw a big cherry tree. I said, 'This is a sign. This house has to be great.' And it was. I must have seen sixty houses, and my friends a lot more – it was very much like casting. We tried to shoot in time for the cherries. Of course, there were no cherries that year because it was too dry, and we had to put false cherries on the tree. We started shooting in June, so we could still get spring light.

PF: *Did Jean-Claude Carrière bring to the film a certain surreal quality, through his experience with Buñuel?*
LM: The scenes you're thinking of were in my original script. I intended, and I'm not even trying to justify it or be rational about it, that the old lady would reappear at the end, when Milou is left alone. She would be there waiting for him. The last words would be, 'Alone at last.' Obviously, Milou was terrified of his mother, but had devoted his life to her and had this passion for her, although she tyrannized him. The owl scene was directly from my memory.

Jean-Claude was against the reappearance of the old lady. He may have been right. I don't know. He thought the film should stand somewhere between Chekhov and Feydeau. He would have liked it to be a little more realistic than it was. I wanted the film to be an accurate, and ironic, portrait of this kind of family. But I also wanted the magic of nature, life in the country. I was not terribly interested in the plot being plausible. I've always been aware of the fact that when they all panic and run to hide in the woods there is a plausibility gap. A lot of people felt this was too much and they didn't buy it. A number of people said, 'We liked the film up till then, then you lost me.' I was not trying to be realistic.

PF: *Some savage exchanges come out at that point, don't they, especially those between the sisters? Real bitterness and familial breakdown?*

59 *Milou en mai:* Milou (Michel Piccoli) going for crawfish

LM: Yes, really ugly. But always within a comedy register. I know where the business of the mother reappearing comes from. Again, it comes from my own mother. She died in 1982. She was a little bit like Paulette Dubost in *Milou* in the sense that she was a very strong personality, she held the family together. She could be adorable, but she could also be tyrannical. She was really the power in the family. After she died, I kept dreaming about her; she reappeared constantly in my

60 *Milou en mai:* Milou (Michel Piccoli) sees an owl on his window sill
in the small hours

dreams. Half of my dreams have my mother as one of the characters. In a
way it's great; it's as if she's not dead. I still see her, she's around in my
dreams.

I think it came from that. I made sure that when she reappears she's
younger, she is certainly not in black, she wears one of those summer
dresses, she's like a representation of herself twenty years before. She
appears to her two faithful followers, Léonce the handyman, who does
everything in the house, and Milou. I had in the script that she also
appeared to the little girl, Françoise; I shot it, but I cut it. It didn't work,
it wasn't a good idea, suddenly it became gratuitous. I like the scene
when she appears to Léonce, who's for ever digging the grave at night; he
does a double-take, shrugs and continues.

When I came up with the character of Françoise – of course, I had to
put a little girl in this story – I was very tempted to make her the central
character and to see the rest of the family through her eyes. I'm sure it
would have worked very well and it would have been a continuation of
my previous films. But I was afraid it would become repetitious, because I
have done that so many times. I did something I'd never quite
approached before, except maybe in *Le Voleur*, which was to have a real

ensemble of actors, as in Chekhov's plays. It's always difficult to do and takes an enormous amount of concentration for the director. We had twelve characters, who were all important enough to evolve throughout the story, to come into the foreground often – all of them active and important in the story at some point.

PF: *You are constantly testing the audience, pushing them, challenging their tastes, seeing if they are prepared to be shocked by the mother laid out in death with the people coming in and dancing around her. There's this scene where Milou sees his granddaughter bending over to kiss his dead mother. He's not entirely awake and he looks up and there's a great flicker of lust on his face when he sees her buttocks. Then there's the scene where the little girl goes into the bedroom of the young female lovers and sees one of them actually tied to the bed. It's not just the frisson when you see this bondage, but when you see the girl's reaction to it, you wonder what will she think, and then she starts asking questions. You are intending to undermine the audience, or wrong-foot them emotionally.*

LM: I've always done that from the beginning – pushing my luck. It comes naturally to me. It's really my sensibility; maybe my peculiar sense of humour. I like to surprise people, to catch them on the wrong foot. It's sometimes a little childish, but it's part of what I've been trying to accomplish: to offer people always another view, or a different angle; to encourage them, force them sometimes, to re-examine, to look at things differently, to rethink what they take for granted. To say that behind what is routine, there's something else. I'm obsessed with showing the subjectivity of our judgements. I've always been convinced, and tried to have people share my belief, that there's no such thing as Truth with a capital T, the revealed truth. In the beginning I started by rebelling against religion, especially our monotheist religions, which come with such rigid views and a set of values that are untouchable and cannot be re-examined.

I would like my spectator to be on a permanent double-take, to see something and then say, 'Oh my God! Well, that's not what I expected, it's something else.' That's what I suppose I've always attempted to do. *Zazie*, for instance, was pure provocation in a way, visual provocation; but since it was a comedy it was supposed to make them laugh. I remember when we finished *Les Amants* and it was shown to the distributor, they tried to convince me to take out a shot, the one where Jeanne Moreau was leaving the house at the end and she stopped to say

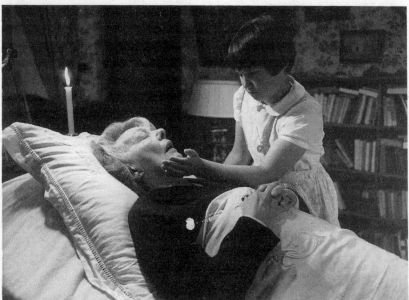

61 *Milou en mai:* with Grandma dead in the next room, her possessions divided up and labelled, the party begins – Bruno Carette, Miou-Miou, François Berléand, Dominique Blanc, Michel Piccoli, Harriet Walter
62 *Milou en mai:* Milou's niece Françoise (Jeanne Herry-Leclerc) examines her grandmother (Paulette Dubost) as she lies in state

goodbye to her daughter. They said, 'Why don't we forget about the daughter?' The moment is so romantic, and then suddenly you remember that she is also a mother, that she is doing something horrible by abandoning her child. To leave her husband, Alain Cuny, is all right, but to abandon her four-year-old child – they thought it was going to turn off the audience. I said, 'I'm sorry, but this is exactly the point. If I take that out, it becomes meaningless. If she didn't have children she'd just drift from lover to lover and then come back to her husband. But the fact that she makes the choice to abandon her child means her decision is much more important. To ask me to cut that makes the end of the film not serious, but heavy.'

PF: *You talk about rebelling against the reactionary church in earlier films. The reverse is the case here in* Milou, *in that the priest is a source of humour because of his left-wing and very fashionable opinions. He leads the local youth, and tries to get the revolution going among them.*
LM: The French Catholic Church has always been split between those who are fiercely reactionary and the worker priests and supporters of liberation theology. In the 1960s there were quite a number of radical priests. Again, I was trying to give it a comic dimension, because you wouldn't expect a country priest to be like that.

PF: *On the question of the ensemble acting, were there opportunities to develop the characters in discussion with the actors and actresses and have them contribute to it by improvisation during rehearsal?*
LM: I'm very proud of the casting of *Milou*. For me it's almost perfect casting. I would not change anything if I was to do it again. I was happy with everybody – with the possible exception of one, because perfection doesn't exist. When I started working on the screenplay and, even more so, when Jean-Claude and I finished the screenplay, we had certain actors and actresses in mind. From the very beginning I wanted Michel Piccoli to play Milou. It was really written for him. As for Camille, it was Jean-Claude's idea – I was a little surprised, then I thought it was a wonderful idea, the best example of counter-casting – to put Miou-Miou in this part of a very tight and conventional reactionary bourgeoise. When we gave her the script, she called us and laughed, 'How could you possibly have thought of me for this part? It's miles away from me – I've never done anything like that, I don't know anything about the character.' Of course she wanted to play it, but she said, 'I'll have to do a certain amount of research.' But I knew she'd be great in this part. Some of the

others, like Dominique Blanc, we also thought of early on.

As we were polishing the screenplay during pre-production, little by little, like a puzzle, we started putting the pieces together. Because it was an ensemble it was important not to cast separately, but to keep thinking about the chemistry between all these people. Two months before shooting, we started getting together at Jean-Claude Carrière's house in Paris. We would meet and have lunch. It was great. Even before the cast was completed. We would read the screenplay and actors would ask questions and make suggestions. Some of them were excellent. I remember a suggestion Miou-Miou made about her character. At some point the Dominique Blanc character, Claire, confronted with her dead grandmother, says, 'I didn't like her – she made us wash our hands all the time.' Miou-Miou said, 'Maybe I would have taken that from the grandmother,' and so a few times in the film she tells the twins, 'Go and wash your hands.' We met and worked together regularly, and each time a new member of the cast would be present. Early on I cast Paulette Dubost, whom I had worked with in *Viva Maria*. I loved Paulette.

PF: *Was there an association there with* La Règle du jeu – *as you'd had Gaston Modot from* La Règle du jeu *in* Les Amants?
LM: Oh definitely. The circle was completed. She would play the matriarch of the family instead of playing the soubrette. Although she dies in the first scene, she is a crucial character – ever present, so powerful for the rest of the family, a constant reference point. My only problem with Paulette, although I think she's past eighty, was that she's in such great shape. When she was on her deathbed we had to make her look older. She looks frightfully young! I was not sure she would be plausible as Piccoli's mother.

And then we all got together in this marvellous place where we shot the whole film. It was full spring and we were all very happy to leave Paris and be in complete isolation. And everybody got along surprisingly well, which is not always the case. We spent a whole week rehearsing on the spot. In costume, too. Because the film was an ensemble, it was essential to get all these people, who were from very different backgrounds, to know each other, to become a family, before we started. The result was possibly my most exhilarating memory of shooting. The script really worked well. I was having a great time – to the point that it scared me. Jean-Claude Carrière was in Paris and would get phone calls from the location saying how great it was, what a wonderful time everyone was having. So he called me and said, 'Louis, you're in trouble. Comedy is difficult. When things go too well on the set it's usually not a good sign.' I said, 'I know, I know, I'm trying to keep my concentration. It's hard.'

Because most of the scenes were inside or outside the house, we were able to shoot more or less in sequence, which rarely happens in a normal shooting schedule.

It was very intense, but everyone was having fun. It didn't seem like work. The actors were very creative. We had many scenes with ten people in the frame. Each one had something to do, in line with his or her character. I could trust them. For instance, in the first few days I understood that although Michel Piccoli is such a professional that he can do twenty-five takes and be excellent in each of them, yet he gives something special, something extra, a sense of inventing his lines, in the very first take. In the key moments of his character, I nearly always edited the first takes. Some other members of the cast, because they were less experienced or because they had to warm up, took more time to get it right. So when they had scenes together, I had a problem!

The making of a film is such an incredibly intense relationship; it's like a passionate love affair over a short period of time. It's eight, nine, ten weeks, but seems like a lifetime. And it's about birth, the birth of this thing we are making together, this film. It takes on a life of its own. Then, suddenly, we were in the middle of August and the shooting was over. It's always very hard, after such intensity, when people say goodbye to each other and pack and leave to go and do something else. You, the director, stay with your hundreds of cans of film, trying to make sense of them. You feel abandoned, almost betrayed. If the experience has been happy, or even unhappy – it's the same in a way, just a different emotion – it's difficult to imagine how empty it leaves you when it's over. It's almost like experiencing death each time.

Milou was an especially gratifying experience. Today we still keep seeing each other in Paris; we have become a sort of veterans' association: *les anciens de Milou en mai*. We maintain that, which is unusual. We go back to the location when we have a chance.

PF: *There are very few French films set in England. There aren't that many French films with English characters. You have an English character, the second wife of the son who works for* Le Monde *in London, played by Harriet Walter. How did you come to cast an English actress when, if you'd been looking for an obvious angle for foreign distribution, it would have been an American you should have cast, with the husband working for* Le Monde *in Washington or New York?*

LM: The character was originally American, but then I thought it would be fun to evoke the 'Swinging London' of that time. It seemed like London in those days was pretty much ahead of the rest of us, very trendy and hip, the flower generation, the music, the fashion. So she became a not-very-young hippy, which was fun. I remembered that from the period. Some of the things Harriet wears came from Alexandra Stewart who used to wear them in the early 1970s – the Afghan coat and those Tibetan necklaces and belts. Fortunately, she had kept them. I was very happy to cast Harriet, especially when I discovered she spoke impeccable French. It was very hard for her because speaking perfectly in a language and acting in that language are quite different.

This is something else I'd seen with Léa Massari in *Le Souffle au coeur*, and was to experience with Juliette Binoche in *Damage*. But Harriet pulled it off extremely well. It would have made no sense in the middle of this very coherent ensemble to introduce an American star. Harriet fitted in very well with Michel Duchaussoy, who plays her husband – the London correspondent of *Le Monde* who keeps dropping bits of English into his conversation.

PF: *The music by Stéphane Grappelli – given the setting, it would inevitably produce in most people's minds echoes of the use of Django Reinhardt on the soundtrack of* Lacombe, Lucien. *Was this choice purely accidental?*

LM: Of course not! I love Grappelli, and I found it surprising that he had scored only one other film before – Bertrand Blier's *Les Valseuses*, also with Miou-Miou, way back in the 1970s. It was an excellent score which was hardly noticed – the best compliment one can make about a score. You couldn't say that about a John Williams[4] score! I always had Grappelli in mind. Early on, trying to come up with the Milou character, I put a note in the margin: 'Milou is Grappelli's violin'. I also had source music in the film, quite a bit of it, such as Claire playing Debussy and Camille singing Mozart, and, of course, that absurd song that Jean-Claude Carrière remembered – 'La fille du bédouin' ('The Bedouin's Daughter').

PF: *The one they dance to – is that a traditional French song? I had never heard it before.*

LM: It's the best-known song of an operetta which was quite famous in the 1930s called *Le Comte Obligado*. A silly operetta. And by a bizarre coincidence Paulette Dubost had created the operetta on stage and then on film. So I thought, this is a sign.

Before I worked with Grappelli, I took from his many albums various pieces that I felt would fit the mood of the film, and cut them into the scenes. So Grappelli came to a screening of the film with his own music. Of course, it had to be something else, because some of the themes didn't work. But we started from that, and made adjustments. Stéphane, greater than ever at eighty-two, was bursting with ideas.

We ended up in the studio doing something that was quite similar to what I had done with Miles Davis. Basically, it was done with the musicians Grappelli always works with, playing two guitars and a piano. It was not a written score, but it was all very prepared, over several weeks of choosing and discussing. But when we got to the studio, then it became an improvisation.

PF: *In the picnic sequence, when intoxicated by wine, ideas and a little pot, they become revolutionaries and talk of their commune. As they go off walking, Grappelli strikes up a very comic swing version of the 'Internationale', which always gets, every time I see the film, a considerable laugh. Whose idea was it to use it at that point?*

LM: It was my idea from early on. Before I worked with Grappelli I had a waltz version of the 'Internationale' that a friend of mine had made on a synthesizer just to see if it worked. It was very pretty and funny. I'll tell you where it comes from. When I was shooting *Le Souffle au coeur* we had very little money and we needed a lot of extras for the scene of the ball of the Fourteenth July that precedes the incest scene. My assistant was a very active member of a Maoist group, so I said, 'Fernand, why don't you bring in your friends. We'll either pay them or give money to the cause.' Actually, it was a devious way to beat the extras' union; also, I wanted a very young crowd. They came and very quickly realized that being an extra in a film at night takes for ever. And is boring. They got restless. We had this musette orchestra, this typical Fourteenth of July band, and they started insulting the musicians, saying, 'What you play is shit. Why don't you play "L'Internationale"?' To tease them, or perhaps to calm them down, the band suddenly started playing 'L'Internationale' as a waltz. I thought it was wonderful. I actually thought of using it right on the spot, but of course it was inconceivable in *Le Souffle au coeur*, in this spa, in 1954.

But it stayed in the back of my mind. And it occurred to me that *Milou* would be the perfect occasion, especially at the moment when they all dream of changing the world. Stéphane was reluctant to do it. He said, 'In 1939 we did a recording of "La Marseillaise" in jazz with Django,

63 *Milou en mai:* the tipsy picnickers advance to the strains of the 'Internationale' – Dominique Blanc, Michel Duchaussoy, Jeanne Herry-Leclerc, Michel Piccoli, Harriet Walter, Renaud Danner, Rozenn Le Tallec

and we got into a lot of trouble.' I said, 'You don't have to worry, especially these days; I think people will get the joke.' So he agreed to start the piece as a waltz, and, of course, it quickly turned into a jazz piece. I'm only sorry that because the dialogue is funny and important at the time, I had to lower the music. On the album it's just great.

Notes

1 Gilles Jacob: French critic and documentary film-maker. Since 1977, Délégué Général (Executive Secretary) and chief selector for the Cannes Film Festival.
2 The 1968 Cannes Jury: André Chamson (President), Monica Vitti (Italy), Claude Aveline (France), Boris von Borrezholm (West Germany), Veljko Bujalic (Yugoslavia), Paul Cadéac d'Arbaud (France), Jean Lescure (France), Louis Malle (France), Jan Nordlander (Sweden), Roman Polanski (USA), Rojdestvensky (USSR), Terence Young (GB). Among the films in the aborted competition were Richard Lester's *Petulia*; Albert Finney's *Charlie Bubbles*; Mai Zetterling's *Doctor Glas*; Milos Forman's *The Firemen's Ball*; Alain Resnais's *Je t'aime, je t'aime*; and the three-part Edgar Allan Poe film

Histoires extraordinaires, though presumably only Fellini's and Vadim's segments were eligible for the *Palme d'Or*.

3 André Chamson (1900–1983): French novelist, essayist and art historian, born in Provence of Protestant stock. Much of his fiction (e.g. *Les Hommes de la route*, 1927) was inspired by peasant life in the Cévennes mountains, where he grew up. He was president of PEN International in 1956 and in the 1960s Director of the French National Archives.

4 John Williams (b. 1932): American pianist and composer, he entered films in the 1960s and came into his own a decade later with rousing scores for disaster movies, epics and the films of Steven Spielberg. He won Oscars for *Jaws*, *Star Wars* and *E.T.*

CHAPTER 6

Damage

PF: *Any student of your work reading Josephine Hart's* Damage,[1] *and knowing you were planning to film it, would notice certain pre-occupations of yours in her novel – the upper-middle-class background, incest, suicide, the surrender to an overwhelming passion. How did you discover the book and what attracted you to it?*

LM: I read *Damage* before it was published because Josephine Hart had the proofs sent to me. I was working at the time on a modern adaptation of Henry James's *What Maisie Knew*[2] and was having great difficulties. When I read *Damage*, there were themes, visual moments and characters that really intrigued me; I was very compelled. I quickly optioned the book through my French company. As it turned out, several American studios were expressing an interest – that was in January 1991. I'd been sick, I'd had surgery, and I was supposed to be taking things easy in Los Angeles. For the lead, I thought at once of Jeremy Irons, and when he read the novel he was immediately enthusiastic. So I had the book and I had Jeremy. I did a first structure. Then I realized it was much more difficult than I expected. The novel is written in a first-person narrative; it's all about him, how he feels at every moment, his memories, his emotions, it's all a long voice-over. I started by keeping the voice-over, but it was very dangerous. The story became so subjective it was going to be difficult to make the other characters exist. I worked for a while with Jean-Claude Carrière, trying to tell the story more objectively, though it was still centred on the novel's narrator.

PF: *In some ways this short, spare, emotionally analytical novel is close to a certain French tradition – one thinks of Raymond Radiguet's* Le Diable au corps, *Marguerite Duras's* The Lover, *and perhaps even books you've filmed –* Vivant-Denon's Point de lendemain *and Drieu La Rochelle's* Le Feu follet.

LM: Yes, I think so. Reading it I thought immediately of *Les Amants*. It's the same kind of milieu; it's about somebody discovering that his life (or, in the case of *Les Amants*, her life) is very empty; something happens which brings about the collapse of the conventional world in which he lives. It seemed interesting for me to revisit this theme, plus I was fascinated by Anna, this very disturbing woman who wants to share the father and the son. The book in a way is in a French tradition, but it is a Gothic tale too, and very operatic.

Anyway, I felt I had a lot to do on the book. For instance, the stylized and sometimes very beautiful dialogue would be difficult for actors to speak. But in the first draft that I did with Jean-Claude we went too far away from the novel. I felt we'd lost what I really liked about the book and I decided I had to work with an English writer. At some point I thought of moving it to France or the States, but the Englishness of the background was terribly important, so that's how I came to work with David Hare.[3] He had read the book and liked it. Not everybody did. We worked pretty fast and came up with a thirty-five-page synopsis. We made some changes in the plot because I felt that the moment the hero becomes completely obsessed with this woman, which happens early on in the book, the narrative becomes very linear. We developed events, contradictions, a dramatic progression. I was very happy when I read David's first draft, which was in the autumn. We did not shoot until February because of the weather.

In the meantime I had thought of Juliette Binoche for the role of Anna Barton. It was a part that many actresses wanted to play. In the book she's an intriguing and rather opaque character. I'd met Juliette with Jean-Claude Carrière and when David Hare came to Paris I had him meet her. Little by little the part was written for her. When we started rehearsing we produced another draft that tried to get closer to the book, while preserving the additions we had come up with. The script has a strong dramatic quality; in a way, it's a classical tragedy. There is a sense of fate, of something inexorable: you know that it's going to end tragically as we get deeper into the relationship. Yet in a story of a woman pursuing a Utopia there should be a hope – or fear – that it just might work out.

PF: *The tragic outcome arises from the consequences of a distant (by some fifteen years) experience of incest on Anna's part and an immediate grand sexual passion on Stephen's. To what extent are you now confronting the consequences of acts that in* Le Souffle au coeur *and* Les Amants *issued in apparently happy endings?*

LM: *Les Amants* didn't really have a happy ending. I left the end open. In *Damage* the huge difference is that Anna's brother commits suicide at sixteen and that she had to deal with that. She was very young and it was a tremendous trauma. The interesting idea of the book is that because she's survived she's become dangerous; survivors know that they'll get by, whatever happens.

PF: *This is the first time you've made a film set in contemporary Europe since* Le Feu follet *twenty-seven years ago. Did you feel compelled to look at present-day European society – or perhaps you don't regard Britain as Europe for that purpose?*

LM: I was happy to make a contemporary film after having recently explored my past – yet *Damage* brings back many things I've covered during my lifetime and in my work, as you've said. The fact that it takes place in contemporary England makes it a bit like my American films in that it has to do with a certain state of society, a certain moment. It's terribly interesting and sometimes difficult. I'm trying to observe English behaviour. I don't think, though, that it's going to be just another British film.

PF: *Surprisingly few French directors have worked in this country or made films set in Britain – in the 1930s, René Clair (*The Ghost Goes West*) and Marcel Carné (*Drôle de drame*); since the war René Clément (*Knave of Hearts*), François Truffaut (*Fahrenheit 451*), Jean-Luc Godard (*Sympathy for the Devil*) and most recently Bertrand Tavernier (*Death Watch*). All of these films were fantasies or futuristic pieces, with the exception of Clément's movie.*

LM: Strangely enough our two countries are only forty minutes apart, but there are tremendous cultural differences – even today with Europe and all that. For me, it is essential to try to understand how people react emotionally. It is important for me that Anna is half French and is played by a French actress, because she does have a different sensibility. I always wanted her to be not English – as she is in the book – so that she can be a strong contrast to the other characters, who are rooted in their English background. Because she's a diplomat's child, because she's travelled a lot, because her mother's French, when she appears in the story she's from elsewhere. I was, of course, slightly worried that American and British audiences might dismiss her by saying, 'Well, of course, she's French.'

PF: *There was a tradition in British movies in the 1950s and 1960s of casting continental actresses in the roles of women conscious of their sexuality or sexually liberated – even when in the novels on which the films were based they were clearly British. One thinks of Simone Signoret being brought over to appear as the middle-class Yorkshirewoman in the film of John Braine's* Room at the Top *or the sensual wife of the Welsh businessman in* Only Two Can Play *(the film of Kingsley Amis's* That Uncertain Feeling*) being turned into a Scandinavian and played by Mai Zetterling.*

LM: These are cultural areas that are very difficult to understand. There is something about Juliette that is Mediterranean, let's say, not necessarily French, which sets her apart from this fairly conventional English family. I didn't want to make her a *femme fatale*, a destroyer, but she had to be different.

PF: *But the way in which you present Stephen, he is less parochial, less insular, than the politicians surrounding him, who are constantly making jokes about their ignorance of French and who, on the visit to the European Commission in Brussels, remark on the tedium and unintelligibility of continental politicians. He is ready for an experience of a kind that they are not.*

LM: Yes. I didn't want to make him a caricature Englishman. And also I hope this is a story that has a value beyond the fact that the character is British. Like the new generation of politicians these days, he is more open. Stephen is a Conservative, but not a right-wing Conservative. He's someone who cares; he's not ambitious. His wife seems more ambitious than he is, but politicians who say they are not ambitious are the ones you have to be careful about.

PF: *How did you find working with David Hare? Presumably you share certain social attitudes about the middle classes, but he's politically some way to the left of you.*

LM: Yes. But I don't think that has played much of a part in this. He accepted from the beginning it was not going to be a satire on the ruling class. It was going to be an observation of their mores. Jeremy was very concerned about that: he felt that because David was a left-wing intellectual he would ridicule the character of Stephen, but this is not the case.

PF: *But over the last decade he's been particularly associated with the so-called theatre and cinema of Thatcher's Britain: state-of-the-nation plays and films, invariably of an adversarial kind. That Britain is now in the past, at least to the extent that it bears her name, and presumably*

there isn't much mileage left in a picture of that sort.
LM: Well, the novel belongs to a different genre, and David felt good about it. From the beginning I had a most interesting relationship with David. As you know, I like to work closely with writers and this had never happened to him before for the simple reason that whenever he wrote plays, or screenplays or teleplays, whether he directed them or not, they were always original stories and his own creations. For the first time he was adapting a book (which I believe he had always refused to do) for a director who brought it to him and had lots of notions about what the film was to be like. So it's been an unusual collaborative effort for him. I think he enjoyed it.

PF: *What have been the problems in bringing the script to the screen?*
LM: Well, the characters are always on the edge. Stephen's behaviour is very self-destructive, and you could easily think of Anna as a real monster. I'm always on this thin line, which makes the shooting very difficult because I must maintain a balance. What happens is very shocking, but I would have failed if the audience dismissed or rejected the characters. I hope they'll understand the character of Anna. She's enigmatic, and she should be. But she's pursuing this Utopia which is, I suppose, a fantasy of many women – to have a double relationship that fulfils different needs, to find happiness between these two men. But because of her past, consciously or unconsciously she brings disaster.

PF: *In preparing* Damage *were you conscious of any British films or writers – other, of course, than Josephine Hart or David Hare – that have guided your thinking on matters of style and behaviour?*
LM: I've read a great many novels and seen films, but I didn't conduct any special research apart from technical matters like the routine of a British politician. I trusted David for the Englishness. I ended up spending a year, on and off, in England before we started shooting and feel much better acquainted with the way things are here. But there haven't been any recent British films about this milieu, have there?

PF: *There's David Hare's own movie* Paris by Night, *oddly enough, which takes a female Conservative MP over the channel to be destroyed in France. Working with a largely British cast, to what extent have you been reliant upon your actors and actresses for guidance on matters of behaviour and what they might and might not do? Have you admitted them as collaborators?*

LM: Well, I always do so, except in the case of something like *Au revoir les enfants*, when I'm drawing on my own memories and on research. But let me say that when I work with Jeremy or Miranda Richardson or Rupert Graves, I'm always very interested in what they have to say about their characters. *Damage* has been one of my most collaborative enterprises. I used to work that way in America; when I had actors I trusted, I would often feel they knew more about the characters than I did. In the case of *Damage*, I sometimes disagreed with them, but it was very much a dialogue. Sometimes I try things different ways – it's tentative, but when we do the scene it seems to take its place, and find its truth. And so far it's been pretty good.

PF: *In the American films, with the exception of* My Dinner with André, *you're dealing with a blue-collar milieu – not with the background in which you grew up or the one you frequent in the States.* Damage *takes you into the English equivalent of the* haute-bourgeois *world in which you were reared.*

LM: In that sense, yes. But there are lots of differences and these differences are subtle and very fascinating. In terms of the surface, manners and behaviour, this is a world that I'm quite familiar with on the other side of the Channel. I think I know better than the actors do about the behaviour of these characters. It is a very specific world, but I hope that people outside England will find it interesting, not only because it's a portrait of a particular class, but for wider reasons – because it's about emotions that could be experienced anywhere.

PF: *At the end of Josephine Hart's novel the unnamed narrator, whom you call Stephen Fleming in the film, retreats from the world following his disgrace to an unnamed town. In the movie he settles in Caylus, not far from the stamping ground of Lucien Lacombe, the setting for the civil war in* Black Moon *and the crumbling mansion of Milou, not to mention your own country house. Whose decision was this?*

LM: That was mine completely. I wanted to finish in one of these little towns of the French South-West, which are very austere, a bit like Spain. It's not as if he retires to Saint Tropez. Josephine Hart was very worried: 'Is he going to retire in Provence?' 'No, no, no, no,' I assured her. 'When you see this little town he retires to, you'll see how medieval it is. It's like becoming a monk, in a way.'

64 *Damage:* an exchange of glances between Stephen (Jeremy Irons),
Ingrid (Miranda Richardson), Martyn (Rupert Graves) and Anna
(Juliette Binoche), as Sally (Gemma Clarke) looks on
65 *Damage:* as Martyn (Rupert Graves) sleeps beside her in a Parisian
hotel, Anna (Juliette Binoche) takes a call from his father

Notes

1   Josephine Hart: the Irish-born wife of the advertising tycoon Maurice Saatchi, she has worked in publishing and as a theatrical impresario, producing Lorca's *The House of Bernarda Alba* and Coward's *The Vortex*. *Damage* is her first novel.

2   *What Maisie Knew*: Henry James's short novel, published in 1897, was a product of his involvement with the theatre and he wrote a detailed scenario before embarking on the book itself. It is among the first works of fiction to deal with the effects of divorce upon a child and the setting is upper-middle-class England. Like Anna Barton in *Damage*, Maisie Farange (from whose point of view the novel is largely written) is a child when her parents part and remarry, and there is a bizarre exchange of partners when her parents' second spouses go off together. In Malle's film Stephen Fleming makes a surprise visit to Anna's mews house while she is entertaining an ex-lover and she pretends that Stephen has come to pick up a book. She gives him a copy of *What Maisie Knew*.

3   David Hare (b.1947): British playwright and film-maker and Associate Director of the National Theatre. For the cinema he adapted his own play *Plenty* (directed by Fred Schepisi, 1985) and has written and directed *Wetherby* (1985), *Paris by Night* (1990) and *Strapless* (1991).

CHAPTER 7

Coda

PF: *Now that we have come to the end of this journey through your career, do you have any final thoughts?*

LM: I'm always very wary of making 'statements' – especially when they appear in print, since they then take on the aspect of '*pensées*'. However, I do feel that it is essential for an artist to create a world, a world defined by a style and a vision. At the same time, I admire artists who move on, who don't stick for ever to the same technique, the same expression.

Take a painter like Georges de la Tour. He was obsessed by a certain technique of lighting and kept repeating that same effect over and over again. You can say that de la Tour has a world, but my preference is for artists who are constantly trying to open up and enlarge their experience. And so for me the supreme artist is Matisse. I say Matisse rather than Picasso because Picasso was always such a virtuoso; he really was the ultimate chameleon. I like Matisse for his patient, reflective approach to enlarging his vision, always going towards more simplicity, towards the essential.

As far as my own work is concerned, I'm always ready for something new or drastically different. One French critic said to me, 'When I go to see a new film of yours, I always feel uncomfortable. I'm sort of suspicious, and I ask myself, "What is he going to come up with this time?"' When people say, 'You've made all those films in so many different directions – what do they have in common?' all I can answer is, 'Me.' Personally, I tend to think that I repeat myself, so I try to resist the temptation to return to what I have already explored.

In the beginning, it was all so exciting – partly because cinema, especially in France, was such an enormously popular medium. Through the 1960s we, the young directors, were the cultural heroes of France. *Hiroshima mon amour*, *Les Quatre cent coups*, *Les Amants* were tremendously important events. These days, because of television and the incredible saturation of images, I'm not sure this would happen any more. Cinema has become – I don't want to say obsolete, but somewhat marginal.

66 Louis Malle 1992

We live in a culture of the disposable. A film can be an event, be huge at the box office, win all kinds of awards, and then in a couple of years be pretty much forgotten. Anyway, we film-makers don't work for posterity. We create with celluloid and chemical pigments that don't last very long. They fade away. In 200 years there will be nothing left of our work but dust.

PF: *But if you had to nominate three of your films for a special archive where they would be certain of preservation, which three would you choose?*

LM: It's really not up to me to do that. Instead, let me just mention the films of mine that I like.

Of my early films, I would say *Zazie* and *Le Feu follet*. From my films of the 1970s, I would definitely single out *Lacombe, Lucien*. Although I like *Le Souffle au coeur*, I think *Lacombe* is somehow a more important film. And in this last decade, I would say *Au revoir les enfants*.

So, maybe *Au revoir les enfants*, *Lacombe, Lucien* and *Le Feu follet*. Strangely enough, they are three pretty dark films, but I'm very attached to them. I could give you an alternative list, in a lighter vein: *Zazie, Le Souffle au coeur* and *Atlantic City*.

But ultimately I think I'm most proud of *L'Inde fantôme*. I think it's unique among documentaries.

In the end, I guess, my films always had a lot to do with where I was at that point in my life. I'm still very enthusiastic and excited by the medium. Film-making is incredibly difficult and contains so many elements you must keep under control. I like to think that I am getting better at mastering what I do, but there's still room for improvement. After all these years, I'm still finding out about the medium and discovering new possibilities. The longer I live, the less I trust ideas, the more I trust emotions.

Filmography

1956

Le Monde du silence (GB/US, The Silent World)

A documentary film covering two years of underwater exploration in the Mediterranean, the Red Sea, the Persian Gulf and the Indian Ocean by the pioneer oceanographer Commandant Cousteau and the crew of his expeditionary ship the Calypso. At times going down to a then unprecedented depth of 247 feet, the divers use experimental equipment like aqualungs and an electric underwater scooter and survive various tight spots and hazards. They swim along with shoals of fish, examine coral reefs and investigate sunken wrecks. The Calypso is caught in a monsoon storm, engages in a bloody encounter with sharks and a school of whales, and its crew go ashore on an island in the Indian Ocean where the ship's dog plays with giant turtles.

Production company: Société Filmad et Requins Associés
Directors: Jacques-Yves Cousteau, Louis Malle
Cinematography: Edmond Séchan (Technicolor)
Underwater photography: J.-Y. Cousteau, Louis Malle, Frédéric Dumas, Albert Falco
Music: Yves Baudrier
Editor: Georges Alépée
Special effects: Noël Robert
Commentary (English version): James Dugan
86 mins (UK version 82 mins)

1957

Ascenseur pour l'échafaud (UK, Lift to the Scaffold; US, Frantic; a.k.a. Elevator to the Gallows)

Julien Tavernier, ex-paratroop officer and veteran of colonial wars in Indo-China and Algeria, is in love with Florence, the wife of his boss, the munitions manufacturer Carala, and they plan the perfect murder. Just before the company's office closes for the weekend, Julien enters Carala's office unobserved, shoots him and arranges the death to look like a suicide. But he forgets to retrieve the grappling hook he'd used to scale the wall outside his victim's office, and returning to get it he is trapped in the lift when the power is turned off for the night. For the next twelve hours he makes desperate efforts to escape. Meanwhile Véronique, the teenage girl in the flower-shop across the road, and her boyfriend Louis steal Julien's American convertible and go off for a joyride. Florence, who has seen the car drive past and mistakes Louis for Julien, waits in vain for her lover to join her at a café and later walks anxiously around town. Véronique and Louis check into a smart motel using Julien's name. They meet a wealthy middle-aged German and his wife, take photographs using

Julien's camera and give a roll of film to be developed at the motel. During the night Louis attempts to steal the German's Mercedes and when its owner appears with a gun he kills him and his wife using a revolver he found in Julien's glove compartment. The young couple drive off, dump the car and, back at the girl's flat, realizing that Louis could be executed, they enter into an unsuccessful suicide pact. Florence is taken into police custody with a drunken friend she's met in a bar, but is soon released, though not before Inspector Chérier brings up the name of Tavernier. By the time the power is switched on in the office building, Julien's photograph is on the front page of the newspapers as prime suspect in the motel murders and he is arrested shortly after he leaves. Under interrogation by Chérier and his assistants, Julien cannot reveal his alibi without admitting to the murder of Carala. While he is being held, Florence confronts the young couple at Véronique's flat, then follows Louis when he goes by motorbike to retrieve the incriminating film at the motel. Inspector Chérier is waiting in the dark room and arrests him. He then shows Florence the photographs developed from the same reel of her and Julien Tavernier, taken in happier times, which provide the evidence of the plan to murder her husband.

Production company: Nouvelles Éditions de Films
Producer: Jean Thuillier
Director: Louis Malle
Screenplay: Louis Malle, Roger Nimier (from the novel *L'Ascenseur pour l'échafaud* by Noël Calef)
Dialogue: Roger Nimier
Photography: Henri Decaë (black and white)
Editor: Léonide Azar
Art directors: Rino Mondellini, Jean Mandaroux
Music: Miles Davis
Sound: Raymond Gauguier
Assistant directors: Alain Cavalier, François Leterrier
Cast: Maurice Ronet (*Julien Tavernier*), Jeanne Moreau (*Florence Carala*), Georges Poujouly (*Louis*), Yori Bertin (*Véronique*), Lino Ventura (*Inspector Chérier*), Ivan Petrovich (*Horst Bencker*), Elga Anderson (*Frau Bencker*), Jean Wall (*Simon Carala*), Félix Marten (*Subervie*), Charles Denner (*Inspector Chérier's assistant*), Jean-Claude Brialy (*chess player at motel*)
90 mins

1958

Les Amants (GB The Lovers)

Jeanne Tournier, the bored wife of a wealthy newspaper proprietor in Dijon and mother of a small child, contrives to spend as much time as possible in Paris, staying with her smart friend Maggy and seeing her handsome polo-playing lover Raoul. One day she is driving home to her mansion, where the weekend guests will be Maggy and Raoul, when her chic convertible breaks down on a country road. Bernard, a young archaeologist, gives her a lift in his 2CV. After he stops to visit an old friend, they arrive late at the Tournier's grand house and Bernard is invited to stay overnight. After a tense dinner of brittle conversation in which Raoul is put out by Henri Tournier's apparent concern for his wife, the company retire to bed. Unable to sleep, Jeanne goes into the moonlit garden, where she meets the equally restless Bernard and they go for a long walk around the estate and take a rowing boat along the river. Realizing they are in love they return to her room to spend the rest of the night in bed together. The following morning Jeanne packs and, to the astonishment of

Maggy, Raoul and her husband, leaves with Bernard in his car. They stop for coffee at a bar in a nearby town and then continue on their way into an uncertain future.

Production company: Nouvelles Éditions de Films
Director: Louis Malle
Screenplay: Louis Malle, Louise de Vilmorin (freely adapted from *Point de lendemain* by Dominique Vivant, Baron Denon)
Dialogue: Louise de Vilmorin
Photography: Henri Decaë (Dyaliscope, black and white)
Editor: Léonide Azar
Art directors: Bernard Evein, Jacques Saulnier
Sound: Pierre Bertrand
Music: First and second movements of Brahms String Sextet No. 1 in B Flat Major (Opus 18)
Cast: Jeanne Moreau (*Jeanne Tournier*), Alain Cuny (*Henri Tournier*), Jean-Marc Bory (*Bernard Dubois-Lambert*), Judith Magre (*Maggy Thiébaut-Leroy*), José-Luis Villalonga (*Raoul Florès*), Gaston Modot (*Coudray, the Tourniers' manservant*), Claude Mansart (*Marcelot*), Georgette Lobbe (*Marthe*), Patricia Garcin (*Catherine*)
88 mins (in original UK version 87 mins)

1960

Zazie dans le Métro (UK, *Zazie*)

Zazie, a self-assured ten-year-old from the country with a colourfully obscene vocabulary and an ability to disconcert adults, comes to Paris with her mother. At the Gare de l'Est she's dumped on her hapless uncle Gabriel while the mother goes off to spend thirty-six hours with her lover. Zazie's greatest wish is to travel on the Métro but it is closed down due to a strike and she is driven to the uncle's home in the taxi of his friend Charles. Gabriel and his wife Albertine live above a café, owned by Turandot, run by the waitress Madot and in the process of modernization. Gabriel does a drag act in a night-club and is dressed by Albertine for his performance. Next day Zazie goes out on the town and, after humiliating Turandot in public by alleging that he's a child-molester, she meets the chameleon-like Trouscaillon, who takes her to the flea market to buy her American jeans and a fancy meal. He chases her around Paris by bike and car, throwing bombs around, with jump cuts and in slow motion, suddenly ending up back home, where Zazie introduces Trouscaillon as a policeman. He falls instantly in love with Albertine and outrages Gabriel by suggesting that he is homosexual. Gabriel then takes Zazie for a vertiginous visit to the Eiffel Tower, after which they encounter the widow Mouaque, who develops a passion for Gabriel. He, however, becomes involved with a busload of Danish tourists. Zazie and Mouaque meet Trouscaillon, now in police uniform, and they follow him in his pursuit of Albertine to the night-club, where Gabriel performs with a top-hatted chorus line. Everyone then goes off to a café for a meal of onion soup but a drunken fight develops between the restaurant staff and the guests and the place is totally destroyed, though a sleeping Zazie is oblivious of the uproar. Finally Trouscaillon heads an attack by an army of black-shirted fascists (with back-projections of machine-gun fire and Stuka dive-bombers). But Albertine leads everyone to safety by a lift to the cellars, which open out on to the Métro, which is running once more. Zazie wakes up and at last gets her subway ride. In the morning she is reunited with her mother at the station for her journey home.

Production company: Nouvelles Éditions de Films

Director: Louis Malle
Screenplay: Louis Malle, Jean-Paul Rappeneau (from the novel by Raymond Queneau)
Photography: Henri Raichi (Eastmancolor)
Art director: Bernard Evein
Sound: André Hervé
Editor: Kenout Peltier
Music: Florenzo Carpi
Artistic adviser: William Klein
Cast: Catherine Demongeot (*Zazie*), Philippe Noiret (*Uncle Gabriel*), Carla Marlier (*Aunt Albertine*), Vittorio Caprioli (*Pedro Trouscaillon*), Hubert Deschamps (*Turandot*), Jacques Dufilho (*Gridoux*), Annie Fratellini (*Mado*), Antoine Roblot (*Charles*), Yvonne Clech (*the widow Mouaque*), Odette Piquet (*Mme Lalochère*), Nicholas Bataille (*Fédor*), Marc Doelnitz (*M. Coquetti*)
92 mins (UK release version 88 mins)

1961

Vie privée (UK, *A Very Private Affair*)

Jill, spoilt daughter of a wealthy upper-middle-class family, enjoys a life devoted to parties and boyfriends beside Lake Geneva. But after falling in love with the Italian theatre designer Fabio, the husband of her best friend Carla, she defies her mother and goes to Paris with her current lover Dick, a choreographer. They soon split up and Jill takes a succession of jobs as a dancer, a photographer's model and an actress, as well as an endless succession of lovers. Within a couple of years she has become a movie star, notorious for her promiscuity and constantly in the public eye. To find some privacy after a breakdown (partly brought on by being taken to task for her lifestyle by a charwoman in a lift), she returns incognito to Geneva. Her mother is no longer there, but she takes up again with Fabio, who has split with Carla, and he saves her from suicide. The press still pursue her, and when Fabio leaves for Spoleto to produce *Catherine von Heilbronn* at the Festival, Jill follows him, accompanied by her mother's courteous, aristocratic lover Gricha. The attention of the gossip writers and *paparazzi* distracts Fabio from his work, the couple quarrel and separate. Before leaving town Jill climbs on to a high roof to see the première of Fabio's open-air production. A photographer spots her and, blinded by the flash from his camera, she loses her balance and falls to her death in the street below.

Production company: Progefi, Cipra (France), CCM (Rome)
Producer: Christine Gouze-Rénal
Director: Louis Malle
Screenplay: Louis Malle, Jean-Paul Rappeneau, Jean Ferry
Photography: Henri Decaë (Eastmancolor)
Editor: Kenout Peltier
Designer: Bernard Evein
Sound: William Robert Sivel
Music: Fiorenzo Carpi. With the poem *Sidonie* by Charles Cros set to music by J. Max Rivière and Jean Spanos
Cast: Brigitte Bardot (*Jill*), Marcello Mastroianni (*Fabio*), Eleonore Hirt (*Cécile*), Ursula Kubler (*Carla*), Dirk Sanders (*Dick*), Gregor von Rezzori (*Gricha*), Jacqueline Doyen (*Juliette*), Antoine Roblot (*Alain, the photographer*), Paul Sorèze (*Maxime*), Nicolas Bataille (*Edmond*), Gloria France (*Anna*), Jeanne Allard (*charwoman in lift*), Jacques Gheusi (*Bazy*)
103 mins (English dubbed UK version 94 mins)

1962

Vive le Tour (a.k.a. Twist encore)

An impressionistic documentary on the annual Tour de France bicycle race concentrating on the spectators, the press entourage and the ordeal of the competitors as they struggle up mountains, collapse with cramps and become involved in pile-ups.

Director: Louis Malle
Photography: Ghislain Cloquet, Jacques Ertaud, Louis Malle (black and white)
Editor: Kenout Peltier and Suzanne Baron
Music: Georges Delerue
18 mins

1963

Le Feu follet (UK, A Time to Live and a Time to Die; US, The Fire Within)

Alain Leroy, an upper-middle-class thirty-year-old Parisian, is nearing the end of six months' residence at a private clinic for alcoholics in Versailles. He spends his days reading, chain-smoking, keeping a diary, fondling his Luger pistol and cutting out news-paper items on death and dying to decorate the walls of his room alongside pictures of Marilyn Monroe. His American wife is in New York and he spends a night with Lydia, a friend of hers, at an hotel. She drives him back to Versailles and he accepts money from her. Dr La Barbinais, who has been caring for Alain, believes he has been cured of his addiction and urges him to adopt a positive attitude to life. To test the doctor's views Alain hitchhikes into Paris and sets about revisiting old friends and former drinking companions. They have all betrayed themselves socially, intellectually and politically. His old chum Dubourg has become a complacent bourgeois husband and father and is obsessed with Egyptology. Jeanne is into drugs and is surrounded by pretentious pseudo-intellectuals. The society hostess Solange and her rich husband Cyrille invite him to dinner, where Alain is shocked by the right-wing politics and cynicism of his hosts and their smart guests. His disgust with society and with himself starts him drinking again. The next day he wakes up with a hangover. He asks not to be disturbed and while he is clearing up his room and packing his bags Solange calls to say they're expecting him for lunch. He finishes reading a Scott Fitzgerald novel and shoots himself in the heart with his Luger.

Production company: Nouvelles Éditions de Films
Director: Louis Malle
Screenplay: Louis Malle (from the novel by Pierre Drieu La Rochelle)
Photography: Ghislain Cloquet (black and white)
Editor: Suzanne Baron
Art director: Bernard Evein
Music: extracts from *Gymnopédies* and *Gnossiennes* by Erik Satie played at the piano by Claude Helffer
Cast: Maurice Ronet (*Alain Leroy*), Léna Skerla (*Lydia*), Yvonne Clech (*Mlle Farnoux*), Hubert Deschamps (*d'Averseau*), Jean-Paul Moulinot (*Dr La Barbinais*), Mona Dol (*Mme La Barbinais*), Pierre Moncorbier (*Moraine*), René Dupuy (*Charlie*), Bernard Tiphaine (*Milou*), Bernard Noël (*Dubourg*), Ursula Kubler (*Fanny*), Jeanne Moreau (*Jeanne*), Alain Mottet (*Urcel*), François Gragnon (*François Minville*), Romain Bouteille (*Jérôme Minville*), Jacques Sereys (*Cyrille Lavaud*), Alexandra Stewart (*Solange*), Claude Deschamps

(*Maria*), Tony Taffin (*Brancion*), Henri Serre (*Frédéric*)
110 mins (UK version 107 mins)

1964
Bons baisers de Bangkok
Documentary for French television on everyday life in the Thai capital.

Production company: ORTF
Director: Louis Malle
Photography: Yves Bonsergent
Editor: Nicole Lévy
15 mins

1965
Viva Maria
For fifteen years Maria O'Malley (Maria II), a pretty Irish girl, assists her Republican terrorist father to plant bombs to blow up British soldiers and policemen in Britain and around the Empire. He is finally killed in 1907 while they're blowing up a bridge in a British colony in Central America, but she escapes through the jungle. At a travelling circus she observes a lovelorn young woman, Janine, commit suicide. The dead woman was the partner in a double-act with another woman, also called Maria (Maria I) and after stowing away in her caravan Maria II crosses with the company into the Republic of San Miguel and replaces Janine in the act. The new team become a great success when they accidentally discover striptease. In addition to her initiation into show business, the naïve Maria II also learns about sex. Travelling the country, the circus people come across evidence of terrible exploitation of the peasants by a military dictatorship. They encounter the captured revolutionary leader Florès, and Maria I falls passionately in love with him when the circus is taken captive by the followers of the sadistic Rodriguez. The seductive Marias hypnotize Rodriguez and the circus's cockney gunsmith Rudolpho leads an escape from the dictator's hacienda during which Florès is mortally wounded. Maria I swears to the dying revolutionary that she will carry on the struggle and stirs his native village to action by delivering Mark Antony's speech from *Julius Caesar* over Florès's body. Drawing on the Irish Maria's skills as a bomb-maker, the two Marias become legendary heroines as they lead the people to victory after victory. The local Catholic bishop, shocked by the people worshipping the two Marias, contrives their arrest and they are brought before the Inquisition, though the priests can't get the ancient instruments of torture to work. Once more Rudolpho and his circus colleagues lead an attack on the gaol and the two Marias are rescued seconds before they are to be shot by firing squad. The revolution succeeds and the circus leaves the town through cheering crowds.

Production company: Nouvelles Éditions de Films/United Artists (Paris)/Vides (Rome)
Producers: Oscar Dancigers, Louis Malle
Director: Louis Malle
Screenplay (and lyrics): Louis Malle, Jean-Claude Carrière
Photography: Henri Decaë (Panavision, Eastmancolor)
Editors: Kenout Peltier, Suzanne Baron
Art director: Bernard Evein
Sound: José B. Carles

Colour consultant and costumes: Ghislain Uhry
Music: Georges Delerue
Cast: Jeanne Moreau (*Maria I*), Brigitte Bardot (*Maria II*), George Hamilton (*Florès*), Gregor von Rezzori (*Diogène*), Paulette Dubost (*Mme Diogène*), Claudio Brook (*Rudolfo*), Carlos Lopez Moctezuma (*Rodriguez*), Poldo Bendandi (*Werther*), Francisco Reiguera (*Father Superior*), Jonathan Eden (*Juanito*), Adriana Roel (*Janine*), José-Angel Espinoza (*El Presidente*), José Baviera (*Don Alvaro*), Fernando Wagner (*Maria O'Malley's father*), José Luis Campa, Roberto Campa, Eduardo Murillo and José Esqueda (*The 'Turcos'*)
115 mins (UK version 120 mins)

1967

Le Voleur (US, *The Thief of Paris*)

Between midnight and dawn as he ransacks an unoccupied haut-bourgeois mansion some miles outside Paris of its precious possessions, Georges Randal recalls his career as a gentleman-thief in *fin-de-siècle* France. Orphaned as a child, the gullible Georges was raised by his cynical uncle in Paris and grew up expecting to marry his cousin Charlotte. But, returning home from a long absence at school and in the army, he discovers that his considerable fortune has been lost (or embezzled) by his uncle and that Charlotte is about to marry a well-off neighbour. At the engagement party, Georges seduces a servant girl as a means of stealing the family jewels. The engagement is called off, and though Charlotte knows that Georges committed the crime for which others (for social reasons) were accused, he gets away with his swag. At the party, Georges has met the Abbé Margelle, and they meet again in a railway carriage. The priest reveals himself as a criminal king-pin operating from Brussels, fencing stolen goods and using the proceeds to finance missionary work in China. The Abbé introduces Georges to a world of international crime throughout Europe and the ace-burglar Roger-la-honte instructs him in the intricacies of the profession. He meets prostitutes, unfaithful wives and mistresses, who provide him with information that makes him a leading member of the underworld. He also sees his uncle taken up by a demi-mondaine. Invited by a right-wing deputy to attend a right-wing political gathering in Dieppe, George meets the celebrated anarchist thief Canonnier, a friend of the Abbé and a recent escapee from Devil's Island. Georges is impressed by his cool demeanour, his smoothly articulated ideology and the skill with which he enables the two of them to gather up all the concealed valuables from the room in which a rich woman is lying in state. Meanwhile, within earshot in the hotel's grand banqueting room, the deputy is delivering a reactionary speech at a political dinner to an appreciative audience. But, leaving the hotel, Canonnier is recognized by the police and shot dead virtually at Georges's feet. Subsequently Georges is joined at his London base by Charlotte and they become lovers. When her father, Georges's uncle, has a stroke and is dying, Georges – in league with the Abbé Margelle – forges a will. They cut the mistress out (but the Abbé arranges for her to go off with a rich suitor) and the estate is left to Georges and Charlotte. Disillusioned by bourgeois greed, the Abbé declares his decision to leave for China. Georges, however, cannot break with his life as a thief. He is addicted. Finishing off his current burglary, Georges climbs over the wall into the deserted early-morning street and carries his heavy valises towards the station to catch the first train of the day to Paris. His eyes are dead. He seems to suspect that the other ticket-holders on the station are agents of the law. But he is not rumbled. Georges gets the train and lives to commit another robbery.

Production company: Nouvelles Éditions de Films/United Artists (Paris)/Compania Cinematografica Montoro (Italy)

Producers: Louis Malle, Norbert Auerbach
Director: Louis Malle
Screenplay: Louis Malle, Jean-Claude Carrière (after the novel by Georges Darien)
Dialogue: Daniel Boulanger
Photography: Henri Decaë (widescreen, Eastmancolor)
Production designer: Jacques Saulnier
Costume designer and colour adviser: Ghislain Uhry
Editor: Henri Lanoe
Sound: André Hervée
Cast: Jean-Paul Belmondo (*Georges Randal*), Geneviève Bujold (*Charlotte*), Julien Guiomar (*l'Abbé La Margelle*), Marie Dubois (*Geneviève Delpiels*), Christian Lude (*Georges's Uncle Urbain*), Paul Le Person (*Roger-la-honte*), Françoise Fabian (*Ida*), Marlène Jobert (*Broussailles*), Martine Sarcey (*Renée*), Roger Crouzet (*Mouratet*), Fernand Guiot (*Van der Bush*), Charles Denner (*Canonnier*), Bernadette Lafont (*Marguerite, the maid at the home of Charlotte's fiancé*)
120 mins

Histoires extraordinaires (Italy, *Tre passi nel delirio*; GB, *Tales of Terror*; US, *Spirits of the Dead*)

A Franco-Italian co-production featuring three films freely adapted from short stories by Edgar Allan Poe. The first, *Metzengerstein*, directed by Roger Vadim, stars Jane Fonda as a wilful Hungarian countess who causes the death of a young baron and then becomes obsessed with a fierce black stallion in which the spirit of the baron lives on. The third film, *Toby Dammit* (based on the story *Never Bet the Devil Your Head*), directed by Federico Fellini, stars Terence Stamp as a drunken British movie-star brought to Rome to appear in 'the first Catholic Western' in exchange for a Ferrari and being lured to his death on a motorway by a demonic little girl.

In the central story, *William Wilson*, directed by Malle, an officer serving with the Italian army in nineteenth-century Italy runs through the streets and forces his way into a confessional at a Catholic church and insists upon being heard by the priest though he is in fact a Protestant. He gives his name as William Wilson and in flashback he explains the circumstances that led up to his committing murder. He recalls persecuting another boy at school and setting about performing a horrendous operation on a young woman at medical school and how on each occasion his double, also called William Wilson, turned up to expose him and get him expelled. Later in the army, the cold, arrogant Wilson gets into a game of cards with the aristocratic Giuseppina, wins all her money and then, after playing double-or-quits, strips off her clothes to beat her. But his *Doppelgänger* arrives once more to denounce him as a cheat and Wilson is called on to resign his commission. Subsequently Wilson confronts his double and kills him in a duel. Having told his story and blasphemed before the priest, Wilson rushes from the confessional to the church bell tower and throws himself off. He is found in the street below, a dagger in his stomach.

Production company: Les Films Marceau-Cocinor (Paris)/PEA Cinematografica (Rome)
Director: Louis Malle
Screenplay: Louis Malle, Daniel Boulanger, Clement Biddle Wood (from the story 'William Wilson' by Edgar Allan Poe)
Photography: Tonino Delli Colli (Scope, Eastmancolor)
Editors: Franco Arcalli, Suzanne Baron
Art director: Ghislain Uhry
Music: Diego Masson

Cast: Alain Delon (*William Wilson*), Brigitte Bardot (*Giuseppina*), Danièle Vargas (*the professor*), Renzo Palmer (*the priest*), Marco Stefanelli (*Wilson as a child*)
121 mins (*Histoires extraordinaires*); 40 mins (*William Wilson*)

1968–9

Calcutta

A documentary portrait of India's second-most populous city, capital of West Bengal, showing a bustling world of worshippers, beggars, packed streets, crowded trains. At the time the state was under martial law and the film observes non-violent demonstrations against the curtailing of civil rights. There is a visit to Mother Teresa's hospital and the extravagant preparations for a religious festival are recorded. The anglophile ruling class is seen at the exclusive Calcutta golf club, separated by a wall from one of the poorest parts of the city. A left-wing student protest march expressing solidarity with Chairman Mao and North Vietnam is confronted by 10,000 soldiers and police, and the demo stops to let a religious procession pass through. A representative of the large leper community explains their status as outcasts, and acrobats perform astonishing feats from the top of bamboo poles. An extended sequence reveals the city's lack of hygiene – filth pouring into the streets from animals, pigs everywhere, no garbage collection in the slums for months, dried cow dung used as fuel. In the final scene a succession of street urchins look straight at the camera.

Production company: Nouvelles Éditions de Films
Co-producer: Elliot Kastner
Director: Louis Malle
Narrator: Louis Malle
Photography: Étienne Becker, Louis Malle (16mm Ektachrome)
Sound: Jean-Claude Laureux
Editor: Suzanne Baron
105 mins

L'Inde fantôme: Reflexions sur un voyage (GB, Phantom India)

A seven-part TV series, each episode fifty-four minutes long (total 378 minutes), shown in France in 1969 and then in Britain (with Malle delivering his commentary in English). In 1975 the series was shown in European and American cinemas. The credits are as for *Calcutta*.

1: *La Caméra impossible* (or *Descente vers le Sud*) (GB, *The Impossible Camera*)
2: *Choses vues à Madras* (GB, *Things Seen in Madras*)
3: *La Religion* (GB, *The Indians and the Sacred*)
4: *La Tentation du rêve* (GB, *Dreams and Reality*)
5: *Regards sur les castes* (GB, *A Look at the Castes*)
6: *Les Étrangers en Inde* (GB, *On the Fringes of Indian Society*)
7: *Bombay* (GB, *Bombay – The Future India*)

1971

Le Souffle au coeur (GB, Dearest Love; US, Murmur of the heart)

In the spring of 1954 when the French army is being besieged at Dien Bien Phu and the victory of the Viet Minh insurgents is imminent, the fifteen-year-old Laurent, youngest of three brothers, is growing up in Dijon. Their father is a successful gynaecologist; their free-spirited mother Clara, the daughter of Italian fugitives from Fascism, is some years younger than her husband. A gifted scholar, Laurent attends an oppressive Catholic day school (where the priests impress on the boys the sacrifices being made in the Indo–Chinese war against Communism) and is devoted to jazz and literature. But he's worried about his sexuality, disturbed by the discovery that his mother has a lover, and (partly as a result of reading Camus' *The Myth of Sisyphus*) contemplates suicide. His wild brothers instruct him in sexual matters, introduce him to smoking and drink while their parents are away in Paris, and later take him to be initiated in a brothel, though they brutally interrupt him just as he's about to lose his virginity. Shortly after returning from boy-scout camp Laurent develops a 'heart murmur' and is confined to bed for a month. To help him convalesce his mother takes him to a fashionable spa hotel, where a mix-up in the bookings forces them to share a room. Their relationship becomes very close, and Laurent is resentful when Clara flirts with an older boy and when her lover comes to visit. But he makes friends with two girls, Daphné and Hélène, and listens to jazz. The mother returns distraught and tells him she and her lover have broken up. At the hotel's Fourteenth of July dance that night, Clara gets drunk and back in their room he undresses her and they make love. Afterwards, she says, 'I don't want you to be ashamed or to regret this. It was a beautiful moment. It will never happen again . . . it's a secret between us.' Laurent gets dressed and goes to Hélène's room, where he is repulsed, and then to Daphné, who takes him in. Next morning, carrying his shoes, he returns to his own room to find his father, mother and brothers waiting for him. They all roar with laughter and have breakfast.

Production company: Nouvelles Éditions de Films/Marianne (Paris)/Vides Cinematografica (Rome)/Franz Seitz Filmproduktion (Munich)
Producers: Vincent Malle, Claude Nedjar
Director: Louis Malle
Screenplay: Louis Malle
Photography: Ricardo Aronovich (Eastmancolor)
Editor: Suzanne Baron
Art director: Jean-Jacques Caziot, Phillippe Turlure
Sound: Jean-Claude Laureux, Michel Vionnet
Music: Charlie Parker, Sidney Bechet, Gaston Frèche and Henri Renaud
Cast: Léa Massari (*Clara, the mother*), Benoît Ferreux (*Laurent*), Daniel Gélin (*the father*), Michel Lonsdale (*Père Henri, the priest*), Fabien Ferreux (*Thomas*), Marc Winocourt (*Marc*), Ave Ninchi (*Augusta*), Gila von Weitershausen (*Freda, the prostitute*), Corinne Kersten (*Daphné*), Jacqueline Chauvaud (*Hélène*), Micheline Bona (*Aunt Claudine*), Henri Poirier (*Uncle Léonce*), François Werner (*Hubert*), Lilianne Sorval (*Fernande*), Eric Burnelli (*hotel manager*), André Zulawsky (*Clara's lover*). Jacques Gheusi (*hotel receptionist*), Yvon Lec (*Father Superior*)
110 mins

1974

Lacombe, Lucien

June 1944, the Allies have landed in Normandy. Down in south-west France, the seventeen-year-old peasant Lucien Lacombe works as an orderly in a nursing home for the elderly in a small town. Revisiting his native village on a limestone plateau south of the River Lot, he finds out that his mother, whose husband is a prisoner of war in Germany, is living with the landlord and that the family farm has been let to strangers. Lucien takes some dead rabbits to the local schoolmaster, Peyssac, and asks if he can join the Resistance. He is rejected, but cycling back to town he has a puncture and, being out after curfew, he is arrested outside a hotel used as the headquarters by French auxiliaries assisting the occupying forces and the Gestapo. They treat him in a friendly manner and after being plied with drink he talks about his village. The following day, Peyssac the schoolteacher is arrested and tortured. Lucien remains at the hotel, and falls under the influence of the attractive collaborators: Aubert, a former cycling champion, Jean-Bernard de Voison, a handsome dandy from an aristocratic family, and Jean-Bernard's mistress Betty Beaulieu, a one-time movie actress. He becomes a fellow-collaborator, acquires a gun and is taken by Jean-Bernard to get a suit made by Albert Horn, a famous Jewish tailor from Paris who's hiding out in the town with his twenty-year-old daughter France and his elderly mother. As Lucien gets deeper and deeper into nefarious Militia activities against the Underground, he pursues an initially unenthusiastic France. But after taking her to a dance at the hotel, where she is subjected to anti-Semitic insults, Lucien becomes her lover and moves into the Horn household. As the Allied forces move south, the Resistance becomes increasingly bold, and Jean-Bernard and Betty are killed. Lucien's mother, who has been receiving anonymous threats, urges her son to flee, but he says he likes it where he is. Horn, however, can no longer stomach Lucien's presence, delivers himself up to the vicious anti-Semitic collaborator Faure and is taken away by the Germans. Subsequently Lucien comes with a German NCO to arrest France and her grandmother. On the spur of the moment as they leave the house, he kills the soldier and spirits the two women away into the countryside. After their car breaks down, they take refuge in a deserted farm and begin to live an idyllic rural life with Lucien trapping animals and shooting birds to feed them. A final caption appears over his face one hot summer day: 'Lucien Lacombe was arrested on 12 October 1944. Tried by a military court of the Resistance, he was sentenced to death and executed.'

Production company: Nouvelles Éditions de Films/UPF (Paris)/Vides Film (Rome)/ Hallelujah Films (Munich)
Producer: Louis Malle, Claude Nedjar
Director: Louis Malle
Screenplay: Louis Malle, Patrick Modiano
Photography: Tonino Delli Colli (Eastmancolor)
Editor: Suzanne Baron
Art director: Ghislain Uhry
Costumes: Corinne Jorry
Sound: Jean-Claude Laureux
Music: 'Minor Swing', 'Nuages', 'Manoir de mes rêves', 'Fleur d'ennui', 'Douce ambience' and 'Lentement Mademoiselle' performed by Django Reinhardt and the Quintet of the Hot Club de France; 'Ah! c'qu'on s'aimait' and 'Mon coeur est un violon' performed by André Claveau; 'Mademoiselle Swing' by Irène de Trébert
Cast: Pierre Blaise (Lucien), Aurore Clément *(France),* Holger Löwenadler *(Albert Horn),* Thérèse Giehse *(Grandmother),* Stéphane Bouy *(Jean-Bernard),* Loumi Jacobesco *(Betty Beaulieu),* René Bouloc *(Faure),* Pierre Decazes *(Aubert, the barman),* Jean Rougerie *(Tonin),* Cécile Ricard *(Marie, the hotel maid),* Jacqueline Staup *(Lucienne),* Pierre Saintons *(Hippolyte, the black collaborator),* Gilberte Rivet *(Mme Lacombe, Lucien's mother),* Jacques Rispal *(M. Laborit, the Lacombe family's landlord),* Jean Bousquet *(Peyssac, the schoolteacher),* Ave Ninchi *(Mme Georges)*
137 mins

Humain, trop humain

A documentary about the manufacture of an automobile on the production line at the

Citroën factory at Rennes, Britanny in July 1972, and its presentation to the public at a Paris Motor Show in October. The first part observes the workers operating as a team to choral music. The second part looks at the same process emphasizing the tedium, discomfort, oppressive noise and grinding hard work.

Production company: Nouvelles Éditions de Films
Director: Louis Malle
Phtography: Étienne Becker (Ektachrome, 16mm)
Editor: Suzanne Baron
Sound: Jean-Claude Laureux
75 mins

Place de la République

Over a period of some ten days in 1972 Louis Malle and Fernand Mozskowicz observe and talk to people in the Place de la République in Paris, sometimes using concealed cameras and microphones, sometimes with the cameraman and sound recordist in view. At one point a young woman handles Malle's camera and joins them in asking questions.

Production company: Nouvelles Éditions de Films
Director: Louis Malle
Associate director: Fernand Mozskowicz
Photography: Étienne Becker (Ektachrome, 16mm)
Editor: Suzanne Baron
Sound: Jean-Claude Laureux
94 mins

1975

Black Moon

In some imminent, indeterminate near future, the pubescent teenager Lily drives over a badger on the country road and finds herself in the middle of a remorseless civil war between the sexes in which no prisoners are taken. Abandoning her car, she flees from a firing squad across wintry fields towards a bizarre mansion occupied by an old lady who converses with a rat in an unintelligible language. She is accosted by various animals, among them a talking unicorn, she meets an incestuous brother and sister, she becomes involved with a group of naked children devoted to a massive sow. Waves of action from the surrounding war encompass the house. The children sing, the incestuous brother kills an eagle that appears to fly out of an Indian painting on the wall, the old woman passes away, and Lily ends up offering her breast to the unicorn.

Production Company: Nouvelles Éditions de Films/UFP (Paris)/Vides Film (Rome)
Producer: Claude Nedjar
Director: Louis Malle
Screenplay: Louis Malle
Dialogue co-author: Joyce Buñuel
Art director (and screenplay collaborator): Ghislain Uhry
Photography: Sven Nykvist (Eastmancolor)
Editor: Suzanne Baron
Sound: Luc Perini
Music: Richard Wagner, arranged by Diego Masson
Animal advisers: Robert Verbeke, François Nadal

Cast: Cathryn Harrison (*Lily*), Thérèse Giehse (*the old woman*), Alexandra Stewart (*the sister*), Joe Dallessandro (*the brother*)
100 mins

1976

Close Up

Documentary portrait of Dominique Sanda, the fashion model, transformed into a movie actress by Robert Bresson in *Une Femme douce* (1969), who became a major international star.

Production company: Sigma–Antenne 2
Director: Louis Malle
Photography: Michel Parbot
Editor: Suzanne Baron
Music: Erik Satie
26 mins

1978

Pretty Baby (France, *La Petite*)

The twelve-year-old Violet lives with her prostitute mother Hattie and baby brother Will in a brothel in Storyville, the red-light district of New Orleans. The year is 1917, America is on the brink of entering the Great War and the US Navy threatens to close down Storyville. Violet is intrigued by the prissy, baggy-trousered photographer E. J. Bellocq, who visits the house to make portraits of the whores. One night in an elaborate ceremony Violet's virginity is auctioned off to wealthy patrons and she becomes a professional prostitute. Soon afterwards Hattie leaves with Will to marry a rich client from St Louis, and the temporarily abandoned Violet has a row with the madame and moves in with Bellocq. They become lovers, but her inability to appreciate his devotion to photography leads her to smash some of his fragile glass photographic plates and he ejects her. However, when the brothel is closed down, Bellocq proposes marriage and after the wedding they take the expelled prostitutes for a farewell party on the banks of the Mississippi. Some while later Hattie and her husband return to claim Violet so that she can have a proper middle-class upbringing and Bellocq gives her up. As they part at the station, Hattie's boorish husband Fuller takes a photograph of his family with a Box Brownie camera.

Production company: Paramount
Producer: Louis Malle
Director: Louis Malle
Screenplay and associate producer: Polly Platt
Story: Louis Malle, Polly Platt, (based on documentary material in *Storyville, New Orleans* by Al Rose)
Photography: Sven Nykvist (Metrocolor)
Editor: Suzanne Baron, Suzanne Fenn
Production designer: Trevor Williams
Sound: Don Johnson
Music: adapted and arranged by Jerry Wexler from numbers by Jelly Roll Morton, Scott Joplin, Louis Chauvin, the Original Dixieland Jazz Band, Mamie Desmond and others, and performed by the New Orleans Ragtime Orchestra, the Jazz Combo, the Trio and Bob Green (piano)

Cast: Keith Carradine (*E. J. Bellocq*), Susan Sarandon (*Hattie*), Brooke Shields (*Violet*), Frances Faye (*Nell, the madame*), Antonio Fargas (*Claude the brothel pianist*), Matthew Anton ('*Red Top*'), Diana Scarwid (*Frieda*), Barbara Steele (*Josephine*), Laura Zimmerman (*Agnes*), Miz Mary (*Odette*), Don Hood (*Alfred Fuller*), Gerrit Graham (*Highpockets*), Mae Mercer (*Mama Moseberry*), Pat Perkins (*Ola Mae*), Eric von Thomas (*Nonny*), Don K. Lutenbacher (*Violet's first client*)
110 mins (GB, 109 mins)

1980

Atlantic City USA

The unscrupulous Canadian hippy Dave steals a consignment of Mafia cocaine in Philadelphia and drives to Atlantic City, New Jersey, with his pregnant flower-child mistress Chrissie to visit his estranged wife (and Chrissie's sister) Sally. Sally is working at the fish bar of one of the newly licensed casinos in a town undergoing transformation from decaying resort to a flashy East Coast Las Vegas, and she is training as a croupier under the instruction of the Frenchman Joseph. Living in the same seedy apartment block as Sally, and secretly in love with her, is Lou Paschall, an elderly crook with delusions of grandeur. The kept man of the hypochondriac widow Grace, Lou fears that his shabby livelihood as a numbers runner is threatened by legal gambling. In the belief that Lou is a major underworld figure, Dave uses him to sell the cocaine. When Dave is killed by two Mafia hitmen, Lou is left with the drugs and wins Sally's confidence by handling the funeral arrangements. He takes her out to an expensive restaurant and they sleep together. For her association with Dave, Sally is fired by the casino, and to protect her Lou kills the two gunmen and drives off with her in the direction of Florida. At a motel Sally steals some of Lou's loot so she can get away to fulfil her dream and become a croupier in Monte Carlo, and he lets her go with his blessing. After phoning Grace to boast of being the killer the cops are seeking, Lou goes back to Atlantic City. He and the revived Grace walk jauntily along the Boardwalk after she has helped sell the rest of the cocaine.

Production company: Cine-Neighbour (Montreal)/Selta Films-Elie Kfouri (Paris)
Producers: John Kemeny, Joseph Beaubien, Denis Heroux
Production co-ordinator: Vincent Malle
Director: Louis Malle
Screenplay: John Guare
Photography: Richard Ciupka (colour)
Editor: Suzanne Baron
Production designer: Anne Pritchard
Sound: Jean-Claude Laureux
Music: Michel Legrand (extract from Bellini's *Norma* performed by Elizabeth Harwood and the London Philharmonic)
Cast: Burt Lancaster (*Lou Paschall*), Susan Sarandon (*Sally*), Kate Reid (*Grace*), Michel Piccoli (*Joseph*), Hollis McLaren (*Chrissie*), Robert Joy (*Dave*), Al Waxman (*Alfie*), Robert Goulet (*singer in hospital*), Moses Znaimer (*Félix, hitman*), Angus MacInnes (*Vinnie, hitman*), Louis Del Grande (*Mr Shapiro*), Cec Linder (*president of hospital*), Wallace Shawn (*waiter*), Joyce Parks (*Queenie*)
105 mins

1981

My Dinner with André

Two old friends, Wallace Shawn and André Gregory, meet for the first time in years to have dinner at an expensive, old-fashioned French restaurant in Manhattan selected by Gregory. The balding, gnome-like Shawn (son of the then editor of the *New Yorker*) is in his late thirties and ekes out a living in Greenwich Village as an actor and playwright. The handsome, aquiline Gregory, some ten years Shawn's senior, is a celebrated avant-garde director, well off, successful, socially at ease, married with two children. While Wally has been grubbing along in the everyday reality of New York, André has dropped out of a society he despises and has spent five years wandering the world. Under Wally's increasingly sceptical questioning, André recounts his experiences with a variety of mystical searchers after truth on four continents – communing with priests in Tibet, preparing a production of *Le Petit Prince* in the Sahara with a Japanese monk, working with Grotowski's company in a Polish forest, being buried alive in a Halloween ritual at Richard Avedon's Long Island estate, meeting a brilliant Scottish mathematician who talks to fauns in an Edinburgh park, discussing with friends the creation of a conference centre to welcome extraterrestrials and so on. Representing totally opposed approaches to life and to the theatre, the products of different strands in the American life of the 1960s and 1970s, the romantic mystic André and the down-to-earth, pragmatic Wally discuss their different positions while getting through a fine meal. Neither is convinced by the other's argument. When they part, Wally, who at the beginning had come uptown by subway, decides to take a taxi home to tell his companion Debbie about his dinner with André.

Production company: The André Company. For George W. George in association with Michael White
Producers: George W. George, Beverley Karp
Director: Louis Malle
Screenplay: Wallace Shawn, André Gregory
Photography: Jeri Sopanen (Colour–Movielab)
Editor: Suzanne Baron
Art directors: David Mitchell, Stephen McCabe
Sound: Jean-Claude Laureux
Music: Allen Shawn (extract from *1st Gymnopédie* by Erik Satie performed by Joseph Villa)
Cast: Wallace Shawn (*Wally*), André Gregory (*André*), Jean Lenauer (*waiter*), Roy Butler (*the barman*)
111 mins

1983

Crackers

In San Francisco's impoverished, racially mixed Mission District, the redundant security officer Westlake works as a guard at a run-down pawn shop owned by the elderly Garvey. The black pimp Boardwalk informs him that the unemployed white electrician Dillard and his Hispanic sidekick Ramon are planning to follow up the installation of a burglar alarm in the pawnshop by robbing Garvey's safe. Westlake accordingly appoints himself leader of the gang and brings in his ever hungry assistant Turtle and Boardwalk to assist. The date chosen for the heist he has masterminded is the night Garvey is away celebrating his mother's ninetieth birthday. The feckless quintet are variously distracted on their way to the scene of the crime, the explosive fails to work. While they are gathered around the safe, Garvey unexpectedly returns. His mother has died. Then the explosive goes off. However, as Garvey explains, the safe was unlocked and empty. Instead of turning them over to the police Garvey gives them a little talk about friendship and shares with them the salmon he'd bought for his mother's birthday.

Production company: Universal
Producers: Edward Lewis, Robert Cortes
Director: Louis Malle
Screenplay: Jeffrey Fiskin (based on the 1958 Italian comedy *I soliti ignoti* – GB, *Persons Unknown*; US, *Big Deal on Madonna Street*; France, *Pigeon* – scripted by Agenore Incrocci, Furio Scarpelli, Suso Cecchi d' Amico and Mario Monicelli)
Photography: Laszlo Kovacs (Technicolor)
Editor: Suzanne Baron
Production designer: John J. Lloyd
Music: Pal Chihara
Cast: Donald Sutherland (*Westlake*), Jack Warden (*Garvey*), Sean Penn (*Dillard*), Wallace Shawn (*Turtle*), Larry Riley (*Boardwalk*), Trinidad Silva (*Ramon*), Christine Baranski (*Maxine*), Charlaine Woodard (*Jasmine*), Tasia Valenza (*Maria*), Irwin Corey (*Lazzarelli*), Edouard DeSoto (*Don Fernando*), Anna Maria Horsford (*Slam Dunk*)
91 mins

1985

Alamo Bay

Dinh, a young Vietnamese refugee, hitchhikes into the small fishing town of Port Alamo near Corpus Christi in southern Texas. It is the late 1970s and he has come to join the growing community of fellow Vietnamese fishermen who have settled there since the fall of Saigon in 1975. There is considerable hostility on the part of the locals towards the newcomers because of the long hours they work and their lack of respect (through ignorance) for laws and codes of practice governing fishing – especially at a time when the shrimps in the vicinity are being exhausted by over-fishing. Some of the antagonism is being directed against Wally Scheer, the kindly middle-aged owner of the packing plant that deals with the local catch, who employs Vietnamese and is sympathetic to the newcomers. Wally's daughter Glory has returned from the big city to help her threatened and ailing father, and she renews her old affair with Shang Pierce, a handsome fishermen married with three children. The embittered Pierce (the nickname refers to Shanghai Pierce, a legendary post-Civil War Texas cattle-drover) is experiencing hard times and his fishing boat, *American Dream Girl*, is about to be repossessed.

Ku Klux Klan organizers move into Alamo Bay to exploit the unrest and Pierce emerges as the leader of the disgruntled xenophobic locals. He cuts Vietnamese nets, shoots at them with a rifle, and leads a band of whites in motor boats to force the Vietnamese out of the harbour at gunpoint. A Klan cross is burnt outside the newcomers' shantytown, nicknamed 'Slope City', with placards reading 'Death to the Gooks' and 'Death to the Cong'. Dinh, after unsuccessful attempts to make friends with the Texans, emerges as leader of the resistance, though the majority of the intimidated Vietnamese quit. As the result of the pressure put on him, Wally has a heart attack and dies, but Glory joins forces with Dinh to keep her father's business going and to defy the blockade set up by Pierce and his followers. In a final showdown, Pierce leads a night-time raid on the packing factory, which is being guarded by Dinh and a friend. He's just about to kill the young Vietnamese when Glory turns up and shoots him dead.

Production company: Tri-Star-Delphi III Productions
Executive producer: Ross E. Milloy
Producers: Louis Malle, Vincent Malle
Director: Louis Malle
Screenplay: Alice Arlen (inspired by a series of *New York Times* articles by Ross E. Milloy)
Photography: Curtis Clark (Metrocolor)
Editor: James Bruce
Production designer: Trevor Williams
Sound: Danny Michael
Music: Ry Cooder
Cast: Amy Madigan (*Glory*), Ed Harris (*Shang Pierce*), Ho Nguyen (*Dinh*), Donald Moffat (*Wally Scheer*), Truien V. Tran (*Ben*), Rudy Young (*Skinner*), Cynthia Carle (*Honey*), Martino Lasalle (*Luis*), William Frankfather (*Mac*), Bill Thurman (*Sheriff*), Khoa Van Le (*Father Ky*), Buddy Killen (*Rev. Disney*), Callaway Nugent (*Rev. Disney's wife*)
99 mins

1986

God's Country (France, *Le Pays de dieu*)

A documentary about Glencoe, an agricultural town with nine churches (seven Protestant, two Catholic), no synagogue and a population of 5,000, some 60 miles west of Minneapolis. Malle and his crew visit Glencoe in 1979 to observe the people mowing lawns, a girls' softball team practising, a marriage at a Lutheran church and so on, and to talk with farmers, a banker, the police chief and others. In August 1985 Malle returns to Glencoe to see what has happened to the town over the past six years and how its inhabitants have been affected by the recession and the depression in farming.

Production company: PBS (with grant from National Endowment for the Arts)
Producer: Vincent Malle
Director: Louis Malle
Commentary: Louis Malle
Photography: Louis Malle (colour)
Sound: Jean-Claude Laureux (1979), Keith Rouse (1985)
Editor: James Bruce
95 mins

1987

And the Pursuit of Happiness (France, *La Poursuite du bonheur*)

A documentary, commissioned as one of a series of TV programmes to mark the centenary of the Statue of Liberty. Malle travels around the United States, observing and talking to recent immigrants. Among them, Cambodians arriving at Kennedy Airport via Thailand and Italy; a Russian actor teaching the Stanislavsky Method; Cubans in Florida; Vietnamese in California; a Hispanic astronaut who became an American citizen in 1977; a Vietnamese doctor in rural Nebraska treating a labourer who arrived from Greece in 1907; Egyptians in Los Angeles complaining of being stereotyped as Arab terrorists; a Pakistani schoolteacher turned beautician; the West Indian poet Derek Walcott worrying over an ambience of mediocrity; an ex-Laotian army officer working for the Colt arms company; a Hindu running a chain of motels from a palatial home in California; the son of the Nicaraguan dictator Somosa living in luxury in Miami. Malle discovers that a third of all immigrants at the turn of the century returned home and he explores the current American anger over illegal immigration from Mexico and Latin America.

Production company: Pretty Mouse Films Inc (New York)
Director: Louis Malle
Script: Louis Malle
Photography: Louis Malle (colour)
Editor: Nancy Baker
Sound: Danny Michael
80 mins

1987

Au revoir les enfants

In January 1944, the wealthy middle-class mother of the twelve-year-old Julien Quentin and his sixteen-year-old brother François sees them off at Paris's Gare de Lyon as they return after the Christmas vacation to their exclusive Catholic boarding school run by Carmelites at a small town in the Île de France. Three new boys enter the school, and one of them, Jean Bonnet, is introduced to Julien's dormitory by the head of the school, Father Jean, and assigned to the adjoining bed. Julien, a bright, popular, somewhat insolent lad, at first joins in teasing the newcomer. But gradually their interest in music and literature draws them together and one evening after confession Father Jean asks Julien to be kind to him. Their friendship is sealed when they are stranded out in the forest at night after getting lost during an adventure exercise and are brought back to the school by kindly German soldiers, Catholics from Alsace. Bonnet claims to be a Protestant whose father is in a prisoner-of-war camp in Germany and his mother in Vichy France. Julien, however, has discovered that he is in fact a Jew called Kippelstein, and confronts him with this when they're in the school infirmary after their escapade in the forest. When Julien's mother comes one Sunday to visit the school with other parents, she takes Jean along with her sons to a smart restaurant where some French militiamen enter the dining room and demand that an elderly Jew eating there be expelled. François and another diner come to his defence and a German officer, to impress Mme Quentin, orders the intruders to leave. Subsequently Julien and François tease their mother about having Jewish relatives in Alsace, but she insists they're Catholics, though adding that she has nothing against Jews. Jean, François and some other boys have been involved in a little black-market dealing (exchanging food from home for cigarettes and stamps) with Joseph, the surly, limping orphan who works in the school kitchen. When this is revealed the pupils are punished and Joseph is sacked. A little later the Gestapo descend on the school, arresting Jean Bonnet in the classroom and rounding up the two other Jewish boys, and it transpires that they have been informed on by the disgruntled Joseph. The school is closed down, and in front of the assembled staff and pupils the three Jewish boys and Father Jean are led off. Malle, on the soundtrack, states that the three boys died in Auschwitz and the priest in Mauthausen.

Production company: Nouvelles Éditions de Films/MK2 Productions/Marin Karmitz (Paris)/Stella Film and NEF (Munich)
Producer: Louis Malle
Director: Louis Malle
Screenplay: Louis Malle
Photography: Renato Berta (colour)
Editor: Emmanuelle Castro

Art director: Willy Holt
Sound: Jean-Claude Laureux
Music: Extracts from 'Moment Musical No. 2 in A Flat' by Schubert; 'Rondo Capricioso' by Camille Saint-Saëns
Cast: Gaspard Manesse (*Julien Quentin*), Raphaël Fejtö (*Jean Bonnet*), Francine Racette (*Mme Quentin*), Stanislas Carré de Malberg (*François Quentin*), Philippe Morier-Genoud (*Father Jean*), François Berléand (*Father Michel*), François Négret (*Joseph*), Peter Fitz (*Müller, Gestapo officer*), Pascal Rivet (*Boulanger*), Benoît Henriet (*Ciron*), Richard Leboeuf (*Sagard*), Xavier Legrand (*Babinot*), Arnaud Henriet (*Negus*), Jean-Sébastien Chauvin (*Laviron*), Luc Étienne (*Moreau*), Irène Jacob (*Mlle Davenne*), Jacqueline Paris (*Mme Perrin*), Jacqueline Staup (*nurse*)

1989

Milou en mai (GB, *Milou in May*; US, *May Fools*)

The sixty-year-old widower Émile Vieuzac, known as Milou, lives with his aged mother in the family's once grand mansion surrounded by run-down vineyards in Le Gers in south-west France. It is May 1968 and the student revolution in Paris is spreading through the country, though these events scarcely impinge on Milou as he goes quietly about his life, keeping bees and neglecting his estate. When his mother suddenly dies, he calls the family together for the funeral – his brother Georges, a journalist on *Le Monde*, currently writing a book on the Côte d'Azur, and his young English wife Lily; his niece Claire (who has a lover, Marie-Laure); his right-wing, Catholic bourgeois daughter Camille, her doctor husband and young children (twin boys and the ten-year-old Françoise) from Bordeaux; and Georges's son Pierre-Alain, a student in Paris. Because of the strike by public transport workers and a shortage of petrol, all have difficulty in making the journey. Pierre-Alain arrives in the middle of the night, having hitched a ride with Grimaldi, a self-employed working-class lorry driver who was turned back outside Paris with his load of Spanish tomatoes bound for Les Halles. The family lawyer, an old flame of Camille's, reads the will, revealing that a fourth part of the estate has been left to Adèle, Madame Vieuzac's devoted servant. When it proves impossible, owing to a gravediggers' strike, to go ahead with the funeral, the body is left lying in state in the house, while at the insistence of Camille they set about dividing up the mother's possessions and (to Milou's dismay) discuss selling off the house. A decision is made to dig a grave on the estate. During the long hot days and nights, the group dine, drink, talk, form alliances, attempt seductions, and – high on wine, pot and revolutionary fervour at a picnic – they even contemplate turning the estate into a Utopian commune. That night as they dance around the house and embark on sexual games, Monsieur Boutelleau, a wealthy, middle-aged factory owner and his wife from the neighbouring estate, arrive stating that de Gaulle has fled, the revolution has succeeded and that soon hordes of vengeful Communists will be at their door. A radio transmission, broken off by a power failure, seems to confirm this news and they hastily pack and head for the hills. Mistaking a party of hunters for revolutionaries, they abandon their meal and camp fire and end up sheltering from the rain in a cave, demoralized and fighting among themselves. Next morning Adèle tracks them down, bringing the news that de Gaulle has returned and the threatened revolution is no more. They return dishevelled to the house and go ahead with the funeral. When everyone has gone his or her way, Milou finds that Boutelleau has polluted the local river and killed the fish, taking advantage of the strike to drain the vats at his factory. After cursing the industrialist as he rides by, Milou returns to the house, now denuded of furniture. In the drawing room, his mother, looking much younger than at the time of her death, is playing the piano. The music continues, when she gets up to dance with him.

Production company: Nouvelle Éditions de Films/TF1 Films (Paris)/Ellepi Film (Rome)
Producers: Louis and Vincent Malle
Director: Louis Malle
Screenplay: Louis Malle, Jean-Claude Carrière
Photography: Renato Berta (colour)
Editor: Emmanuelle Castro
Art director: Willy Holt
Sound: Jean-Claude Laureux
Music: Stéphane Grappelli (plus Cherubino's Aria from Mozart's *Marriage of Figaro*, Prelude '*Général Lavine*' by Claude Debussy and the song 'La fille du bédouin' from *Le Comte Obligado*)
Cast: Michel Piccoli (*Émile Vieuzac, 'Milou'*), Miou-Miou (*Camille*), Michel Duchaussoy (*Georges*), Dominique Blanc (*Claire*), Harriet Walter (*Lily*), Bruno Carette (*Grimaldi*), François Berléand (*Daniel, the family lawyer*), Martine Gautier (*Adèle*), Paulette Dubost (*Mme Vieuzac*), Rozenn Le Tallec (*Marie-Laure*), Renaud Danner (*Pierre-Alain*), Jeanne Herry-Leclerc (*Françoise*), Benjamin and Nicolas Prieur (*Camille's twins*), Marcel Bories (*Léonce*), Étienne Draber (*M. Boutelleau*), Valérie Lemercier (*Mme Boutelleau*), Bernard Brocas (*Priest*), Serge Angeloff (*Adèle's fiancé*)
108 mins

1992

Damage

Dr Stephen Fleming has had a happy, unruffled and successful life. A former GP, he is now a Conservative Member of Parliament and Minister of State in the Department of the Environment and lives in Hampstead with his beautiful wife, Ingrid, and their two attractive children, the thirteen-year-old Sally and the twenty-five-year-old Martyn, who has just been appointed deputy political editor of a leading national newspaper. Ingrid is the only daughter of the widowed Edward Lloyd, a rich, influential ex-Tory MP with a country house that has been in his family for over 200 years. It is Edward who encouraged Stephen to enter politics. But Stephen's idyllic existence is shattered by a sudden (and reciprocated) passion for his son's new girlfriend, the thirty-year-old Anna Barton, who works for a London auction house, and they become lovers. The daughter of a British diplomat and his French wife, Anna was raised in various world capitals and her parents' marriage broke up following the suicide in Rome of her brother at the age of sixteen. It transpires that the brother had a deep, incestuous love for Anna, a year his junior, and slashed his wrists when he realized that she would not be his for ever. His death made Anna terrified of possessiveness and she cautions Stephen, 'Damaged people are dangerous, they know how to survive.'

Stephen's obsession leads him to slip away from a European Commission meeting in Brussels to spy on Anna and Martyn in Paris, where he makes love to her against a wall in a side street. While in Paris he sees the art dealer Peter Wetzlar, who turns out to have been Anna's first lover after her brother's suicide. Back in Britain at a weekend party for Ingrid's birthday at her father's country estate, Martyn and Anna announce their engagement. The news proves a great shock to Ingrid, who has doubts about Anna's suitability for her beloved son, and to Stephen. Elizabeth Prideux, Anna's four-times-married mother, comes from her home in Palm Springs for the wedding and, sensing Stephen's obsession, issues a discreet warning. This initially persuades him that the affair should end. But Anna assures him that she wishes it to continue and she sends him a key to a flat in West London where they can have love trysts. On the day that Stephen is arranging a visit to Downing Street to be confirmed as the new Minister of Health he meets Anna at the flat. Through accidentally receiving a message intended for Anna, Martyn arrives there while his father and fiancée are making love. He recoils from the sight before him, topples over the rails on the landing outside and falls four storeys to his death.

Observed by neighbours in the hall, the naked Stephen cradles his dead son as Anna quietly leaves to find refuge in her mother's suite at a Mayfair hotel. Stephen is questioned by the police, pursued by the press and turned upon by his distraught wife, who suggests he should have committed suicide when he felt possessed by his passion. He resigns from the House of Commons and leaves the country to travel, eventually settling into a lonely routine existence in the medieval town of Villefranche de Rouergue in south-west France. On the wall of his spartan apartment is a large blown-up photograph of himself with Anna and Martyn taken the day their engagement was announced. In voice-over at the end he remarks upon having seen her unobserved once at the Paris airport with her husband, Peter Wetzlar, and their child.

Production company: Skreba (UK)/Nouvelles Éditions de Films (France)
Producers: Vincent Malle, Simon Relph
Director: Louis Malle
Screenplay: David Hare (based on the novel *Damage* by Josephine Hart)
Cinematography: Peter Biziou (colour)
Editor: John Bloom
Production designer: Brian Morris
Music: Zbigniew Preisner
Sound: Jean-Claude Laureux
Cast: Jeremy Irons (*Stephen Fleming*), Miranda Richardson (*Ingrid Fleming*), Rupert Graves (*Martyn Fleming*), Juliette Binoche (*Anna Barton*), Leslie Caron (*Elizabeth Prideux*), Ian Bannen (*Edward Lloyd*), Julian Fellows (*Donald Lindsay, MP*), Peter Stormare (*Peter Wetzlar*), Gemma Clarke (*Sally*), Linda Delapena (*Beth, the Fleming's housekeeper*), Susan Engel (*Miss Snow, Stephen's secretary*), Raymond Gravell (*Raymond, Stephen's chauffeur*), Jeff Nuttall (*Trevor Leigh Davies, MP*), Roger Llewellyn (*Palmer, Anna's boss*), Henry Power (*Henry, Sally's boyfriend*), Benjamin Whitrow (*elderly civil servant*), Frank Shelley (*old man in hall of apartment block*), Francine Stock (*TV interviewer*)

Select Bibliography

Books

Armes, Roy, *French Cinema since 1956*, vol. 2: *The Personal Style*, A. Zwemmer, London (rev. edn 1970)
– *French Cinema*, Secker & Warburg, London (1985)
Beylie, Claude, and Jacques Pinturault, *Les Maîtres du cinéma français*, Bordas, Paris (1990)
Chappier, Henri, *Louis Malle*, Seghers, Paris (1964)
Malle, Louis, *Au revoir les enfants* (with Patrick Modiano) and *Lacombe, Lucien* (introduction by Philip French), Faber & Faber, London (1989)
Malle, Louis, and Jean-Claude Carrière, *Milou in May*, Faber & Faber, London (1990)
Mallecot, Jacques, *Louis Malle par Louis Malle*, Éditions de l'Athanor, Paris (1979)
Predal, René, *Louis Malle*, Edilig, Paris (1989)
Roud, Richard (ed.), *Cinema: A Critical Dictionary* (essay by James Monaco), Secker & Warburg, London (1980)
Thomas, Nicholas (ed.), *The International Dictionary of Films and Filmmakers*, vol. 1: *Directors*, St James Press, Chicago and London (2nd edn 1991)
Thomson, David, *Biographical Dictionary of the Cinema*, Secker & Warburg, London (rev. edn 1980)

Articles and Reviews

René Predal's *Louis Malle* contains an extensive bibliography of interviews, reviews and published screenplays in French up to *Au revoir les enfants*. John Baxter's essay in Nicholas Thomas's *Filmmakers*, vol. 1 is accompanied by a bibliography of English-language writings on Malle. The following is a short list of reasonably accessible reviews in English, virtually all but my own available in books or bound volumes in reference libraries.

Le Monde du silence
Monthly Film Bulletin, 1957, p. 12 (unsigned); *Variety*, 6 June 1956

Ascenseur pour l'échafaud
Monthly Film Bulletin, 1960, p. 62 (Penelope Houston); *Variety*, 7 May 1958

Les Amants
Monthly Film Bulletin, 1959, p. 154 (Eric Rhode); *Variety*, 17 September 1958; *Sight and Sound*, 1959, p. 21 (Richard Roud)

Zazie
Monthly Film Bulletin, 1963, p. 20 (Tom Milne); *Variety*, 23 November 1960; Dwight Macdonald in *On Movies*, Prentice-Hall, New Jersey (1969), p. 384; *Sight and Sound*, 1963, p. 37 (Geoffrey Nowell-Smith)

Vie Privée
Monthly Film Bulletin, 1962, p. 152 (Tom Milne)

Le Feu follet
Monthly Film Bulletin, 1964, p. 114 (Peter John Dyer); *Variety*, 11 September 1963

Viva Maria
Monthly Film Bulletin, 1966, p. 40 (Tom Milne); *Variety*, 8 December 1965; *Sight and Sound*, 1966, p. 90 (Penelope Houston)

Le Voleur
Variety, 15 March 1967

Histoires extraordinaires
Monthly Film Bulletin, 1973, p. 76 (Tony Rayns); *Variety*, 5 June 1968

Calcutta
Variety, 14 May 1969

L'Inde fantôme
Monthly Film Bulletin, 1975, p. 13 (Jan Dawson)

Le Souffle au coeur
Monthly Film Bulletin, 1971, p. 203 (Philip Strick); Pauline Kael in *Deeper into Movies* (1973), p. 305; *Variety*, 14 April 1971

Lacombe, Lucien
Monthly Film Bulletin, 1974, p. 149 (Jan Dawson); *Variety*, 30 January 1974; *Sight and Sound*, 1974, p. 176 (Tom Milne); *The Dilys Powell Reader*, ed. Christopher Cook, Carcanet (1991), p. 180; Pauline Kael in *Reeling* (1976), p. 447

Black Moon
Variety, 24 September 1975; Pauline Kael in *When the Lights Go Down* (1980), p. 82

Pretty Baby
Monthly Film Bulletin, 1979, p. 231 (John Pym); *Variety*, 5 April 1978; *Sight and Sound*, 1979, p. 261 (Tom Milne); *Observer*, 28 September 1979 (Philip French)

Atlantic City
Monthly Film Bulletin, 1981, p. 3 (Tom Milne); *Variety*, 3 September 1980; *Sight and Sound*, 1981, p. 137 (Tim Pulleine); *Observer*, 25 January 1981 (Philip French); Pauline Kael in *Taking It All In* (1986), p. 173

My Dinner with André

Monthly Film Bulletin, 1982, p. 109 (John Pym); *Variety*, 16 September 1981; *Observer*, 9 May 1982 (Philip French); Pauline Kael in *Taking It All In*, p. 286; *Sight and Sound*, 1982, p. 118 (Wallace Shawn, '*My Dinner with André* – A Collaboration'), p. 208 (Julien Jebb)

Crackers

Monthly Film Bulletin, 1985, p. 19 (Tom Milne); *Variety*, 25 January 1984; *Observer*, 27 January 1985 (Philip French)

Alamo Bay

Monthly Film Bulletin, 1986, p. 5 (Richard Combs); *Variety*, 3 April 1985; *Observer*, 2 February 1986 (Philip French)

Au revoir les enfants

Monthly Film Bulletin, 1988, p. 296 (Louise Sweet); *Variety*, 2 September 1987; *Sight and Sound*, 1988 p. 283 (Philip Kemp); *Observer*, 9 October 1988 (Philip French); Pauline Kael in *Hooked* (1990), p. 435

Milou en mai

Monthly Film Bulletin, 2 September 1990 (Jill Forbes); *Variety*, 14 February 1990; *Sight and Sound*, 1990, p. 201 (Richard Mayne); *Observer*, 2 September 1990 (Philip French)

Note. In addition to the collections of *New Yorker* columns by Pauline Kael cited above, there is a revised edition of her *5001 Nights at the Movies* (Henry Holt, New York, 1991) which contains capsule versions of all the reviews, together with short pieces on *Ascenseur pour l'échafaud*, *Zazie*, *Vie Privée*, *Viva Maria*, *Le Voleur*, *Calcutta* and *Humain, trop humain*.

A Note on the Editor

Philip French was born in Liverpool in 1933 and, after serving as an officer with the Parachute Regiment in the Middle East, he studied law at Oxford and journalism at Indiana University. For over thirty years he was a producer and scriptwriter in the Talks and Documentaries Department of BBC Radio, where he created and edited *The Arts This Week* and *Critics' Forum*. Throughout this time he wrote on theatre, books and the cinema for a variety of newspapers and magazines (including *Sight and Sound, Movie, London Magazine, The Times*, the *Financial Times*, the *New Statesman*, the *Listener*) and since 1978 has been film critic of the *Observer*. His books include *Age of Austerity 1945–51* (co-edited with Michael Sissons), *The Movie Moguls, Westerns: Aspects of a Movie Genre* and *Three Honest Men: Edmund Wilson, F. R. Leavis and Lionel Trilling*. In 1972 he was a visiting professor at the University of Texas and in 1986 he was a member of the jury at the Cannes Film Festival.

Index

NOTTINGHAM UNIVERSITY LIBRARY